Endorsements

'Morning coffee' for most is the ritual that starts the day. They cannot effectively launch the day without it. It picks them up, gives them focus and stamina. It gives them the fuel to face the day. Some people say that it's addictive. *Morning Coffee* definitely has the same effect on its readers. The online *Morning Coffee* readers are eager for their morning email to give them the focus and fortitude they need for the day. When you ingest the positively nourishing, smoothly blended sips of *Morning Coffee* served up by our literary Barista, you will get a clarity that is addictive. The clever guidance delivered in the daily messages is like a gift from the writer via the Writer.

I am fortunate enough to have a personal line to Mr. Watson who has helped me get my personal line with God connected; and it all started one message at a time. It is like Espresso for a person just embarking on a new, long walk. These personal stories of God in action followed by his daily reminders of who God is and what He can do are what have brought me to where I am. I can only hope that through these pages, he intends to share with all what he has shared with me which is this gift that He has given to him.

I am not too much of a coffee drinker but I have a big cup of *Morning Coffee* every morning. Honestly I go back and have more than one helping depending on how the day is going. Readers should feel fortunate and consider this book their very own big ol' pot of coffee.

Brandi -J. Johnson
Owner
Strategic Urban Marketing

The Morning coffee is a book I would pick up and read because it reminds me of how God gets me started on my day every morning. I am not a coffee drinker, but it reminds me when I spent three years away from my family-training Soldiers in the Military during Operation Iraqi Freedom, and Operation Enduring Freedom. Before heading out to the ranges every morning we had training, we all had to stop by the PX store for those that wanted to get a snack for the day. Most of the Training Unit would get a cup of coffee. If they didn't have their cup of coffee they would be cranky all day. This book would be my cup of coffee to prevent me from being cranky all day. The best part of waking up is the Word of God in your cup.

SFC Wynn, Bruce Lee
US Army Reserves

I am inspired by Jesse's ability to take the ancient truths of the Bible and apply them to our modern times so that we can be guided by the gospel of Christ in our time. He takes examples from his own life to show us exactly how the timeless truths of the gospel of Jesus Christ will always be a solid foundation to rely on.

Brooke Poppinga
Friend and Wife of Brady Poppinga of
The World Champion Green Bay Packers

"I consider Morning Coffee one of the tender graces and mercies that God grants me daily. This book is a reminder that my Heavenly Dad is with me and I face my trials and tests with Him...and we've won!" "Watch, fight and pray...and read this book to get your day started!"

Holly Harris
Engineer/Chevron

"I recommend for your spiritual growth a daily dose of Morning Coffee. This is a very insightful God inspired book."

Olus Holder
Executive Pastor
Fallbrook Church

Jesse Watson's Bible based "Morning Coffee" is a must read for anyone who desires a stimulating dose of practical application of God's word that's a lot like caffeine ...it gets you going in the morning, evening or night.

Talulah Ruger, CEO/Founder, Talulah Ruger Ministries, LLC

"In getting to know Jesse, it's been a tremendous blessing to see how the powerful, yet practical wisdom he offers is born out of his own experiences. 'Morning Coffee' provides the fuel necessary to embrace the daily battles of being a Christ follower." - **Malcolm Marshall**

Associate Minister of Connection & Community Lead Chaplain for NBA's Houston Rockets Overseer of Joined at the Hip Ministry

Editing this book was a tremendous blessing! No price tag can be placed on the priceless and spiritual empowerment gained by ingesting the scriptures and stories. Morning Coffee is a perfect title, because it is addictive, awakening readers, giving them a spiritual boost of energy with no harmful side effects!!! Reverend Watson fearlessly blended both scripture and personal experience to inform, encourage, and most importantly, remind us that God's word is the best Nourishment for our hungry souls. I can't wait to reread my purchased, autographed copy, which will be given to friends and family as gifts. I am also highly anticipating his future works, which will line my shelves.

Shanedria Wagner
Editor
Morning Coffee

I have observed Jesse since I was a teenager and his discipline is admirable, he has been my closest advisor for many years and there is no one I trust more as it pertains to living up right and abiding by the laws of God. He is a constant inspiration and an extremely valued friend.

Terrance J. Koontz/ Founder of
Community Alive

Jesse Watson has implemented a way of touching an individual's heart and challenging them to excel in Christ through his morning coffee emails. Morning coffee has rejuvenated my spirit every morning through its biblical references, and has inspired me mentally through its practical editorials, which help shape my day through spiritual thinking and faith walking.

Elder Gene A. Moore, Jr.
St. Agnes Baptist Church

LETTER OF ENDORSEMENT

As I awake each morning, I am very grateful to my Heavenly Father for breathing His breath of life into my nostrils. Because He is so faithful, I am given another day to get this thing that we call life right. After I thank Him for this opportunity that He has presented me, my next mission is to secure my "Morning Coffee". Contrary to most, it is not the Folgers's brand that I seek or the nearest Starbucks franchise. I can honestly admit that it is the spiritual writings and teaching by Minister Jesse R. Watson, Jr. entitled "Morning Coffee" that provides the spiritual lift that I need to make it through the day.

As the Founder and Director of Business Operations for Full Potential Academy/ Sports Trainers, it is indeed my pleasure to endorse Minister Jesse R. Watson, Jr. and his Morning Coffee endeavors. I am an advocate reader of his material and am thoroughly impressed with the quality and deliverance of his material. The teachings are easy to understand and very applicable to situations many face on a daily basis. The teachings engage and foster spiritual growth to all readers regardless of how strong your walk with God may be at the initial juncture.

With our Full Potential Academy/ Sports Trainers entity, our main goal is the overall development of student athletes and the moral growth of our youth. We have adopted the Morning Coffee provided by Minister Watson as a philosophy to start our initial process in the Holistic development of the youth in our program. To say that the teachings have been well received by the students in our program is an understatement. We are looking forward to building a greater relationship with Minister Watson and utilizing his writings/ teaching to help further produce productive people.

We believe that together, Full Potential Academy/ Sports Trainer and Minister Jesse R. Watson, Jr. are in the ideal position to offer high quality developmental strategies at all levels.

Joseph M. Lane
Director of Business Operations
Full Potential Academy/ Sports Trainers

Morning Coffee

Jesse R. Watson Jr.

Copyright © 2011, 2014 Jesse R. Watson Jr.

All rights reserved. No part of this book may be used or reproduced by any means, graphic, electronic, or mechanical, including photocopying, recording, taping or by any information storage retrieval system without the written permission of the publisher except in the case of brief quotations embodied in critical articles and reviews.

Watson Publishing books may be ordered through booksellers or by contacting:

Watson Publishing
www.jessewatsonjr.com

Because of the dynamic nature of the Internet, any web addresses or links contained in this book may have changed since publication and may no longer be valid. The views expressed in this work are solely those of the author and do not necessarily reflect the views of the publisher, and the publisher hereby disclaims any responsibility for them.

Cover art by Ladarwin Cumby IDG Company

Edited by Shanedria Wagner

ISBN: 978-0692642849

Library of Congress Control Number: 2011962990

Printed in the United States of America.

Watson Publishing rev. date: 11/03/2014

Dedication

To God, thank you for trusting in me to deliver this project to your people. Please continue to use me as a conduit to draw others to you. I will continue to be a beacon of light in this world for your glory.

To my wife Rhonda and our three boys, Joshua, Jason and Judson I thank God for your patience and understanding especially throughout this process. Your support and belief in who God has called me to be, is priceless. Thank you for praying and understanding the long nights and the time missed. I love you all dearly and know that your love and support encourages me to stay on course.

To my family and friends your continued support and prayers have been felt. Thank you for all of the communication over the course of this project encouraging me to finish the assignment.

To you all, I dedicate this book.

Foreword

There are encouraging signs that our culture still recognizes the value and power of character. Some businesses even require a level of character training as a part of its employee orientation. There are so many pressures in the every day world pulling us in the wrong direction that all of us need a reliable source for true character choices. Even when our lives are going the right direction we still need daily encouragement to stay on the path.

Morning Coffee is a great resource for helping you to begin each workday morning with just the right foundational thought to keep your life on track that day. Each morning, Jesse takes a core Biblical principle and places it into a real life application. You'll relate to his stories and through them he will get you thinking about how you can use *today's* principle of character, faith, encouragement, and love to make the right choices.

As you drink your coffee, consume just one key thought that can improve your day – how you can respond to the situations you are about to face in a winning way. *Morning Coffee* challenges you to set yourself apart from the norm and shows you how to do it. This is a perspective you shouldn't do without.

This book comes from the heart of a man I have watched in our church be *the real deal*. He walks his talk and now he provides all of us an opportunity to peer inside the heart of a man who has learned a great deal about how to live *real life* through the most powerful principles of the ages.

Walk through *Morning Coffee* for a year and it will be one of the best investments you have ever made.

Mark S. Hartman
Lead Pastor, Sugar Creek Baptist Church

Preface

'Morning Coffee' is a practical approach to reading and applying the word. Many people have a hard time getting going in the morning so the potential to make the week long, is a possibility. So the devotions are to give people the edge they need to motivate them to make it through the day and ultimately through the week. If our Spirit is satisfied daily the rest of our body will fall in line. Everybody feels like they need a morning cup of Joe and by the power of the Holy Spirit I submitted my will to the Lord's to be used to brew up the flavor of the day.

Most cups of coffee when brewed just right are warm and goes down smooth to hit all of the right spots to perk you up and help prepare you for the day. Every day we wake, we receive God's grace and mercy irrespective of the day before. God does not discriminate because He loves us all and extends His grace to us as He apportioned it according to the scriptures. Since God provides for us daily, even though we don't deserve it, you can say our blessings are tailored specific to each individual. Everyday, you choose your flavor or brand of coffee; you drink what is going to give you what you need to get going. In the same way God serves you a fresh cup; overflowing with what you need as well. You may have had a long night and need something strong to wake you or you may want something really smooth, you can get the Word of God daily through the Morning Coffee served to fit your need in Grande or Venti.

Inspired by my desire to read the word daily so I could stay in line, is how this journey began. I wanted to challenge myself to constantly dig into the word of God so I have plenty stored into my spiritual library. Being full of God's word is important to me because I knew; I had to put something in me in order for the Holy Spirit to have something to work with. How can anyone or I say they trust God and believe in His word if you don't hide the word in your heart? Mark 1:35, the text this bookstands on and should be the inspiration for us all to start our day off the right way. With Jesus Christ being the standard and not the exception we are called to live like Him. In the text, the word says Jesus Christ got up very early while it was still dark, went to a quiet place to spend time with the Lord. It hit me that we should be doing the same thing so this text affirmed the birth of 'Morning Coffee.' We are called to go out and make disciples and to duplicate ourselves. If our lives aren't measured by the word, what are we teaching others who are watching us? Jesus Christ was the perfect example and we should strive to be more like Him daily because nearby are more people following us than we know. The only way to be sure we are leading others in the right way, the only way to be accountable is to spend quality time daily with the Lord. 'Morning Coffee' will allow you to spend that quality time with the Lord. This is a practical approach to reading and learning God's word and everyday you read you will be able to apply something to your life right away.

So as the sun rises, find you a quiet place to make time for the 'Morning Coffee.' This is the right way to start your day. When you are empty, He will fill your cup.

Save Yourself

> "Then he said to them all: "If anyone would come after me, he must deny himself and take up his cross daily and follow me. For whoever wants to save his life will lose it, but whoever loses his life for me will save it."- **Luke 9:23-24**

For many this text may be a little difficult to swallow when you look at what it is saying. I am not going to get too deep with this one however I do want you to understand what is being said.

Here Jesus is talking with the disciples and He asks the question, "Who do you say I am." Peter immediately answers the Messiah or the Christ of God. So they were clear whom they were with. Christ then told them that He had to suffer, die, and be raised on the third day; that alone was tough for the disciples. Then Jesus shares the text for today with them.

As followers of Christ, we must be aware and confident in His identity and purpose. We have to know that He went through a lot on our behalves and if we are going to follow Him, we have to know that it won't be easy. Following Christ requires that we let go of our sinful desires, look past material gain for Christ, deny exalting ourselves before man, and be willing to live for Him by being examples for Him daily. We have to get past our own selfish desires in order to seek Jesus. We are seeking to preserve our own lives by following the Biblical model of Christ. Surrender and trust are the way of the disciples and we have to be willing to do the same thing for Christ-sake. When we surrender to Christ we are denying ourselves and saving our lives in an eternal sense.

It doesn't mean that we won't get the desires of our heart or that we have to suffer and live without. God wants us to live in abundance; however He wants us to be disciplined. Following Christ's example puts us in better positions to live the lives that we always wanted. The Bible is very clear that if we focus and follow the word of God, we will be prosperous and successful. The key is seeking first the kingdom of God and His righteousness. God wants the best for our lives, more than we do. He is just asking us to trust Him and allow Him to lead the way.

We must have faith that God is going to do what His word says. Our way of showing that Faith (trust and confidence in the Lord) is submitting our lives fully to God. In order to save ourselves, it requires us to follow Christ and in doing that we can't allow the temptation of acquiring material things or status to be our downfall. The Bible says that the humble shall be exalted, so all we have to do is submit to His power, will, and authority. He will do the rest. The only way to do that is to follow Christ by denying ourselves daily.

God Bless

Salt and Light

> "Be wise in the way you act toward outsiders; make the most of every opportunity. Let your conversation be always full of grace, seasoned with salt, so that you may know how to answer everyone."- **Colossians 4:5-6**

Since we are the salt of the Earth and the light of the world, we have to be careful how we act towards others, especially those who don't know Christ. If you think about it, light, once it enters, it is all consuming. It enlightens and informs, so without light we can't see. We have to be careful what people see when they look at us because we don't know how many people are modeling themselves after us. The Bible says that we have to season our words with grace. We have all been given grace, so we know what that means. However, we don't always show that to others. Salt creates value and it has a major impact; it is used to preserve, so when we speak to others we have to say something that will have a positive impact on their lives. We have to speak as if we are preserving their lives for a right relationship with Christ.

God Bless

Root Cause

> "Consider him who endured such opposition from sinful men, so that you will not grow weary and lose heart."
> **- Hebrews 12:3**

When you think about being successful at anything you know that there are obstacles that come along with it. These obstacles will do one of two things; they will trip you up and cause you to stumble and fall or they will propel you to greatness by strengthening you during your journey. I have always been one to model myself after successful people. One of the general rules of being successful at anything is finding someone who is willing to give guidance.

I have learned that it is very difficult to do almost anything by oneself. If for nothing else, we need someone to encourage us along the way. When facing new obstacles, we become helpless if nobody (experienced in our areas) can help us. We must humble ourselves to consult others for guidance and wisdom. What we often don't realize is that there is almost always some difficult time that we face that causes us to break down and ask for help or guidance. The thing that stops us from being successful after that is that we never deal with what drove us to seek that assistance.

In walking with Christ, we know that Jesus Christ has walked the walk for us and before us. We have heard about His story and what He had to endure. When we first came to Christ it was His story that inspired us to want to follow Him. As a result of our own hardships, instinctively we get excited about being in Christ because now we have someone in our lives who loves us unconditionally. To know that we have that kind of support gives us the fortitude to endure our hardship with hope and confidence. In most situations, we find that we don't get weary or lose heart. In fact we get stronger to the point that we strengthen others as well.

There is one thing, though, that we lost focus of and it always seems to come back up, the reason we went to the Lord in the first place. Some were just tired of fighting challenges by themselves. However for many, there was something specific that drew us towards the Lord. Often when we accept Jesus Christ we feel so relieved, (like the burden has been lifted) that we loose focus of the issue that got us there. Soon after, we get caught up with the excitement about living for the Lord that we never go back to deal with our issues, which causes us to go on an emotional roller coaster later in our walk with the Lord. Jesus Christ had an issue before He committed His life forever and it was being separated from His Father. However, before He allowed Himself to be crucified, He dealt with His issue. As a result of His facing His issue, Jesus let it go and moved forward with confidence. Jesus Christ showed us this when He was in the Garden of Gethsemane and He said, "Not my will but your will be done." We have to make sure that while we are on our journey with the Lord that we allow Him to help us deal with our root cause of choosing to follow Him in the first place. Deep down inside, it will continue to be an obstacle that will stunt our growth because something familiar will always bring it back to our remembrance. Don't forget the enemy is an opportunist who will wait until you are really high in the Lord to try to knock you back down. Any fall that you make means that he was successful at his attempt. In order for us to ensure our successful growth in Christ, we must follow His example. The weapons may form, but because we dealt with our internal struggle, it will not prosper in our lives.

God Bless

Right Thinking

> "Finally, brothers, whatever is true, whatever is noble, whatever is right, whatever is pure, whatever is lovely, whatever is admirable—if anything is excellent or praiseworthy—think about such things."- **Philippians 4:8**

In the first sermon the Lord gave me and used me to preach, one thing that He said through me was the outcome of your crisis is a reflection of how you dealt with your issue. That statement is still so timeless today. Normally in our minds we already play out the entire scenarios before anything happens and try to draw our own conclusions. The main point that we tend to forget is that God is really in control. So what we tend to do is push ourselves toward what we envision because of negative thinking or stinking thinking.

Paul is telling us here to hold on to positive thoughts. Think on anything that will lead to a more fruitful outcome. It is interesting because vs. 6 and 7 are the verses that I used. It simply says not to worry about anything. Instead pray about everything. We have to understand that with praying we have to acknowledge the power of God and believe that our situation will work out for our good.

We had to have an intervention last night with one of our neighbors well into 2 this morning. To make a long story short, she doesn't like the decisions her 12-year-old-daughter is making and thinks that sending her away is the only solution. After much discussion, she agreed to allow her daughter to stay with us a few days to work on restoring their relationship as much as we can. If this mother holds on to those negative thoughts and keep feeding them to her child, it is inevitable that some of that (if not all of her thoughts) will come to pass.

We are going to share with her today that if she changes her mind, she can change her and her daughter's lives. Their issue is not resolved, however there is hope.

It is so important that we turn our attention to things above and not those things below because God is able to protect our minds and our hearts, and turn our situations around to work out for our good.

Whatever is admirable—if anything is excellent or praiseworthy—think about such things. Again, if you change your mind, you can change your life.

God Bless

Rest

"Come to me, all you who are weary and burdened, and I will give you rest."- **Matthew 11:28**

How many times have you found yourself exhausted on all levels: physically, mentally, emotionally, and most importantly, spiritually? It can be very draining. There is so much going on in the world today that can cause one to absolutely loose it. There are so many people who are looking for that peace; they are looking for that safe place to get away from it all. The only catch is wherever many people turn; relief is only temporary. Before they know it they find themselves right back in that same place fighting for their lives once again.

The only safe place where we can get rest and never worry about those issues again, the only place where we can leave our problems to get taken care of, is with Jesus. The Lord's word is very clear and definitive, meaning that it is said with confidence. It is guaranteed. No matter what you are dealing with, cast your cares upon the Lord. Take it to Jesus and by the power of the Holy Spirit; you will have peace.

God Bless

Respect Elders

"Teach the older men to be temperate, worthy of respect,
self-controlled, and sound in faith, in love and in endurance."
- **Titus 2:2**

When I was younger, I was always told to respect my elders or someone older, especially if they were in positions of authority. I would always do as I was told. Now in my growing process, there were some folks who really didn't deserve the respect that they got.

The interesting part about this is that children today are not all being raised the way we were in our day. Simply stated, they are more disrespectful and concerned about the idea that you have to give respect to get it. To a certain degree, they are right. The Bible clearly says it here; however, there are many adults who feel that they should be respected just because. The only way for these young folks to get a true picture of how it should go is to show them. We have to learn to respect their space, mind, time, and their lives. The only way to connect with this younger generation these days is to create a relationship with them and that starts with respect. The only way to get them in a position to possibly change is to show them everything that this text is saying; we have to live it in order for them to see it and want it for themselves.

The saying the children can only be what they see is true. In order to see the fruit of our investments for a better tomorrow we have to make the right deposits today. We have to live lives worthy of respect in order to receive it and by doing so we then model for the youth today and will possibly make a major impact in their lives.

Michael Jackson said the he was looking at the man in the mirror and asking him to change his ways. I am starting with me and only with the power of the Holy Spirit can I be consistent in living a life worthy of respect. When the son shines on me, my shadow should be a reflection of HIM.

God Bless

Remain in His Love

> "If you obey my commands, you will remain in my love, just as I have obeyed my father's commands and remain in his love."- **John 15:10**

Some of us may be familiar with the phrase, "If, if was a fifth, we would all be drunk." Some of you are being exposed to this for the first time. The point is that so many of us use this expression to justify our own action, basically using it to say once someone else does something, you will.

"If" as a noun means a stipulation or a condition or covenant. It is the premise upon which the fulfillment of an agreement depends.

God is true to His word and no matter what will come through, period. The reason "IF" is so big here is that the agreement that will be fulfilled is staying in God's love. Who wants to be outside of His love? I know that I don't. I don't want to be viewed as an enemy of God. The Bible says that God is love; so in essence, Jesus is saying that if we remain in His love we remain in God. It all comes down to being obedient. In our day that is a BIG IF.

It is so easy for us to sit back and throw "if" around as a condition on whether we do our part when it comes to dealing with someone else, whatever it is. Most of the time we want everything to be just right, on our terms before we agree to do our part. In other words, we often hold others to a high standard before we jump in to help them. If whomever you are doing work with doesn't put their best foot forward then that is the premise that we don't either.

So what if God view us in the same manner?

I'll give you an even better example. God does look us at the same way. He holds us to a high standard because He paid such a high price for us. God expects and deserves excellence in all that we do. Now we don't always give Him that excellence, however He still loves us and provides for us regardless.

Don't let IF be the reason that you don't give your all in everything that you do. "If" has caused wars, death, divorce, sin, and so much more.

Do your best in everything, knowing that the condition that comes with if takes care of itself. We must get in to the habit of doing this with others and in turn we will please God and remain in His love.

God Bless

Reconciled

> "Wash and make yourselves clean. Take your evil deeds out of my sight! Stop doing wrong, learn to do right! Seek justice; encourage the oppressed. Defend the cause of the fatherless, plead the case of the widow."- **Isaiah 1:16-17**

The Lord is pretty intense here in this verse and it is because of what was happening at the time.

Side note: Whenever you read a verse from the Bible it is good to always read the verses before and after so that you can really get the context of the message.

Here the Lord was speaking to the people of Israel, His chosen people. They had rebelled against the Lord and because of their sinful acts, had been compared to Sodom and Gomorrah. This city was destroyed because of its wickedness.

There are a lot of people around us today who are caught up in a world of sin. Some are so caught up that they think there is no way out. Just like the Lord spoke to the Israelites, He is speaking to His people today. It is possible to cleanse yourself of the sin in your life. In verse 18, it speaks about meeting the Lord right where you are, and discussing the issues that you have been dealing with. He says that even though it seems that you can't be forgiven, you can. It is just like wasting cranberry juice on your carpet or clothes; it is hard to get that stain out. But God says that He will wash you as white as snow.

The key to it all is verse 19 where it says IF YOU are willing, you will eat the best from the land. God still shows compassion, no matter how much sin you have in your life if you are willing to let it go and turn your life around. However, for those who rebel the Bible says in verse 20 you will be devoured by the sword. In other words, you are fighting a winless fight. Your arms are too short to box with God; instead, have the Lord fight your battles for you.

God Bless

Quick to listen, Slow to Speak, Slow to get Angry

> "My dear brothers, take note of this: Everyone should be quick to listen, slow to speak, and slow to become angry,"
> - **James 1:19**

These days it is very easy to misunderstand or misinterpret what someone says to you. Often as a result, tension gets high quickly and before you know it, there is potential for a major confrontation to take place. In the same breath, a lot of times there are people in that very situation who have heard enough or only heard what they wanted to hear before they are ready to give you a piece of their mind. This comes of course many times without them getting a full understanding of what is being said.

This can happen with friends, strangers, coworkers, bill collectors, and family. Something as simple as taking the time to listen could change everything. Many of us have been accused of selective hearing at some point in our lives and I have to admit that I have suffered from it before. Effective communication not only requires us to express our thoughts clearly, it also requires us to listen carefully as well. This is a matter of self-control and simply choice.

How often is someone trying to tell you something and before you know it, you cut him or her off or vice versa? The scenario can open the door to a major confrontation, all because someone thought he or she knew it all and didn't want to listen. If we all condition ourselves to be great listeners, we may discover that there is a lot more to what is being said and maybe we won't be so quick to go off on people. When we are communicating we should not always be in defense mode, because that causes us to react quickly to the first thing that doesn't sound right. Quite honestly, everyone is not out to get over on you so you don't have to be so willing to cut a person up with your words, body language, and attitude.

Jesus always showed compassion and He displayed that He was a great listener because He already knew the outcomes. When people would come to speak with Him, He would listen to their full requests and get an understanding of their state of mind and sincerity to assess their level of faith to help them overcome.

Hebrews says that it is impossible to please God without faith because whoever comes to Him must first believe that He exists and that He will reward those who diligently seek Him. God has to listen to your words and your heart to understand where you are in your walk with Him.

What if you go to God after you have made the same mistake five times asking to be restored and God cut your request off and told you to get out of His face because he'd grown sick of your excuses? What if you were really on your last leg or at your wit's end on life and God never took the time to listen to you heart?

Just in this brief devotion I have been convicted because I don't always apply this principle when getting on my five-year-old. As a result, I now see how sometimes he feels that what he has to say is not important. Thank you God!! Apply this principle in your life; you'll never know whom you may be pushing away or how you could be crushing their feelings. You may be creating an environment that they no longer want to deal with. Your relationship with that person is more valuable than your being quick to release your frustration due to a lack of listening. It is not always going to be easy, but you have to choose to change. Change starts today for me.

God Bless

Put it in His Hands

"As for me, I am in your hands; do with me whatever you think is good and right."- **Jeremiah 26:14**

Here the Lord spoke to Jeremiah and told him to go to speak to the cities of Judah and deliver a message where Josiah was the king at the time. The message was simply to follow the Lord's commands and turn from their evil ways. If they were to listen then the Lord said that He would not bring on the disaster He was planning for them. The Lord told Jeremiah not to omit one word because He wanted His message to be clear. He didn't want Jeremiah to dumb down the message to appeal to the people. The interesting thing is that they had been warned before. Jeremiah did exactly as the Lord commanded and the priest, prophets, and all the people didn't like it at all. They seized Jeremiah and wanted him to die because of the words the Lord told him to speak. Jeremiah's last appeal was to tell all the people that the Lord did in fact send him to tell them that message and that they should take heed to the words of the Lord. Then he said as for him they can do what they think is the right thing to do but if they kill him, they should know that he is telling the truth and the Lord did send him.

Jeremiah was confident in the Lord's will and was obedient to God. As a result of his obedience the people let him go and began to reflect on the other times the Lord had warned them before. As a result of Jeremiah's boldness to stand for the Lord the people listened and received grace from the Lord.

Many of us have tried doing things our own way and if you tell the truth about it the results were not always favorable. From this day forward, let's put everything in God's hands. Let's wait to see what He does. Let us give up trying to control everything and recognize that God is in control.

Today is a very special day. Two of my old students' lives will change forever because they trust God much like Jeremiah in this story. Between today and tomorrow, we are praying for today, he will be drafted into the NFL and life for them will never be the same. After talking with them it is clear that they trust God and always have. They are willing to accept whatever God's will is for their lives. I am even more excited because, once drafted, they will get the opportunity to be a beacon of light to so many others who try so hard to maintain control over their lives instead of trusting God. The best way for them to have a major impact is to carry the message, just as Jeremiah did; by the way they live and carry themselves. When the opportunity presents itself, they should not be ashamed to tell how God blessed them. The blessing in this is that they have already given everything to God and when we spoke last they said that they were not worried, but praying. So, in other words, Roger Goodell and the NFL teams it is in your hands. Do whatever you think is good and right. We know he is going to be drafted; now we are just trusting God about where he will go.

God has placed a situation in your life that, if you just trust Him, will be taken care of by Him. However, we sometimes make it so hard to release control. What are you fighting to let go? Do you believe that God is big enough to handle it? Why not be like Jeremiah and let go and let God? Try Him today. He won't let you down.

God Bless

Purify Ourselves

> "Since we have these promises, dear friends, let us purify ourselves from everything that contaminates body and spirit, perfecting holiness out of reverence for God."
> - **2 Corinthians 7:1**

God has promised in chapter 6 to live with the Corinthians and walk with them and be their God. He said that they would be His people; He would be a Father to them. This promise comes from the Lord through Paul as he expressed to them that they should not be yoked with unbelievers. The concept behind being yoked is the joining of two to work together harmoniously on one accord. Simply stated, a yoke was a wooden beam used on a pair of oxen back in the day to allow them to work together to pull the load. We all know that in relationships we have to work together to pull the load if we are going to experience any kind of success. I may have to come back to this one later, especially for our married folk.

So when we get to chapter 7 Paul says that now since we have these promises there is something that the people in Corinth have to do. He says, "let us purify ourselves from everything that contaminates body and spirit." Purifying ourselves is a two-fold action. First, we have to be willing to turn away from sin. Then we have to be willing to turn towards God. Let's face it; so many people are comfortable living in sin because it appears to be getting them what they want and where they want to be. They are blinded by their own selfish desires and can't see that their pleasure is only temporary because there is no foundation for it to stand on. It is understandable that when you are faced with a challenge sometimes the easy way out is very appealing. We may even convince ourselves that one time won't hurt and no one will know unless we tell him or her. Then that leads to our justifying for our actions. I only ask one question; where does faith that God got you fit into that equation?

Turning to God really is the easy part. We just don't always realize it though. Think about it. If you choose to take the easy route and you get to the end and it still doesn't work the way you wanted it, whom do you call on? God! Exactly! So why not just go to Him first and save yourself the heartache? The people in Corinth had a hard time grasping that concept and truthfully we do too some times. It is still all a part of the process of purification. God is the only one who knows where the road leads and when it will end. So why not just choose to go to God first?

For the Corinthians perfecting holiness meant having nothing to do with paganism. We too have to disassociate ourselves with evil sinful ways. We all have to make a clean break with our pasts and give ourselves to God alone. The only way to receive the promises of God is to do it His way. We sometimes want to circumvent the system and expect the same results. God is not bootleg and He will not allow us to be either. In order to receive what God has in store for us we have to willingly commit to living our lives according to His will. We should want to do it out of respect and love for God, who has done so much for us. I want what God has in store for me. His vision for my life is far greater than I can ever imagine so I am going to do everything within my power to stay committed to Him. In that effort, everything else will fall in line by the grace of God. So what are you going to do?

God Bless

Prepare a Way

"A voice of one calling: "In the desert prepare the way for the LORD; make straight in the wilderness a highway for our God."- **Isaiah 40:3**

In Chapter 40 of Isaiah we have the people of Israel getting word that their struggle is over. No longer in captivity, they learn that their sins have been paid for. Basically here the Lord is saying that they have received atonement for their suffering; even though they didn't deserve the move from wrath to mercy, God granted it anyway. Here the call was made for God's people to prepare a way for Him to return to them.

Ultimately, God's chosen people rejected Him and they were held captive in Babylon for many years. There are so many people who have turned their backs on God or have never chosen to allow Him to have control of their lives at all, mostly because of something that someone else has said or done. Perhaps they even had a misguided understanding of who God really is. Still, others have been separated from God for too long. This season is a perfect time to prepare a way for the Lord.

During this holiday season we celebrate the memory of the birth of our risen Lord and savior. My son shared with me on yesterday that the scripture taught in Sunday school class was great news. Jesus Christ is born. That was the way it was broken down for them and it just reminded me as I shared with Him how good it really is that Jesus Christ came to save us all.

For those whose hearts have been hardened for whatever reason; now is a better time than any to get into a right relationship with God. As believers, we have to do everything possible to open the hearts of those folks so that they can receive Him properly. Giving shouldn't be associated with Christmas time; it should be a yearlong practice. However, now is the time that it is highly emphasized. So let us commit to participate fully. There are many people who are hurting and hungry for a savior, looking for a way out. We know the only one who can provide. If you don't give any other gifts this year, share the gift of Jesus Christ. Share hope and save a life.

God Bless

Prayer of a Righteous

"Therefore confess your sins to each other and pray for each other so that you may be healed. The prayer of a righteous man is powerful and effective."- **James 5:16**

Even if we have covered this before it is well worth being repeated.

Almost all the time when we do something out of order or respond improperly to a situation, the last thing we want to do is share that information with someone else. We sometimes feel that way because we don't want anyone in our business and definitely don't want to risk half the world knowing what we are dealing with. When we'd rather deal with issues than seek help when life deals us a difficult hand, we also apply the rule of privacy. Honestly there is nothing wrong with being cautious and not wanting to share your information with others.

Here James is telling us that there is a benefit to sharing your information. The Bible says that two is better than one because you get a better return on your work. We have to be really cautious with whom we share our information. However, having a trustworthy person to confide in relieves stress. Likewise, we should cherish sensitive information about others, never playing tit-for-tat by disclosing their personal information to get even. That is not trust; it is more of a bargaining agreement. We should only trust those who guard our secrets like safes; it takes some powerful explosives to get it out of them.

We have already discussed that prayer changes things; the Bible is also clear when it says that when you have two or more gather together, the Lord is also in the midst. Regardless of what you are dealing with, you want the Lord to be present. You also want someone to pray on your behalf especially when you grow weary, and feel like your prayers are not being answered. We should never underestimate the power of prayer and more importantly the power of others praying for us. Let's face it; many of us are who and where we are today because someone was praying for us.

There are certain people that I talk to about what I am going through. I want them to pray for me because it just seems that their prayers reach God. This doesn't mean that we should not pray for ourselves. Jesus did in Mark 1:35 when it says that while it was still very early He went off to a quiet place where He prayed. The key here is that you want someone in Christ whom you can trust to bounce stuff off of. In that process you know that they are going to pray either for you or with you. Often the Lord will reveal your answer through them. Also, you want to have someone as your accountability partner as you continue on this journey to be more like Christ. I honestly don't trust everybody so I am very selective with whom I speak to concerning my private affairs. There are times you may not even have to go into details. Just ask that person to just pray for you. Just like we said yesterday, when you are dealing with something, pray, pray, and pray more. Don't take for granted the opportunity to have someone else interceding on your behalf. The more prayers going up the better, that way you know that the Lord got your request. The prayers of the righteous really are powerful and effective.

God Bless

Pray Through Everything

"Be joyful in hope, patient in affliction, and faithful in prayer."- **Romans 12:12**

Paul is giving instructions to the people in Rome on living Godly lives. Chapter 12 is about being a living sacrifice and here Paul gives us three characteristics to help in that process. Just for face value this text is some really good advice for anyone. I share this word with everyone, from some of the weddings I have done as well as funerals and anything in between. This particular verse is mentioned by Paul in the section where He was talking about how we should love one another more than ourselves.

When we look at being "joyful in hope", one would probably think, "Why wouldn't I be?" We have to make sure we understand what Paul was talking about, though, to answer that question. Joyful is the state of having joy and when we break down joy it is a state of happiness or a source of delight. In Greek, it means to rejoice. Hope, on the other hand, means outcomes with great expectations. So here Paul is saying that we should rejoice in our expectations, believing that the outcome will turn out in our favor. So He is saying that we should express our joy and delight before we ever receive our desires. When you think about it for so many it is hard to get excited about what they don't have. However, having faith in the Lord's promises allows rejoicing, knowing that desires will come to fruition.

To be patient is to be steadfast despite opposition, difficulty, or adversity. It is to be able or willing to bear suffering. Suffering is what pain means in Greek. Affliction means the cause of persistent pain or distress. So here He is saying that we should be willing to stand firm on what we believe, and to endure persistent suffering or distress. This reminds me of the pledging process for fraternities and sororities. The whole thought of the process is to break you down to build you back up. You go into the process expecting to have to push through opposition knowing, however, that there is a greater prize in the end for those who endure. Enduring challenges strengthens the determined, regardless of their nature.

Faithful means to be firm in adherence to promises, to be loyal to the end and conscientious. Of course we all know that prayer is just having a talk with the Lord like you would talk with anyone else, only with a higher regard. So here Paul was saying for us to be consistent and loyal with our conversations with the Lord recognizing what He has promised us. The Lord has made several promises to us if we just remain loyal to Him in prayer. One example is found in 2 Chronicles 7:14 where He promises to forgive sins and restore the land. One of the conditions is prayer. God is true to his word and will do exactly what He said that he would do. Here Paul is displaying for us how all three components in this verse depend on one another. Whenever we start anything in life, job, marriage, parenthood, or a business, we have to have great expectations. We have to be willing to endure hardship or challenges, knowing that adversity will just make us stronger. Honestly, the only way to do that and stay grounded in the process is through constant prayer. So in essence this scripture applies to anything in your life, past and present.

Just remember that there is power in prayer that is why Jesus did it so much. As a result of His praying, things happened. Why wouldn't God do the same thing for us? I am a living witness that prayer changes things and as I apply Romans 12:12 in my life daily, God never ceases to amaze me.

Don't worry about anything. Instead, pray through everything.

God Bless

Praise Him

"Let everything that has breath praise the LORD. Praise the LORD." -**Psalm 150:6**

After doing research I discovered that this psalm was inspired by the promise of God being fulfilled. In Babylon, which is now Iraq, The Jews were forced to move there from Jerusalem and told to make the best of it. God promised that he would deliver them and seventy years later He did. They moved back to their homeland and rebuilt the temple that had been destroyed. Even though the book of Psalms had a few authors, it is said that the Jews put the Book of Psalms together to sing in their new temple.

The Jews spoke in Hebrew and in their book they used the word Hallelujah. Halel means to tell someone that they are great. We translate it to mean Praise. U in Hebrew means "all of you" and we just say "you." Finally, "jah" for them means a name for God that we translate as Lord. So when they say "Hallelujah" we say praise the Lord. The idea here is to tell the Lord how great He is. God made a covenant with His people, He agreed to love them and send them help and they agreed to love Him and obey. As a result of their agreement, the Lord showed Himself to be true.

The Bible says, "**Jesus said, "If people held their peace, the stones would immediately start shouting" (Luke 19:40).** No one wants the rocks to cry out in their place so here we learn a valuable lesson from the Jews today. Let's look at it this way. If you were to try to hold your breath for 30 seconds, after that you would probably realize that all you could think about was how long you had to hold your breath. Your need to breath should always remind you of how great God is and all the things that the Lord gives you. God has promised us all many things and some of them have come to pass and some are still a work in progress. Either way, we have all experienced the grace and mercy of God on some level. I would even be willing to say that we have all seen God move in a situation, whether in someone else's or your own, where you know that only God could have brought you through it. When you think about those moments, it should make any challenge seem small. When you think about your need to breathe, and your need for air, why not praise God for it? After all, when you think about it, if He had not breathed life into you where would you be right now?

Be obedient to the word of God and praise Him every chance that you get. Think about how He came through for the Jews and think about how He came through for you. Don't forget the Jesus Christ is still seated at the right hand of the Lord, interceding on your behalf. He deserves all of the praise and the glory. At some point, you should stop and praise the Lord for every breath.

God Bless

Please God

> "May the words of my mouth and the meditation of my heart be pleasing in your sight, O LORD, my Rock and my Redeemer." - **Psalm 19:14**

Would you change the way you live if you knew that every word that comes out of your mouth and every thought would be examined by God? There are so many people who are so far from caring about this thought. As I travel from one location to the next and catch some people in their natural environments, I normally get an ear full. There is no telling what you may hear in the store, the mall, the barbershop, or the beauty salon.

What about how we sometimes easily adapt to the environments we are in? Sometimes people either consciously or unconsciously find themselves adapting, either because it is still so prevalent in them or they are trying to fit in. Many times we don't think about our witness when we allow this to happen.

David, in this text, asked that God approve his words and his thoughts. David basically admitted that he is not perfect so he needed the Lord to help him. His desire was to please God above anything or anybody else. The best person at some point will still fail so who better to help you in this Christian walk than the sovereign Lord? If we are going to be the light of the world, we have to recognize that we are not perfect. Most importantly, being in Christ, we have everything that we need to represent the kingdom. However there is no way that we can do it by ourselves. This is why the Lord says that He will be with us until the end, because He made us and He knows that we need help. More importantly God wants us to be successful at abiding by His word and leading others to Christ. We may not think about it but what we say and do speak volumes about who we are and how people perceive us. If we willingly allow our character to be flawed, who will believe that we are children of the most high God? If we consistently allow our words and actions to misrepresent our surrendered life to the Lord, our ability to draw others to Christ is weakened.

Let us humble ourselves and consciously recognize that God has assignments for us. As we begin everyday, let us determine that God's love will guide what we say and how we think.

God Bless

Obedience is Better than Sacrifice

"If you obey my commands, you will remain in my love, just as I have obeyed my Father's commands and remain in his love."- **John 15:10**

God is so awesome and very specific with His word. Throughout the Bible we are presented with conditional statements from the Lord. If this then that, basically making it really clear that we have a choice and a chance to see the results of our decisions. One of the greatest gifts that God ever gave us outside of Jesus Christ and life is free will. We have the freedom to choose if we are going to follow the word of God or not. Just like those of us who have children; we give them a command and they have to decide if they will follow it or not. In telling them what we expect out of them we also give them what would be the consequences of their actions.

My five-year-old loves to play video games. That is also something that we enjoy doing together. However, he is very competitive and he does not like to lose. I have been working on teaching him that you can't win every time; sometimes you will lose so, losing should be viewed as an opportunity for improvement. Instead, my little man gets upset and so as a result he finds himself restricted from playing video games sometimes for like six months. I know that is a little extreme for such a young child. However, I use that time to shape and mold his mind because it could be worse.

Here the word says that it is better for us to be obedient to God's command because it keeps us in His good graces. Saul found this lesson out the hard way in 1 Samuel chapter 15. Samuel was charged with blessing Saul as the king over Israel. He gave Saul specific instructions from the Lord. He said for him to lead his people to destroy the Amalekites because of the way they treated the people of Israel when they came out of Egypt. They were to destroy everything and leave no one alive, however they saved the King Agag and what they considered being the best that the city had to offer. Saul and his men saved sheep and cattle to make sacrifices to the Lord and Samuel said to him that obedience is better than sacrifice. What Saul thought was honorable was really out of order and not what the Lord had instructed him to do. It takes more to deny self than to make a sacrifice because you have to humble yourself to glorify God in obedience.

Saul disobeyed the Lord and as a result Samuel told him that God was not pleased and he was replaced as the King over Israel and rejected by the Lord. None of us wants to be outside of the will of God; we don't want to know how it feels to be rejected by Him either. Instead our prayer should be Psalm 51:11 "Do not cast me from your presence or take your Holy Spirit from me." Just like my son doesn't want me to be upset with him we should not want the Lord upset with us. We tend to make obedience so hard because it is so easy to do wrong. However, obedience is a choice we can't afford to overlook. The Bible says that keeping God's commands is what counts so that should always be your goal. Joshua 24:15 says it best:

"Choose for yourselves this day whom you will serve, but as for me and my house we will serve the Lord."

God Bless

Nothing is Impossible

> "For with God nothing is ever impossible and no word from God shall be without power or impossible of fulfillment."
> **- Luke 1:37**

When I look back over this year, I recall a lot of amazing things that happened in my life and in the world. Of course there were a lot of ups and downs. However when you think about what you have been through, you should agree that the good outweighed the bad. Really think back on how many times this year your back was against the wall and you knew that there was no way out. How did you make it through?

In this text we have the angel Gabriel talking to Mary about her blessing of being pregnant with our savior Jesus Christ. We also recognize that even though they thought Elizabeth was barren, she would give birth as well. It's interesting that both situations really appeared to the human eye as impossible, but just like the angel said, with God nothing is impossible. One thing that I have to highlight here is that one of the things that made these situations possible was that these women believed the word that was given them and they built faith and trust in God with what they were told. Even though it was hard, they chose to trust Him at His word. As a result of their belief and trust in God, they both gave birth to what they trusted God for and their lives were never the same.

How many times this year has God told you something that you found hard to believe? How many times this year has God shown up and shown out in your life and you received because you believed? The word here is encouraging us to let us know that even though we may face odds that seem insurmountable, if we just trust God and believe, He can make the seemingly impossible occur. Not your problems, your pain, your past nor your future, is impossible for God. There is nobody greater than God and no one who can handle what you may be facing like He can.

As we close this year out reflect on all God has brought you through this year and allow your faith to be strengthened as you see how God has really worked in your life. Prepare your mind to trust God more and to really walk by faith and not by sight next year. All the victories that you have had this year are a true testament that God is active and still working miracles in your life. You are not exempt from the blessings of God unless you choose to be by not trusting, believing, or following God. I had the opportunity to be used by God to be a major blessing to a lot of people this year. As a result of my surrendering to His will, not only did their seemingly impossible situations disappear, I saw God doing what He does best, making believers out of them and me.

What are you facing this year that may carry over to next year that seems impossible? What obstacle do you see coming next year that you are trying to brace yourself for? We can't afford to live our lives like the Israelites; they saw first-hand what God can do and still had too many moments of doubt. I challenge you as well as myself to trust God at His word more and believe that He can and will make the impossible possible in your life. I have seen what He can do and I am excited about seeing God helping me beat the odds and overcoming the challenges that I know I will face. What about you? Hasn't He done great things in your life that you thought weren't possible? He has plans for us all and they are not to harm us. They will make our future prosperous. I trust God and His word. Will you? Your future depends on it.

God Bless

No Separation

> "Who shall separate us from the love of Christ? Shall trouble or hardship or persecution or famine or nakedness or danger or sword? No, in all these things we are more than conquerors through him who loved us."- **Romans 8:35, 37**

While it is very clear that God Loves us so much that nothing will separate us from His love, what about the rest of this verse? Often, through counseling or encouraging others, I find that some people tend to give up or get upset with God when they are going through trials.

I have heard many times, people saying that they have prayed and it seems as if God is just not answering or listening. Or maybe they have trusted God for something not to happen in their lives and it happened anyway. So they blame God for not protecting them.

What many people fail to realize is that God is a part of everything that happens in our lives. Though some things are really self-inflicted, God is still faithful to us through our situations. We have all heard or read the word that says that we must endure hardship as good soldiers for the Lord. We are even familiar with the word that says that no weapon that forms against us will prosper. We will go through hardships and endure tough situations, but it is all to the glory of God. He has never disconnected from us, especially through the challenging times. We are always protected through His love for us.

My oldest son sometimes gets frustrated when he can't remember how to tie his shoe or he is having a hard time playing a game. My first instinct as a father is to jump right in to help him and show him how to do it again. However, I have come to realize that sometimes I have to sit back and let him figure it out. Since we have already equipped him with the knowledge to be successful, he now has to recall that information and believe enough in himself to accomplish the task. So no matter how much he pouts and stomps his feet, I sit and watch and just say to him, "Take your time. You know what to do because you have done it before."

I believe that God, our heavenly father, does the same with us. Here in the text He says that we are conquerors through him who loved us; in other words we are already more than victorious over comers because He as already equipped us to complete the task at hand. We have to believe that we have what it takes to be victorious. He is always right there with us, watching and encouraging us through it all. We may come out of a situation wounded and that is because of the grace of God. The outcome to any of our situations could be far worse.

So, know today that whatever you face, God is right there with you every step of the way. He is not going to take His hand off of you; instead He is going to encourage you to press through it, so you can see that you are more than victorious through Him. Nothing will ever stop Him from loving you.

God Bless

No room for Complacency

"For the waywardness of the simple will kill them, and the complacency of fools will destroy them" **Proverbs 1:32**

It is already clear that we live in a microwave thinking society where many people want what they want quickly. The media can desensitize us, if we let it, to the point where many people don't fear God anymore. So many of our youth and young adults alike believe that God exists; however He doesn't have any real power (at least not in their lives). So what do they do? They depend on themselves for strength and perseverance. Or they just sit and wait it out, claiming that it was bound to pass sooner or later. All the while they are just allowing a wedge to come between them and the only one who saves.

Here when the Bible mentions "waywardness" it is talking about disobedience. You know when you knowingly go against the grain. I can tell my boys to stop running through the house and five minutes later they are right back at it again. After the third time, three strikes you're out! I become the disciplinarian. After that my tolerance level has decreased so I react sooner, just so that they can understand how serious I am. Don't be fooled! I learned that from somewhere and it wasn't my earthly father, my heavenly father showed me that. God hates disobedience and He has His own way of dealing with it. The text says that your disobedience will kill you and your being foolish enough to think that things are just supposed to go your way will destroy you.

There are some people who have allowed themselves to believe that they are so good at being them that everybody and everything is supposed to jump when they say, "jump." The Bible will forever proclaim that, "For the foolishness of God is wiser than man's wisdom, and the weakness of God is stronger than man's strength." So on God's worst day, if He ever had one, He is still wiser than all of us together on our best day. Moses found out the hard way.

God told Moses (when the Israelites were in the desert complaining about water) to speak to the rock before the people and that it would pour out water for the community and their livestock in the book of Numbers. Instead, Moses raised his hands and not once, but twice and struck the rock and it poured out water. Even in your disobedience, God will still get His Glory. So why not do the right thing and possibly be exalted? God told Moses and his brother Aaron that because of their disobedience they would not be able to take His people into the land that He promised them. They saw it but they never got to it, all because of disobedience. So death was their fate. I'm not saying that God will take us out immediately, but He can if He chooses to. I am not willing to take that chance by trying Him on that one.

I know and understand that nothing goes my way; His way prevails. If what I wanted happens, it had nothing to do with who I am but everything to do with how I am lined up with Him. We can't afford to be complacent and just expect things to happen how we want them too. We have to operate in the power of God, doing our parts. However, staying out of God's way, at the same time is vital. He knows what's best for us and has too much planned for us to be disobedient. Choose to follow the Lord's command; don't go against it, because whoever is against God is an enemy of God. The bible said that keeping God's commands is what counts and I don't want to be overlooked.

God Bless

My Thoughts are not Your Thoughts

"For my thoughts are not your thoughts, neither are your ways my ways," declares the LORD. "As the heavens are higher than the earth, so are my ways higher than your ways and my thoughts than your thoughts."- **Isaiah 55:8-9**

Over the years I can say that I have matured a lot on every level of my life by the grace of God. My maturity process was still something that I had to be willing to undergo. It didn't start until I decided that I was ready to make a change. I do remember though back in the day how I used to be.

If someone said something that I didn't like, it wouldn't take long for him or her to get some kind of crazy reaction or response. I can remember in college a friend of mine (who is like a brother to me) was upset with me. We were in the same place and he chose to express himself and we exchanged words. The words "hit me, then" came out of his mouth and before I knew it, I had honored his request. I am not proud of it at all; however I can see now how far I have come. The point in this little unknown fact about me is that a lot of times we respond without thinking. There may be times that we think about it and still respond in the wrong manner.

One of the things that have helped me to mature and to think before acting is God's patience. What if God thought like we did and responded impulsively like we sometimes do? Just think about the latest thing that you did that you are not so proud of. Think about if God would have responded to you the way you have responded to someone else. How would that picture look? Almost scary, right?

It is a major blessing that this text is true and I, for one, am excited that God's thoughts are not our thoughts. It brings me great joy to know that as high as the heavens are from us that God's ways and thoughts are that much higher. The ways that the Lord deals with us on certain situations may be difficult sometimes to handle, however just know that it could always be worse. Whenever God deals with us, just know that we are getting the lighter sentence, if you will. It is just as if the police pull you over and you get a warning instead of a ticket. Our normal response is to thank the officer and we do our best to prevent another similar incident, knowing that the next time could be worse.

Just know that the Lord loves us so much that He gives us warnings, because we really couldn't handle getting the ticket and going before the judge for the real verdict. Sometimes the jury, just to get our attention and to give us a chance to get ourselves together, may try us. It feels good to know that, to this date, God's verdict has always been "not guilty"; even though we know that where there was smoke there was a fire; so we did do something. As a result, we are left to deal with the consequences of our actions and truthfully that is still better than what it could be. God has a lot invested in us and everyday we should do all we can to grow in our thinking and our ways, considering the sacrifice He made for us. My prayer is that everyday we ask the Lord to help us think how He thinks and respond the way that He would respond. We are not perfect but being human should not be an excuse. Jesus was the perfect example for us; now all we have to do is follow that perfect model.

God Bless

My Shepherd

"The LORD is my shepherd; I shall not be in want. He makes me lie down in green pastures, he leads me beside quiet waters, he restores my soul. He guides me in paths of righteousness for his name's sake."- **Psalm 23:1-3**

This is a well-known passage of scripture, written by David during the time that Saul was trying to kill him in the book of Samuel. We are probably more familiar with the encouraging text from either church or funerals. David was very specific with this psalm, which is very meaningful.

David, having been a shepherd himself, knows what it takes to tend to his flock. He acknowledges that the Lord is his shepherd so; there is not a need (he has or will have) that God won't fulfill. Let us understand a shepherd's role really quickly. A shepherd supplies every need of his flock and protects them at all costs. The shepherd uses his rod to fight off predators, and his staff to guide the sheep. He corrects them and rescues them if they fall into a hole while grazing. Sheep have no defense mechanism against the enemy, so the shepherd has to protect them. In my research, I found that vipers sometimes hid in holes in the ground where the sheep grazed and would pop their head up and bite the sheep on their noses. So the shepherd would walk the land first and pour olive oil on the entrances of the holes as well as cover the sheep's heads and noses with oil to prevent the snakes from biting them. The oil on the holes would cause the snakes bodies to be too slippery, helping with the protection of the sheep. The shepherd is also known as a servant leader because he would always take care of the needs of his flock, even if it meant getting dirty while providing leadership and guidance.

We are in the same position as the sheep because there is no way for us to defeat the vipers in our lives without being anointed and protected by our shepherd. He provides every one of our needs because we can't provide for ourselves. There is nothing that we can do without God; however, with Him ALL THINGS are possible.

David goes on to say how God provides an abundance of what we need, which is represented by the green pastures. This is important because as sheep graze, after a while they have covered the land so more land has to be sought in order to continue to graze. God provides this for us in abundance and He gives us peace and living water; the still, quiet waters represent that. No matter what we have done in our lives, if we just submit to God and repent, He is faithful and just to forgive and restore us.

Just like David, we have to be willing to follow the Lord, our shepherd. Our willingness will allow God to lead and guide us in the path of righteousness daily.

We can't go wrong following God; He has the road map to our lives and knows every twist and turn and the way out of it to get to our set destination. Just know that God has already walked the land and poured the olive oil in the snake holes. He anoints us daily, so we have nothing to fear. I, like David, am willingly and proud to say that the Lord is my shepherd as well, and I shall not be in want.

God Bless

Morning Coffee

My Refuge

"Whom have I in heaven but you? And earth has nothing
I desire besides you. My flesh and my heart may fail, but
God is the strength of my heart and my portion forever."
- **Psalm 73:25-26**

Since we are all human, we of course have moments when our flesh raises up, causing us to act out of character. The Psalmist here says that they have been senseless and ignorant. Israel has been a brute beast before God. This is their way of acknowledging that they are not perfect and they know that God can see everything. However, in verse 23, they come back and say that no matter what, they know that they are with God and that He holds them by their right hands.

This signifies what's called the right hand of fellowship, which is simply an act of acceptance. It is normally seen when a person receives salvation and decides to join a church; then upon approval they would shake the right hand of all of the members of the church. The awesome part here is that the text says that God is holding their right hands. So here, it is acceptance from God.

When we "fall off" in life, some people may be there to support us and some may not. Often times we may receive support from others, even if we don't deserve it. The beauty of it is that God is going to be there for us no matter what. This is why the psalmist says that they have no one in Heaven but God and really, the true relationship that they desire is with God. The reason is that even when our flesh and our hearts fail, (and there will be a time or two when that will happen), God is still right there. It is He who provides strength for us to make it through whatever we are going through. It is He who will restore us if we are willing to do what it takes, in the way that it needs to be done. God will lie out the way it has to be done and provide everything that we need to be restored. Our job is not to deviate from God's plan or we will find ourselves out of His will again. Stay close to God and He will be your refuge.

God Bless

My Help

"I lift up my eyes to the hills— where does my help come from? My help comes from the LORD, the Maker of heaven and earth."- **Psalm 121:1-2**

What a way to end a week? We are all dealing with something that may be a little discouraging or challenging to us. For some reason we tend to exert all of our energy trying to figure it out or make things happen. That too sometimes ends up being very frustrating.

When going through any tough situation, we are often encouraged when we know that we have some support, someone there to help us through. I know it presents a sense of hope for me. Here the text is reminding us that all the help we really need comes from God. Consider His credentials: He is the maker of heaven and Earth, He healed the sick, gave sight to the blind, He raised Lazarus from the dead. This shows that God is fully capable and qualified to help us out.

Isn't it funny how sometimes you have people who want to help; however they really aren't capable to help handle your situation? Today we know that we can take whatever it is to God and He is fully qualified to handle it.

God Bless

Metamorphosis

> "Consider it pure joy, my brothers, whenever you face trials of many kinds, because you know that the testing of your faith develops perseverance."- **James 1:2-3**

In the face of difficult times we normally don't find much joy in the situation. Most of the time, it is virtually impossible to find anything to be happy about either. Often, depending on how bad the situation is; many may find themselves borderline depressed and trying to figure out a way to disappear from it all.

Here James is clear in saying that we should have joy, even when going through, because it is a part of the process to mature us. It is a refining process that tests our ability to believe and fight through what we are dealing with, believing that the result will be well worth the struggle.

I think about the process that a butterfly goes through to become a full adult. They have four different stages as they go through their metamorphosis. This is a Greek word that means transformation. Those phases to reach adulthood are not easy for them at all. However, if they endure, they go from being viewed as insects to beautiful butterflies.

We too go through our own metamorphoses where God is working on maturing us so that we won't lack anything. I have always said to others that progress without struggle is no progress at all. It is inevitable that we all will endure some tough times. Our outlooks should be that its just God's way of taking out of us what we no longer need and putting in us what will be needed for the next stage in our lives. God's vision for us is, in essence, to get to that stage of being beautiful butterflies with much longer lifelines.

Embrace your struggle and know that God is up to something. So with the Lord in control of what you are dealing with, you should be able to consider it pure joy that you are facing trials of many kinds.

God Bless

Membership Intake

"The man without the Spirit does not accept the things that come from the Spirit of God, for they are foolishness to him, and he cannot understand them, because they are spiritually discerned."- **1 Corinthians 2:14**

In college, I had the pleasure of starting an organization as well as joining one. I am one of the Founders for Rho Chi Psi Recruitment and Retention Organization and I am a brother of Alpha Phi Alpha Fraternity Inc. All Greek-lettered organizations (they really aren't Greek, but that's another story) are distinctively different, but one in the same. They are all about brotherhood or sisterhood, working together to make an impact on the community and the world. Most people who aren't in an organization like ours don't understand why we do some of the things we do, especially during our intake process. They hear some of the stories and automatically say that it is foolishness. Some of it is. However, to really understand the function and purpose of the organizations, one really has to be a member.

Here Paul is talking about the differences between those who are in Christ and those who are not. Those who are in Christ can understand those who are not because we were all in their shoes before we got saved. However, those who have never tasted to see that the Lord is good wouldn't be able to understand His sufficient grace and everlasting mercy. They don't understand why we raise our hands or our voices unto the Lord out of praise and worship for all He has done for us. His or her biggest question is how we can love, trust, and fear, someone that we can't see. Just like the text says, that is foolishness to them. According to 1 Corinthians 1:25 "For the foolishness of God is wiser than man's wisdom, and the weakness of God is stronger than man's strength." Until they choose to crossover, they will have a hard time being able to discern anything on a spiritual level. To discern means to detect with senses other than vision and it is only something that you can truly understand by being in Christ.

Before I became a part of my organizations I would hear people saying that membership has it privileges. Now being a part I can understand what they meant. My membership has opened some doors that otherwise would have been closed. It doesn't make it right. Favor is fair, but just not for everybody all the time. Besides there is an honor system (that this nation is built upon) that justifies decision-makers giving others an edge. However, I know a body that "everyone" ought to want to be apart of; there is no application to fill out, nor are fees required. All that is required is your word, your heart, and your mind. This body is the body of Christ and your life depends on your having membership. Though many won't understand it until they join, one of the greatest benefits it offers is eternal security. I don't know anyone else who can put that on the table and mean it, so I guess membership really does have it privileges. Just like we hold interest meetings to increase our membership in our organizations, being a part of the body of Christ should inspire us to do the same. The best part about being in Christ is that we can have membership intake all day everyday, with no campus of student organizations on our back investigating our every move. For those of us who are pros at it, let us do our parts to bring others into the same understanding. Our founding father wants to welcome them personally.

God Bless

Membership has its privileges

> "I saw the Holy City, the new Jerusalem, coming down out of heaven from God, prepared as a bride beautifully dressed for her husband. And I heard a loud voice from the throne saying, "Now the dwelling of God is with men, and he will live with them. They will be his people, and God himself will be with them and be their God. He will wipe every tear from their eyes. There will be no more death or mourning or crying or pain, for the old order of things has passed away."
> **- Revelation 21: 2-4**

Sometimes when I pray, I ask the Lord when the enemy will realize that I am not giving in and that he just needs to leave me alone? This is not to say that when the enemy comes against me that getting through the struggle is a piece of cake, because it's not. I am stronger than I used to be so I hang my hope and faith on the word of God, knowing that I already have victory. Knowing that allows me to hold on through the storm to see the Lord's promise revealed in my life. You may not have worded your question quite the way I did; yours could have sounded like, "When will this end?" or "Lord, is it over yet?"

Today we read that John is saying that he has seen the Holy City, the great promise from God. It paints the picture that one day those who are in Christ will be with God in the New Jerusalem. It goes on to say that God will wipe away every tear from our eyes, meaning that there will be no more reason to cry. It sounds like a place of endless peace and joy. The picture here is that life, as we know it will have passed away and we will essentially live forever with God. If you continue to read, the Bible says that those who are with God will overcome and inherit all things. However, those who don't believe and are wicked in their ways will suffer in the lake of fire. The Bible couldn't phrase it any plainer.

I recall getting recruited to be a part of an organization in college; some of the members told me that membership has it privileges. While that may have been true I chose not to be apart of their organization. However, when the Lord put it on my heart to be a part of His Kingdom Agenda and He said that I could be a joint heir to the throne, without question I was and will always be sold out for Christ. The scripture today paints a very clear picture on that phrase; "Membership has its privileges" and quite honestly being in Christ, I love my odds.

Share this opportunity with everyone and help him or her to understand the benefit of being in Christ. If for whatever reason, you haven't completely made up your mind, considering we don't know the day or hour when Jesus will return, you may want to renew your membership today.

God Bless

Love the Law

"Great peace have they who love your law, and nothing can make them stumble."- **Psalm 119:165**

There is something about recognizing whose you are and your purpose for life. Just as we stated before, there are conditions to God's word. Here He is saying that He will keep you from stumbling and bless you with great peace if you just love His law. Many of you, I pray, have experienced this peace as though something rises up against you. God kept you from stumbling.

It is only when we deviate from God's plan and start trying to accommodate people or please others that we find ourselves in distress. Our lives should not be consumed by a desire to please or impress people. They can't keep a promise like God can. Who else do you know who can say something and really mean it, every time?

Tye Tribbett says," Who else but God?" God is the only one who can promise you peace and mean it, who can say that no matter the circumstance NOTHING can make you stumble.
The Bible is clear in saying, "Keeping God's command is what counts." 1Corinthians 7:19b
Love GOD and His people. However, Love HIS law and keep His command and see how the Lord blesses you.
God Bless

Love for Enemies

> "You have heard that it was said, 'Love your neighbor and hate your enemy.' But I tell you: Love your enemies and pray for those who persecute you, that you may be sons of your Father in heaven. He causes his sun to rise on the evil and the good, and sends rain on the righteous and the unrighteous."
> **- Matthew 5:43-45**

One of the things that bother me most is when someone meets me and (for whatever reason) dislikes me. My initial thought is that "you don't even know me to say that you don't like me." That quite naturally makes me not want to deal with that person at all. I don't want to talk with them, so I avoid them at all costs.

However, the Jesus in me won't let that happen. Even though this may be true for a lot of us, we still have to be willing to be used by God to turn the other cheek. The truth is that we are not really strong enough to do that on our own we really need the Lord to overlook someone's dislike for us and still want to do for them. Persecution is the acid test of spiritual prosperity according to Wil Pounds and what he says is true.

When the Bible tells us that we must deny ourselves and take up our cross to follow Jesus, is the same thing that we must do in this situation. If someone hates on you it is going to take your self-denial to get past that and love on him or her anyway. I say that because self is going to want to do something else besides showing love. The Bible is very clear when it says that we should love others better than ourselves.

I have found that when I apply our text for today, I really do come out stronger spiritually. I have developed a friend in the process. Even if that doesn't happen, just the fact that Jesus died for us even while we were yet still sinners is enough for me. What if the Lord treated us according to the way we treat and respect Him? Where would you be right now? Would your life be the same? We don't have a heaven or a hell to put anybody in so it is not our job to get in God's business. Whoever it is mistreating you, will have to deal with your Daddy. After all, He made them so He knows everything about them. Who can handle them better than God? Nobody! Pray for those who disrespect and talk down to you and let the Lord handle your lightweight, you have bigger fish to fry.

God Bless

Let Peace Rule

"Let the peace of Christ rule in your hearts, since as members
of one body you were called to peace. And be thankful."
- Colossians 3:15

All Christians are called to a certain lifestyle and to live in peace is a major part of it. This verse starts by saying to let the peace of Christ rule in your hearts and as we know, out of the heart flows the issues of life. Here, peace means not having division, but to join or bind that which has been separated. The peace of God gives us that sense of wholeness and we should allow it to be the decider of all things within our hearts.

The Bible is very clear that if we allow the peace of God to rule in our hearts we won't have to worry about anything. It is also very clear that there is a level of God's peace through Jesus Christ that we won't understand. It gives you the ability to stay calm and composed even in the midst of a storm when you normally would lose it. God's peace ruling in our hearts in the text is important because it is reminding us that we are a part of the body of Christ and have been called to live peacefully. If we allow His peace to rule in our lives, we will appreciate each other more. It will allow us all to live in harmony.

Allowing His peace to rule would hopefully stop us from having a short fuse with others and enable us to be more understanding. Some people these days are so quick to lose their tempers and just let others have it, but if peace was in control, we would be more open to compromise. I perform a spoken word piece entitled "Rest in Peace", a collage of scripture that uniquely expresses the peace that I have in Christ. Most people think about death when they hear "rest in peace" but I am talking about life in Christ and in His peace. It starts off like this:

"I rest in peace because the real peace is in me.
Before I had peace, my peace was in a piece,
This had me frustrated and uptight, sometimes staying up all night.
Though there was no danger in sight, Man! I have to get my life right.
I tried with all my might to get the madness to cease
Accepted Christ now I have real peace"

We have to make sure that no matter what we diligently seek God's peace and allow it to rule in our hearts. Even though sometimes we can't comprehend it we can still depend on it to bring us through the ups and the downs. Most importantly, we have been called to live in peace. So let us accept what is for us and be thankful.

God Bless

Joy

> "As soon as the sound of your greeting reached my ears, the baby in my womb leaped for joy." -**Luke 1:44**

When I was younger there were certain times of the year when I would have no problems getting excited by what I anticipated would come to pass. Anytime we would get close to my birthday and Christmas, without seeing anything, my body was filled with joy knowing that something great was about to happen and that I would receive the gifts that I really wanted. It is amazing now watching my boys get excited about what they think is coming; they have a natural instinct to feel something on the horizon.

When you think about it, though, who doesn't get excited when expecting to receive a special gift? While they were still in the womb, John the Baptist got excited and leaped for joy when Mary came into Elizabeth's presence, pregnant with Jesus Christ. It is interesting for the Bible to emphasize this point and paint such a picture of joy and being filled with the Holy Spirit. Even though he was in the womb, John knew that his Savior was present. The Bible says that John the Baptist would be filled with the Holy Spirit, even in the womb. The joy and excitement in this text helps us to see that the spirit is the source of this joy.

For those who see their need for Christ and desire to live a righteous lifestyle He fills and abundantly blesses them so why not get excited. Everyday that you wake up to, the thought of another day should bring this excitement because it is a reminder that Christ died so that you can live. The Christmas holidays should not be the only time we get excited about the birth of Christ because those who are in Christ receive a fresh anointing everyday. This holiday season is a time that we relive the moment that John the Baptist had in his mother's womb, getting excited about the good news of the coming of the Savior of the world. When you break the word down, you have Christ and mass. Mass, when used as an adjective relates to a multitude of people assembled. So Christmas is a time for us to assemble to honor Christ.

When celebrating Christmas this year with your family and friends, don't forget the baby because he is the real reason for the season. There has never been and will never be a greater gift than Jesus Christ.

God Bless

Jesus Wept

"Jesus wept." **John 11:35**

While watching the movie "Barber Shop 2", I saw a scene where Calvin, the main character, played by Ice Cube, was in court fighting to save his shop and to prevent a governmental takeover of the neighborhood. During the scene Calvin had the opportunity to speak. One of the most memorable quotes from the movie was when he said, "Do you know why Jesus wept? Because He cared."

It is interesting this comedy would actually have a Jesus moment, but I'm sure that everyone who saw the movie had that moment. I actually never thought about why Jesus wept until it was brought to my attention in that movie. The other day my Uncle Steve asked about this same topic after having a discussion in his Bible study. Here is what the Lord shared with me.

The awesome part about this particular text is that Jesus Christ gives us a quick glimpse of His human side. He also shows us a tender and compassionate savior. The interesting part is that He already knew what had happened to Lazarus and as a matter of fact, He didn't hurry on purpose. When Jesus did arrive on the scene Mary was so upset that she didn't even want to go out and meet with Him. Martha, on the other hand, had to express her feelings. The emotions shown during this biblical story shows us a few things.

The Bible says in Romans to rejoice with those who rejoice and weep with those who weep, so it is right and natural for a Christian to sympathize with others in their afflictions. Lazarus was Jesus' friend and sorrow at the death of a friend is not improper. Jesus Christ shows us that the expression of nature and religion does not forbid or condemn weeping and sympathizing with others. "All that religion does in the case is to temper and chasten our grief; to teach us to mourn with submission to God; to weep without complaining, and to seek to banish tears, not by hardening the heart or forgetting the friend, but by bringing the soul, made tender by grief, to receive the sweet influences of religion, and to find calmness and peace in the God of all consolation", as stated by Barnes.

Ultimately, Jesus Christ shows us here how much he really cares for the body of Christ. This wasn't just about Lazarus; instead it was a message to all of us that Jesus Christ understands our afflictions as well as our triumphs. It destroys the myth if Jesus Christ was really born into the world and if He was really fully man and fully God. Jesus Christ loves us all dearly and He didn't just die on the cross because He had to He did it because He wanted to. So just know that when you are going through He understands and He really cares that is why it says in His word for us to cast all of our cares on Him because He cares.

God Bless

Jesus on Board

"That God was reconciling the world to himself in Christ, not counting men's sins against them. And he has committed to us the message of reconciliation. We are therefore Christ's ambassadors, as though God were making his appeal through us. We implore you on Christ's behalf: Be reconciled to God."- **2 Corinthians 5:19-20**

Simple thought today.

I used to look at my JOB as Just Over Broke because I worked hard for what seemed like not enough pay. That was until I realized that I was putting all of my hope in my job and the people in position to change that. Now I look at JOB as Jesus On Board because I realize that all of my hope is in Him and He ultimately is the one who is in position to change anything. People ask me what do you do for a living and I tell them save souls because that is my job and I work for the Lord. However, my career for now is the place of business where I work. My mind is now conditioned to understand that I ultimately work for the Lord and have to respect those who are in authority over me at work. The level of commitment that we often find ourselves having with our place of work and those who are in authority should greatly increase when it comes to God. He unclothed and wrapped Himself in the flesh to save and redeem us back to a right relationship with Him. We owe God our all.

God Bless

It's not About me

> "Yet what we suffer now is nothing compared to the glory he will reveal to us later." **Romans 8:18**

Okay. Let's be real with each other today. Not a day or week passes during which the thought "What about me?" doesn't come up when we ponder what we've endured and done for others. The truth of the matter is at some point we all want to be appreciated or praised for helping someone or making it through storms. When we think about suffering or struggling, most tend to picture the hardest of times like eviction, unpaid bills, or sudden unemployment. Actually there is more to it because sometimes it's a struggle just to get up, make yourself go to work, or say the right thing in front of your children (knowing that they will copy your every move). Either way when we stand firm through whatever we struggle with be it a light struggle or a hard one, is it really about us? Do we really deserve to be praised because we made a choice to stay focused and not take the easy road? We don't deserve to be praised because we were made to overcome the struggle. However, others appreciate us for being an example.

What is most important is that God is pleased with us when we stay strong. We position ourselves to receive favor from God and be exposed to the full Glory of God. This life is not about us but it is all about the Glory of God being revealed in and through us. The Glory of God, as stated in Max Lucado's book, "It's Not About Me" is God's strength, ability, and power. In everything that we go through God wants to reveal His strength in us. The scripture says that when we are weak His strength is made perfect in us. A perfect example of this point how we admit not knowing "how we made it through the trials." We can't "make it" through trials alone. The truth is you did by the grace of God strengthening you.

God wants to reveal His ability through us. The Bible says in Matthew 19:26, "With man this is impossible, but with God all things are possible." Ability is the "quality or state of being able" and when you think about just half of what you have had to deal with, you weren't able to pull yourself out. There was no one around who had the ability to pull you through but God.

He also wants to reveal His power in us. Power is "the capacity to do, act or produce." So God's power is a surge of energy so strong that it forces action and produces results. When you feel that you are on your last leg only God can supply the power you need to make it. In the face of adversity, there is something inside of you that is inexplicably strong; it generates the energy you need to push through the opposition and run to the finish line.

God's glory is revealed to us when we sit back and reflect on these moments of unexplained triumphs. His glory is revealed through us when others see us coming out victoriously. We are examples for others and our testimony causes us to become influential and give others the will to endure when they are going through. So God's glory is transferred through us when we allow the Lord to use us. When we realize that God allows difficult situations to occur so that His glory can be revealed, it becomes easier for us to endure the struggle. Changing our minds will change our lives because we will have difficult moments regardless. Knowing that it is for the glory of God makes it all worthwhile. So our struggles are not about us but about God and His glory. Our ability to be able to weather the storm doesn't go unrecognized; it is just overshadowed by the glory of God, as it should be.

God Bless

It's not about you

> "Humble yourselves before the Lord, and he will lift you up."- **James 4:10**

James is speaking to the twelve tribes that are scattered all over the nation and is giving them detailed instructions. This particular section in chapter 4 is about submitting yourselves to God.

So many people get caught up in the gifts that they have been blessed with. Many times people really work on their gifts get really great at them, and start to think that it is all about them: They conveniently forget that it was the Lord all along who blessed and empowered them. I have seen and heard so many people boast about what they can do and how great they are at what they do that it gets irritating after a while. The interesting part is the minute that they are not doing well with that gift; it is all of a sudden God's fault. It is during trials that they suddenly recognize that God blessed them in the first place.

The Bible also says in Matthew 23:12

> "For whoever exalts himself will be humbled, and whoever humbles himself will be exalted." I want you to know this just in case people act like they don't know that God is true to His word. Whatever your gift is, that has made room for you by the Grace of God and the Power of the Holy Spirit, can be the very thing that breaks you down and forces you to humble yourself. One of my young fraternity brothers told me last week (as it pertains to one of my gifts): if I don't use it I will lose it. So I am not saying not to use your gift; however I am saying, be careful not to lift yourself up as if you did it all by yourself.

I don't delight in seeing people being forced to humble themselves by the Lord. Remember that gifts are for God's glory, not ours. After all He is the only one who is really able to lift us up, so we shouldn't let others blow our heads up until we get out of control. Instead, we should thank those who appreciate our gifts before reminding them that God deserves the credit. He made us great. Let's humble ourselves and thank God, every time someone recognizes (or acknowledges) God's excellence in us.

God Bless

It's more than good looks

"Charm is deceptive, and beauty is fleeting; but a woman who fears the LORD is to be praised."- **Proverbs 31:30**

I once dated a young lady in college who was a beautiful girl. However with time a lot of truth began to unfold. It is not that her looks were superficial, however my expectations of the relationship were; they were based on how she looked. At the time I was beginning my journey of getting closer with the Lord so He began to reveal some things to me. I was would ask her to sit and read the bible with me and it would never happen. She never went to church with me and when I would visit her and her family, I realized that she didn't go to church at home either. So I realized that we were going in two directions with our lives. As a result, many other truths revealed themselves, which led me to leave this young lady alone.

Brothers, there is more to being with a woman than just outer beauty alone. Once again, the Bible is right when saying that charm is deceptive and beauty is fleeting. This young lady wasn't a bad person; she just wasn't for me. Trying to stay with her because of her beauty and charm would have been like getting a triangle block to fit in a circle; it just wouldn't work. When choosing the person you want to be with, you have to go deeper than the surface.

When I met my wife, I thought, "Man she is so beautiful." I called her Pocahontas. However, I was more spiritually mature so it was going to take more than her breath-taking looks to win me over. We took time to talk and get to know each other and with that I discovered her love for the Lord. So again, a woman who fears the Lord truly is to be praised and I thank God that He knows what is best for me.

This suggests to my sisters that the time spent getting that right look, hairstyle, scent and smile should be invested on inner beauty and spiritual substance. The man that you are looking for really needs to see the Jesus in you. In fact, your heart should be so close to God that this man has to seek Him to find you. The truth of the matter is that if you really love the Lord, it will make it that much easier to love you and the man that God sends to you.

Let our focus be to form a closer walk with the Lord, and to better prepare us for the mate God has for us. Let's look deeper than what is on the surface and make sure that there is something for them to fall in love with the Jesus in you.

God Bless

Is it really Love?

> "If anyone says, "I love God," yet hates his brother, he is a liar. For anyone who does not love his brother, whom he has seen, cannot love God, whom he has not seen. And he has given us this command: Whoever loves God must also love his brother."- **1 John 4:20-21**

It is interesting how so many people with so much love in their hearts can quickly turn that love to hate. Given the right situation, if rubbed the wrong way, many people would be willing to cut folks off, even if they have been friends for a long time. Family members aren't even exempt from alienation. It amazes me how we could be good or even casual friends with someone and, yet you cringe just from hearing their names. It's ironic that we claim to love God and desire to be more Christ-like.

We should allow nobody to walk all over us and treat us any kind of way. At the same time, if we are striving to be more like Christ we must decide whether to hold grudges or to show compassion. Think about it, there are several things that we all have done that I'm sure didn't sit well at all with God. Yet He still loves us unconditionally and Christ died anyway just to prove it.

Granted, there are some people who don't care if they are forgiven. Let the situation go. That should not stop you from doing it. You still have to free yourself up in that situation. Any disagreement you have with anybody can be worked out if you want it to. We have all been through a time in our lives; when we felt disappointed by God yet, we still love Him though. It didn't take long for us to restore ourselves back to a right relationship with God.

What is stopping you from doing that with your brother or sister, husband, wife, friend, or whomever? I am with John. How can you say that you love God (whom you can't physically see), yet sometimes can't stand brothers or sisters whom we see all the time?

Right now my church has started what's called "The Love Challenge", which is challenging us to show love and compassion to others consistently, even in situations when we would normally cut people off. It is clear in this text that God has stated that it is impossible to say that you love Him and not love others. Today you can pray and ask God to help you LOVE like Christ loves.

God Bless

Imitators

> "Be imitators of God, therefore, as dearly loved children and live a life of love, just as Christ loved us and gave himself up for us as a fragrant offering and sacrifice to God."
> **- Ephesians 5:1-2**

As a father, I am watched very closely by my boys, who catch everything that I do. So I understand that everything that I do is like tutorial for them. I am teaching them, even when I don't mean to be in teaching mode. Its funny how our younger son does everything his older brother does. Just last night I shared with our oldest to be careful what he teaches his little brother because he does everything the oldest does.

Children are great imitators and they are so open and unrestricted they will do exactly what they see without missing a step and sometime they may add a little bit to it. So in essence a parental figure has to be careful of their daily activity because they never know who is watching and what they are teaching them.

God gave us the perfect example to follow in Jesus Christ and here Paul starts off telling us to be imitators of God. They only way to imitate God is the follow the leader who is Jesus Christ. Now trying to make this too long, however the only way for us to get this text this morning is to go back and read Ch. 4 One thing stated in ch.4 is that we were taught to," put off our old self, which is being corrupted by its deceitful desires; to be made new in the attitude of your minds; and to put on the new self, created to be like God in true righteousness and holiness."

In order to be imitators of God through Christ we have to be willing to let some thing go and that starts with an attitude adjustment. Once you make the decision in your mind to be better it lines up with what is already in your heart and that allows change to take place. It is just as simple as my children imitating everything I do. They see it and they decide to do exactly what they see and eventually it becomes a part of who they are.

Our one year old understands that when someone does something for you, he should say Thank You and when the food is ready the first thing he does is stop what he is doing, put his hands together and he says "God".

It is a choice and that choice grows into a lifestyle. I encourage you to read Ephesians ch.4 and you can make your own decision to Imitate God.

God Bless

If My People

> "If my people, who are called by my name, will humble themselves and pray and seek my face and turn from their wicked ways, then will I hear from heaven and will forgive their sin and will heal their land."- **2 Chronicles 7:14**

"If" is a conjunction that presents a condition for us to follow up with specific actions. The main condition here is that this message is for God's people and the action is to put up or shut up. The first half of the first verse requires you to recognize who you are and whose you are. It also requires that you be confident in your identity and willing to make, for some, a major sacrifice for the good of the majority.

Here the Lord is giving Solomon a charge after the temple was completed. All of the Israelites recognized the presence of God because the Bible says that they knelt on the pavement with their faces to worship God saying that He is good and how His love endures forever. So it is not like they didn't know God. They recognized that He was present.

We are living in some pretty tough times, however the Bible says that nothing is too hard for God and we are at a point where we, as His children, have to try Him at His word. To humble yourself is to free yourself from pride. It's about having the right view of God, yourself, and others. The Bible says that pride comes before destruction and from where I sit; there are too many people who have been very prideful for too long. Our land needs healing right now, a lot of our hearts and minds need healing right now, and according to the Lord, the formula is very simple.

Being Christian, doing what God is asking should be simple. We ought to be praying, seeking God's face, and turning away from wickedness everyday. It is time to take a stand; what is happening around us has gotten so out of control that there is really nothing else for us to do but to STAND. That is in the word. It says that when you have done all that you can do you just stand. WHO IS READY for change in YOUR LIFE? WHO IS READY for OUR LAND to be BETTER? God put us on notice a long time ago. So now if you don't understand what is going on in America but desire change, you want more stability. It is time to step up to the plate and do as the Bible says. I am standing on the promise of God and I trust Him. The question is do you trust Him enough to do what He says He will do? When are you going to stop trying to figure this out and just stand?

God Bless

I Will

"[Jesus Comforts His Disciples] "Do not let your hearts be troubled. Trust in God; trust also in me. In my Father's house are many rooms; if it were not so, I would have told you. I am going there to prepare a place for you. And if I go and prepare a place for you, I will come back and take you to be with me that you also may be where I am."- **John 14:1-3**

When, we go to the store and purchase products, they always come with a guarantee. Once it is all said and done we come to learn that the guarantee is not very dependable because of the loopholes that we didn't foresee. By then, of course, it is too late. For once, I would like to purchase something that the manufacturer will honor their guarantee.

Well, the good news is that just as Jesus comforts His disciples here in this text, He is comforting us. Jesus made a purchase with His blood: mankind. Just as the things that we purchase don't always do what they are supposed to do, neither do we. However, Jesus loves us so much that He made a decision to allow us to be with Him in eternity. The challenge is for us to make the same decision and stay the course. We have to declare that we will follow Jesus and mean it, no matter what we are faced with. This is where integrity is at war with opposition. Will you still stand true to your word? Jesus is true to His word.

I declare today that I WILL!!!

Will you?

God Bless

I Used to do it Too

> "If we claim to be without sin, we deceive ourselves and the truth is not in us. If we claim we have not sinned, we make him out to be a liar and his word has no place in our lives."
> **- 1 John 1:8, 10**

I had the privilege to teach our youth and the title of the lesson the Lord gave me was "I used to do it to." The lesson's purpose was to emphasize that no one alive can claim to be perfect because we have all sinned and fallen short of the glory of God. The problem with most people, especially young folks, is that when they commit shameful acts, getting past them and still living a productive holy, and righteous life seems impossible. The other sad truth is that people in the world have a way of making an exposed person feel like dirt, as if they have never done anything sinful.

The truth is we all have a past; we all have skeletons in our closets, so we shouldn't make people feel so guilty that they can't get past what they have done. It is true that none of us are who we used to be. We neither go where we used to go nor do some of the sinful things that we once did. Nothing can change the fact that we did those things that we are not proud of.

I shared with them that the definition of sin is "the act of violating a known moral rule." Christian or not, there are just some standards that anybody would uphold and make you accountable to. Striving to be Christ-like makes others scrutinize our actions and character. When theses shameful acts are not handled the right way we feel guilt, loneliness, pity, and depression. Keep this in mind; the fruit of your ways will be the consequences you experience. Depression and loneliness especially have a way of disconnecting you from God. You think there is no way you could ever get back in God's good graces.

David was a womanizer, yet God said he was a man after His own heart. Paul and Moses were murderers, Jacob was deceitful, and Jeremiah doubted his ability to lead, yet God used them all for a greater purpose. Martha was mad at Jesus when Lazarus died, but she was the first woman at Jesus' tomb. Esther was disobedient to the king and was still used by God to save her people.

The entire Bible focuses on our need for communion with God and for people, especially Christians, to love, help, encourage, and forgive one another. A growing relationship with God and others becomes the basis for any solution to the problem of getting past your past. If we just recognize that God is loving and faithful, we position ourselves to be over-comers. Let us not forget the things that pushed us to get better and instead use some of those moments to help others, especially our young people. They only see us in our new-and-improved state, and may assume that we were never in their shoes. Be honest and open about your involvement so that you'll have an impact.

If we learn to bless our past it will set us free. Just because you are guilty of being a sinner doesn't mean that there is no longer hope for you. Use your past experiences to be a blessing to someone else being empowered and to cement your victory over that part of your life.

God Bless

He will Sustain

"Even to your old age and gray hairs I am he, I am he who will sustain you. I have made you and I will carry you; I will sustain you and I will rescue you."- **Isaiah 46:4**

About a month ago, our washing machine stopped working, so I called the manufacturer, whose customer service rep informed me that the product's limited warranty didn't cover what needed repair. So since our warranty offered limited coverage, our only option was to pay additional fees to increase our coverage; however, purchasing full coverage wasn't even an option.

Isaiah makes it really clear for us here that God says we have full coverage on everything, FOR LIFE. Most warranties expire before our products stop operating properly; the manufacturers anticipate our out-of-pocket payments since they obviously structure warranties to benefit their companies more than the customers. Consider that new vehicles start having major problems when they are paid off, forcing consumers to purchase "extended" warranties or to assume the high expenses of repairs. God knows that we are not going to do right at any given time, yet we are covered FOR LIFE, no matter what. God has paid the price for our warranty (in full) so when something goes wrong, we can rest assured that we can call the MANufacturer to take care of us, EVERYTIME.

God's WARRANTY is TRULY SOMETHING we CAN DEPEND ON.
If I were a gambler, I would bet everything on ETERNITY.
God Bless

He Supplies

"In my anguish I cried to the LORD, and he answered by setting me free. The LORD is with me; I will not be afraid. What can man do to me?"- **Psalm 118:5-6**

In my extreme pain, distress, or anxiety, I cry out to the Lord and He answers by setting me free. The psalmists are is very descriptive in this verse and I believe it is for a very distinct reason. They want us to know that when we are on our last leg we can depend on the Lord. He will come through. So know that he will, in any situation.

The key is to believe it and not being afraid. When I first started learning Martial Arts, I felt invincible; I feared no man. Of course now, years later, I understand that I am not invincible, just better equipped to protect myself than others. However, when you have Jesus, this is a statement that you can make with confidence because He will supply all your needs. The word continues to say in this chapter that God is with us and is our helper so we can look in triumph on our enemies. That Jesus is in control of our lives is fact. The Bible reminds us that we have VICTORY in Jesus Christ. Additionally, the first four verses of this text remind us that God's love endures forever.

When you have that kind of power working in you, why should you fear anything that you are going through?

Accept and recognize that the Lord is with you so you don't have to be afraid of your situation or circumstance.

God Bless

He is the Manufacturer

> "For we are God's workmanship, created in Christ Jesus to do good works, which God prepared in advance for us to do."- **Ephesians 2:10**

When we make a major purchase, it is very clear whom the manufacturer is. That information is very important because it helps us to contact the maker, should the product malfunction or not meet our expectations.

It is very important for us to know who our *man-u-facturer* is as well. That in itself helps us as well as anyone else to understand our quality. That we were created in Christ Jesus to do good works that were prepared in advance says a lot about who we are.

Romans 8:29, is very clear about our being predestined to be conformed to the likeness of Christ and how we were called. God has a great plan already laid out for our lives and He preplanned everything. We often get off track, but that doesn't change God's original plan. As we grow through life, we have to take some bumps and bruises because that comes with the territory. However, those bumps and bruises should not get us off course of what God has in store. When we get out of the business of doing God's work for Him, we won't meet face-to-face with so much resistance.

Our manufacturer makes the top-of-the-line product and everyone is uniquely designed. God has a plan for your life that Christ has already walked out; now you must walk into your destiny. If anything goes wrong, you should always go back to your manufacturer.

God Bless

He is Patient

> "The Lord is not slow in keeping his promise, as some understand slowness. He is patient with you, not wanting anyone to perish, but everyone to come to repentance."- **2 Peter 3:9**

Our God is an awesome God and He is consistent in showing us unconditional love. He gives us grace, mercy, and second chances daily, even though many don't recognize it. Grace is what we receive from God even though we don't deserve it, like more time to get our lives together. Mercy is what we deserve to get but God blocks it. In looking at the meanings of these words hopefully it will cause us to stop and reflect daily to see how God has been at work in our lives.

In this text Peter is speaking of some who have the audacity to mock God, saying that His second coming has been delayed. Peter makes it very clear that God is time so He doesn't operate on a schedule like we do. In fact the Bible says that a day to us is like a thousand years to the Lord so there is no way that we can confine God time to our schedule. God is very intentional with everything that He does so His second coming is not delayed; He is waiting, giving us a chance to get our lives right and repent.

We have to remember that God is longsuffering and we should be working on that. In essence, it means that we are quick to judgment while God shows more patience.

God doesn't want any of us to perish, or to be forever spiritually lost. Salvation for all is God's desire; however we all have free will. Simply put, we all have the freedom to choose to follow God and walk with Jesus Christ or not. Since we don't know the day or the hour, repentance should be a sense of urgency for all who really want to spend eternity with the Lord. Choosing to delay our walk with Christ is like playing Russian roulette; you are playing with your life. There has to be a certain level of discomfort when you are procrastinating. Life is hard enough with Christ so I can't imagine living without Him.

Think about times when you have been extremely patient with people, waiting for them to make decisions. Once you have waited for so long and you realized that they were holding you up from doing what you needed to do. How did that make you feel? Some get really angry and toss patience and reason out the front door. So now, think about God being patient with us. Some are just taking their time, like they have all the time in the world. Will God get as impatient and angry with us? Do you really want to wait to see if He does?

I don't!!! God is going to keep His promise of coming back. He is very patient with all of us and He really wants us all to live eternally with Him. The ball is in our court and we are on His schedule. So what are you waiting for? If you have already made your decision to follow Jesus Christ, there IS someone that you know who hasn't. Why take this journey alone?

Choose Jesus Christ today because He chose you and He died just to prove it. God Bless

He is Able

"I lift up my eyes to the hills— where does my help come from? My help comes from the LORD, the Maker of heaven and earth."- **Psalm 121:1-2**

What a way to end a week. We are all dealing with something that may be a little discouraging or challenging. For some reason, we tend to exert all our energy, sometimes trying to figure it out or make things happen the way we see it. That too sometimes ends up being very frustrating.

When we are going through any tough situation, we are often encouraged when we know that we have some support, someone there to help us through. I know it presents a sense of hope for me. Here the text is reminding us that all of the help we really need comes from God. Then look at His credentials: the maker of Heaven and Earth. This shows that God is fully capable and qualified to help us out.

Isn't it funny how sometimes people who want to help, really aren't capable of handling your situation? Today, we know that we can take whatever it is to God and He is fully able to handle it.

God Bless

He has all Power

"For in Christ all the fullness of the Deity lives in bodily form, and you have been given fullness in Christ, who is the head over every power and authority."- **Colossians 2:9-10**

The Latin root of the word "deity" means god or goddess. It is someone who is held in high regard and seen as holy and is well respected. They are gods with a little g. Most deities are represented in either human or animal form. Some people go too far when they create deities. There is a group called Gnostics that has some beliefs contrary to those of Christianity. Some of them believe that Christ entered Jesus when He was baptized and left Him before He died. While others don't believe that Jesus really died because, in their opinion, He could not be God if He died.

The word of God is so awesome because it offers a picture of how powerful God really is. Let's look at the word "fullness", which in other translations means complete. "Fullness" means containing all that is normal or possible complete in every particular. When fullness and completeness exist, lacking does not. Some people uplift deities, which are incomplete. However, in Christ we have the fullness of God in our Lord and Savior. The awesome part is that we were given the fullness in Christ so we don't have to be anybody special to receive it. Jesus Christ is not out of our reach and we don't have to make an appointment or jump through hoops to get to Him. He is readily available at anytime and Jesus Christ is head over every power and authority. He is God with a capital G. So it doesn't matter whom or what others believe in, their deity still has to submit to our God. Here position and relationship are so important because we are connected to the source of all power and authority.

We have all heard the phrase "it's not what you know but who you know." Well in this situation who you know, (meaning God), is key. Equally important is what you know about whom you know. We all have to know that we serve an awesome God who sent His Son who is full and complete. You are linked to greatness and in this scenario; membership does have its privileges. Think about it this way. In us resides God's Holy Spirit so He is a part of all of us. Since Jesus Christ is head over every power and authority, guess who has an all access pass to all of the power and authority? Position and relationship are critical and in this text it is clear that we have power and authority over our enemy and any stronghold that tries to come against us.

Walk in your authority and use your power wisely.
God Bless

He did it Before He'll do it Again

> "But the LORD said to Moses and Aaron, "Because you did not **trust** in me enough to honor me as holy in the sight of the Israelites, you will not bring this community into the land I give them."- **Numbers 20:12**

The backdrop of this text is centered on the Israelites being freed from slavery and led by Moses. During their travel they arrived at the Desert of Zin and began complaining about not having water. They even had the nerve to say that they should have stayed in Egypt or died instead of following Moses. The Lord spoke to Moses and his brother Aaron telling Moses to gather the people, speak to the rock, and provide the water (that would come from the rock) to the people. Moses got so caught up that not only did he speak to the rock, he hit it, probably to be dramatic. Their disobedience and lack of trust in the Lord resulted in the aforementioned verse.

We have all been entangled before with something. Regardless of whether it was an old relationship, or issues with health or finances, we were at our wits end and God showed Himself true to His word. It is amazing that the Bible says that we move from Glory to Glory, yet we find ourselves up against a new challenge and our faith and trust in God begin to waver. We get to the point of trying to solve the issues ourselves and really mess up even more.

As in the case with Moses and Aaron, God doesn't need our help to do His business. He never has and never will. Our job is to trust in Him and have Faith that He is Lord and has everything under control. As a result of Moses and Aaron's lack of trust, they died and never entered into the land flowing with milk and honey, the place they had been fighting so hard to get to and enjoy.

Don't allow a lack of trust in God and faithless decisions to stop you from enjoying the fruits of your labor. If God has come through for you before, why wouldn't He do it again? He wants to get the Glory out of our lives; we were made to give Him Glory.

The Lord gave Tye Tribet this," **If He did it before, He will do it again. Same God right NOW, Same God back then."**

God Bless

Your Story

"Ah, Sovereign LORD," I said, "I do not know how to speak;
I am only a child." **Jeremiah 1:6-9**

But the LORD said to me, "Do not say, 'I am only a child.' You must go to everyone I send you to and say whatever I command you. Do not be afraid of them, for I am with you and will rescue you," declares the LORD.

Then the LORD reached out his hand and touched my mouth and said to me, "Now, I have put my words in your mouth."

Jesus was very specific in Matthew when He said, "go you therefore." Part of the reason so many have not been successful is fear. Fear will paralyze you and at that point you become stagnant.

God makes it really clear here when He spoke to Jeremiah, who had a lot of doubt that gave birth to fear. The Lord told him not to second-guess himself. He went further to confirm for Jeremiah that He would be there with him and give him the words to say.

We often don't say anything to anyone about our faith because of fear of either not knowing what to say or of not being accepted by others.

You have to know, just like in the poem "Our Deepest Fear" the poet Marianne Williamson said, "When you let your light shine, you unconsciously give others the permission to do the same."

We have to be confident in what we do know and do, just like the Bible says, meditate on the word day and night and study to show ourselves approved unto God.

You don't have to quote every scripture in the Bible or be a preacher to share your story and how good God has been to you. You never know whose life you may be saving by choosing to be used by God.

Trust in Him and share the truth, even if you are going through something.
God Bless

Your Garden

"Do not be deceived: God cannot be mocked. A man reaps
what he sows. The one who sows to please his sinful nature,
from that nature will reap destruction; the one who sows
to please the Spirit, from the Spirit will reap eternal life."
- **Galatians 6:7-8**

Growing up I spent a lot of time in the country in a little town named Bradley, Arkansas. Every summer we would go to the garden and get the corn, peas, cabbage, squash, and everything else my grandmother had planted. Of course some of our stash, like the corn for example, had worms so we had to either clean it or discard it. Either way, we planted many seeds in the garden so that at harvest time, it would be full.

What seeds are you sewing, not just in other people, in your life? When harvest time comes, what will you reap? The Bible says that if you sew sparingly you will reap the same and if you sew generously you will reap the same. Are you sewing love, joy, peace, and happiness? Or are you sewing jealousy, envy, hatred, anger, and self-pity?

If you sew life to please the spirit that you will also reap.

What's growing in your garden?

God Bless

You Talk to Much

"The wise in heart will accept and obey commandments, but the foolish of lips will fall headlong." -**Proverbs 10:8**

If you listen when you talk you will learn more when you listen. There are so many people who fall into the category of the self-proclaimed resident expert. Usually, the one doing all of the talking thinks that he or she is the smart one. Some talk so much just because they love to hear themselves. There are even those who use this platform to exalt themselves in an attempt to appear wise.

The Bible says that we should be quick to listen and slow to speak. In 1 Samuel 2:3 it says, "Do not keep talking so proudly or let your mouth speak such arrogance, for the Lord is a God who knows, and by Him deeds are weighed." Simply put, we should all learn to speak less and do more. No one really enjoys the company of one who is a braggart. So here we have God's way of saying not to talk about it, but to be about it. If many of us put into action the things that we talk about, our lives would look a lot brighter. It is OK to dream and sometimes-even talk about it, however it gets to a point where you have to put those thoughts into action. If we don't learn to be quiet and move to action, we are talking loud saying nothing.

If you are ready to change your life, don't waste a lot of time talking about it because most people really aren't listening. Instead, be obedient to God and move to action because He inspired the idea that you have anyway. With all of that talking, who are you trying to convince anyway? God already knows what you are capable of, so now it is time to move to action.

God Bless

You Must Believe

"And without faith it is impossible to please God, because anyone who comes to him must believe that he exists and that he rewards those who earnestly seek him."
- **Hebrews 11:6**

Consider what is going on with our economy and how it is causing a lot of panic in the world and the industries in which we all work. Consider that we learn of a new disease or epidemic every other month, along with everything else that the news feeds us. All we have to hold on to (in order for us to stay focused and keep on moving) is our faith. Dedicating our lives to Christ should be about pleasing God all the time. Here the scripture tells us that without faith it is impossible to do that. When everyone around you is suddenly being laid off, it is your faith in God and His promises that give you hope. It is your faith that allows you not to panic but to pray, plan, and prepare. It is your faith that allows you to stay the course and not have doubt that you are next; however in the same breath it allows you to deal with the actuality that it could happen to you, and not feel that you are calling it into existence. Believe in the understanding that you can have hope. Hope is outcomes with great expectations in your God, (whom you have never seen, even in the midst of an economic recession) is what will be pleasing to Him.

It is your understanding that instead of losing it you seek God without delay. That will put you in position to see the Glory of God manifested in your life.

Have hope, trust, and most importantly have faith in God.

God Bless

You Can't Hide

"Can anyone hide in secret places so that I cannot see him?" declares the LORD. "Do not I fill heaven and earth?" declares the LORD."- **Jeremiah 23:24**

There is nothing like, a good game of hide and seek. When I was younger we would play this game all day long; sometimes it took all day to find some people. So, we placed limits on how far one could go to hide.

My oldest son has a habit now of hiding every chance that he gets. We sometimes play hide and seek in the house and he plays for hours if allowed. He loves to hide for no reason at all and I have been telling him to cut it out. Maybe it is an old spirit in me but I feel like his hiding all the time will cause him to be sneaky when he gets older. Every time he does it I can still see him. He asked me the other day, "Daddy how do you always know where I am hiding?" My response to him was, "because I am your father and I know all your hiding places." In essence, I was telling him that there is nowhere that he can truly hide.

There are some grown folks who are trying this same thing with God. The Lord is declaring that nobody (non-believers included) can go unfound. The quintessential question here is why anyone would hide from the Lord? The only sensible answer is that you are doing something contrary to God's will. For some reason people who live contrary to God's will feel that God can't see them. I even know people who say that they are going to get serious and get their lives together after they get their playing out first.

God sees everything that we do. He can even see what you feel so there is nothing that we can hide from God. Psalms 33:13 say that the Lord looks down from Heaven and sees all of mankind, meaning everybody. Let us not take for granted how powerful our God really is. In this text God was greatly angered because there were prophets speaking falsely in His name and leading people astray.

God is serious about our living holy, righteous lives. However it is a choice that all people have to make on their own. In this context, if you are hiding it is because you feel that you have something to hide. God already knows. Since God can see your every move, hiding really defeats the purpose. Hide and seek is a game where one is willing to allow you to hide in hopes of finding you. With God, there is nothing new under the sun and since He is Omnipresent, in all places at the same time. Game over.

God Bless

You are Kept

> "I give them eternal life, and they shall never perish; no one can snatch them out of my hand. My Father, who has given them to me, is greater than all; no one can snatch them out of my Father's hand. I and the Father are one."
> - **John 10:28-30**

Jesus says here that He gives us eternal life. What does *eternal* mean? It means forever, without end, and He goes on to say that we shall never perish. "No one can snatch us out of His hands" really refers to our salvation. There are some who believe that once you receive your salvation, that you can loose it by the way you live. It is true that sin can cause you to fall off, however once you are saved, you are saved.

Sin does pull you away from God and there are some in the Bible who denied Christ, yet He still loved them. You have to admit your shortcomings to the Lord and ask for His forgiveness. You also have to forgive yourself of and remove yourself from what has caused you to stumble.

The Bible says that when we received our salvation, the Holy Spirit also sealed us, which is our guarantee until the day of redemption. In other words, we are kept until we reach our destination so heaven should be your focus. God loves us this much. When God said that nothing could separate us from His love, He meant it. Jesus got a thing for you, as they used to say, and died just to show us all. Jesus is establishing that He and God are one and there is no authority greater. So what He says goes.

Just know that you won't loose your salvation. However, that doesn't mean to live any kind of way. We have what is called eternal security in the Lord. Even though many stray from the path, prayerfully that seed of righteousness within them will lead them back home, eventually just like the prodigal son.

The Lord keeps us all.
God Bless

You are Appreciated

"I always thank my God as I remember you in my prayers."
- **Philemon 1:4**

Here we have Paul writing to Philemon and to all those involved with the church that was meeting in his home. Paul was writing to them on behalf of Timothy to let them know how much he appreciated them. He recognized their faith in the Lord and their love for the saints, so it was like giving them roses while they were still alive. His letter was encouragement to keep fighting the good fight of faith and reassurance that they inspired and encouraged him too.

As I think about the people in my life more especially you I too am encouraged. Your faithfulness to receiving this word daily and allowing it to guide and direct your day is so awesome. To know that God birth these devotions in me daily and you are allowing me to fulfill my purpose and to continue to grow in the Lord is so selfless of you and I really appreciate you for it. No one has accused me of trying to start my own church or force what I think and believe on others. Instead you have received these messages and you have meditated on them and even shared them with others and for that we are fulfilling the Great Commission and I want to say Thank you. You all are growing stronger by the day. You have supported God's work through me and given me the opportunity to sharpen some of my spiritual gifts and so today I want to thank God for you and to say I love you as you are in my prayers.

Continue to be a willing vessel for the Lord and know that because of your faithfulness I too am growing stronger in the Lord daily as well. Thank you for taking this journey with me as we all strive to find our identity in Christ and position ourselves for His return. The Lord honors your commitment and your faithfulness and so do I. Take the time out today to thank God for others in your life who have done the same thing for you and let them know how much you appreciate them and LOVE them.

God Bless

Where Does Your Treasure Lie?

> "Do not store up for yourselves treasures on earth, where moth and rust destroy, and where thieves break in and steal. But store up for yourselves treasures in heaven, where moth and rust do not destroy, and where thieves do not break in and steal. For where your treasure is, there your heart will be also."- **Matthew 6:19-21**

What messages does your lifestyle send to the Lord? Are they clear or mixed signals? There is a thin line between taking pride in yourself and getting consumed by what others think of you. In a nutshell, so many people place so much value on their material possessions that they become overly concerned by the superficial. Too many spend time making sure that they have the best of everything and that certain look, which is façade to mask insecurities. God doesn't care about how big your house is, what kind of car you drive, or if you always have the latest in fashion. He cares about you, just the way you are. It is O.K. to want nice things and to take care of you. However, it shouldn't be the most important thing, like it's a second job or something. Lecrea says it in his record "Identity" and I agree: "Identity is found in the God we trust. Any other identity, will self destruct."

Where is your treasure? In stuff? Or in God?

God Bless

We Are One

"You are all sons of God through faith in Christ Jesus,
for all of you who were baptized into Christ have clothed
yourselves with Christ. There is neither Jew nor Greek, slave
nor free, male nor female, for you are all one in Christ Jesus."
- **Galatians 3:26-28**

Here Paul is speaking to the multitude of believers, not just to men in general. What makes you a part of this family is your faith in God and acceptance of Jesus Christ as Lord and savior. Here he is simply saying that the way the Lord looks at us is not separated by our race, gender, or socioeconomic status; we are all one in His eyes.

It is not like filling out an application or taking a test and having to inform the decision-makers of your ethnicity. I have never understood why race matters on employment applications, for example. It seems to be a prerequisite for acceptance or inclusion. I understand that demographics is central to gathering census data. However, it should be so over emphasized if we are all one body.

I do understand that everybody is not saved and in Christ as well as the history of our country, so that is something that we all have to play a role in causing change in the way that we are all looked at.

Again the Bible is very clear when it says that we have to have a child-like faith to enter the kingdom of God. When we were children we didn't see color; we just saw someone to play with and have fun going through life with. What happened, as we got older? I believe that you all are doing a great job with sharing Christ with others and being color blind with His people, helping whoever needs help. Let us continue to be contagious in our efforts to help Christ's view of the world become the world's view.

God Bless

Trust the Teacher

"This is what the LORD says— your Redeemer, the Holy One of Israel: "I am the LORD your God, who teaches you what is best for you, who directs you in the way you should go."- **Isaiah 48:17**

I have been in karate for many years now and by the grace of God I have been given an awesome Sensei to give me leadership and direction. When faced with a challenge of having a belt test, breaking wood or bricks, competing in competitions or just protecting myself, all I have to rely on is what Bruce taught me. He was very specific about what to do and what not to do. I can remember my first competition; he was right there on the outside looking in, directing my next move and because I was obedient (instead of doing my own thing) I won. I have to say that Bruce Lee Wynn is an awesome teacher and he taught me what is best for me when it comes to Tae Kwon Do.

GOD is even better than that because He gives us instruction for life, and not just in certain areas but: in every area of life. What better teacher than the one who knows everything and created everything! According to God's word, He says that we already have the victory. If the one and only true God can give a guarantee and be true to His word, why wouldn't any of us follow Him? Our God, our redeemer, the one who has ordered our steps according to His word, should be your Sensei.
God Bless

True Worship

"God is spirit, and his worshipers must worship in spirit and in truth."- **John 4:24**

Most often when we think of worship we think of church, where most people only worship. There are many who feel that worship is only done in song.

Here in the text it tells us that God is Spirit and according to most theologians, spirit is "an invisible force or power." What is key here is that God is not limited to a certain place. Our worship is our response to God. I can say that when I am in a worship experience at church, I never want to leave because I feel so free and connected to God. What I have realized is that most times I too am guilty of limiting my worship experience to just the first half of the church service.

In reality, worship should happen anytime and anywhere. It is not just limited to song either. The only way to worship in spirit and in truth is to know the truth. We have understanding of who God is through His word. We have to allow our hearts and our minds to connect to the Father through our studying of the word, prayer time, or quite time meditating on the goodness of God. When we worship God it is recognizing that He is truly worthy of Lordship over our lives. Just like the Bible says, we should offer our bodies as a living sacrifice, Holy and righteous unto God; it should be our spiritual act of worship. So to worship God in spirit and in truth, you have to be willing to give Him all of you. Why? Because He gave His all for all.

God Bless

Train a child

"Train a child in the way he should go, and when he is old he will not turn from it."- **Proverbs 22:6**

Everyday when my family and I get in the truck, our oldest son asks to listen to "Go Hard or Go Home" by Lecrea, a Gospel rap artist. If not, he asks to hear "How Great is our God" by Chris Tomlin. The youngest son just follows his brother. They pray before they eat; it's always yes ma'am and yes sir, thank you, and you're welcome. It is so awesome for my children to reflect who we are and give us a snapshot everyday of what they see.

I agree with the widely-used phrase that children can only be what they see. It is true. Just know that the way you live your life is a tutorial for not only your children, also for any child who may be observing you from a distance as well. If we want this world to become a better place, we must lead by example.

This generation is fading fast. Many don't know how to get better. Neither are many of the youth today looking for a way to improve. What they see is what is on T.V. and in the streets, which is an equation for destruction. We have to become more involved in the lives of not only our young ones, we have to get involved with their friends and other youth as well. We have to be that beacon light for them.

Look at the definition of train: to form by instruction, discipline, or drill; to teach so as to make fit, qualified, or proficient to make prepared (as by exercise) for a test of skill.

So what do we have to do? We have to get these young people ready for kingdom living, and from where I sit; there is a lot of work to do.

God Bless

To Live and Die

"For to me, to live is Christ and to die is gain."
- **Philippians 1:21**

Here Paul is talking to the church at Philippi and to all of us as well about his serious commitment to Christ. He has gotten to a point where his life and walk are Christ-centered. There isn't anything that he won't do for Christ. This is a part of what we know as the Pauline Epistles. He is in chains as he writes. You have to have a serious level of love and commitment to go through being jailed and treated horribly for the love of Christ. He expresses in this text that he would rather die and be with Christ because that is far better. However, he expresses to them that he lives because it will bring glory to Christ by helping them progress in their faith in God.

We all may not be at the point where Paul was. He was willing to die for Christ. However, working towards a serious level of commitment to follow Christ and obey His commands is something we should aspire to. Spiritual growth is vital, especially today. For all of us, spiritual growth makes a difference on whether we make it through a storm and continue to believe in God.

The Bible says that keeping God's commands is what counts and we must do better in our commitment to live for Christ.

God Bless

There is No One Greater

"Before the mountains were born or you brought forth the earth and the world, from everlasting to everlasting you are God. For a thousand years in your sight are like a day that has just gone by, or like a watch in the night."- **Psalm 90:2, 4**

This particular text is simply expressing the eternal existence of God and His Kingdom. We serve a God who literally created everything. The Psalmist is very descriptive here when saying "before the mountains were born" or before we were ever thought of God has and will be King of Kings forever. His glory and majesty will reign from everlasting to everlasting. There is nothing that God doesn't know, down to the smallest detail and the Bible even talks about every hair on our head being numbered, no one knows that but God.

We serve a God who can give us an everlasting reward in living with Him forever in eternity.

Other cultures even recognize the eternal existence of God. In West Africa there is an Adinkra Symbol that means "except for God." It is considered the symbol of the omnipotence and omnipresence of God. It simply means, in reference to life and the world, "No one has seen its beginning and no one will see its end Except God." The theme behind this text is that we serve and awesome God and there is no one greater than He. "Acknowledge the Lord in all of your ways and He will direct your path." Proverbs 3:6. Let's not be fair-weather Christians, allowing God into our lives at our convenience. God deserves more than that considering what He has done and is still doing for us. Accept God's open invitation and walk with Him daily. He is the only one who can truly protect us until the end.

God Bless

The Way

"Jesus answered, "I am the way and the truth and the life. No one comes to the Father except through me."- **John 14:6**

Picture yourself driving with a set destination in mind. You have been driving for miles just to realize that you have been headed in the wrong direction down this one-way road. After you get past the frustration your first thought is to find a U-turn so that you get on track, headed in the right direction. Even though it will take you longer to get to your destination, you still have the satisfaction that something gave you the sense of knowing you could have still been on the other road headed in the wrong direction.

Life is the same way. Many people, who question how to get to the Lord and into heaven, will find the answer in this text.

There are so many people headed down the road to destruction they keep passing the sign to turn everything around, but their vision is blurred. That is, until one day they realize that they have gone far enough not realizing that they were almost at a dead-end. There is one sign left, Jesus Christ. All they have to do is take the U-turn. Repent and turn towards Jesus, the way, the truth, and the life. He is the only way to the father.

Don't allow anything or anyone to sidetrack you from arriving to your set destination. Stay focused on the finish line, not the sideline. God has already paved the way; stay the course and finish strong.

God Bless

The Source

> "I am the vine; you are the branches. If a man remains in me and I in him, he will bear much fruit; apart from me you can do nothing. This is to my Father's glory, that you bear much fruit, showing yourselves to be my disciples."- **John 15:5, 8**

Growing up in the country I have seen a lot of things: observing wildlife in its natural environment, taking care of farm animals, and even tending to my grandmother's garden. I remember having to pick peas, corn, and green beans (we called them snap beans at the time). She grew everything, including tomatoes. We even had a pear tree so that she could make pear preserve. We were really country because we even had a slop bucket for the pigs.

I can remember picking some of those vegetables or fruit and how if we waited too late to get them, some would fall off and disconnect from vines or branches. When this happened, the life span of that fruit or vegetable shortened without the proper care. If it was taken care of properly, we could even use its seeds to bear more.

We are a lot like those vegetables and fruit. As long as we are connected to the vine, we are connected to the source of life. However if we ever get disconnected, our life spans could be jeopardized. Nothing lasts forever. Even some of those fruits and vegetables got rotten while still connected to the vine. When that happened, we had to tear that branch off and throw it away.

As long as we are connected to God and we are serving Him, we create the opportunity for more fruit to grow from our branches. When we serve God by our actions, words, and lifestyles, we plant seeds for others to grow. We also add water to those who may be growing. Either way, we contribute to the life cycle. Part of everyone's purpose is to bear more fruit. There is a saying that goes like this: "You can tell a tree by the fruit it bears."

Are you bearing any fruit? Is it ripe and capable of bearing more fruit?

We have to stay connected to God and grow in Him so that we can produce more disciples to share the gospel of Jesus Christ. I challenge you today (as well as myself) to bear more fruit. Read, study, and live the word more. Being examples for others. Inspire and motivate others to be examples, to model for Christ so they too can lead someone else to the father.

God Bless

Speak Life

"Reckless words pierce like a sword, but the tongue of the wise brings healing." **Proverbs 12:18**

The most dangerous weapon in the world is the human tongue. Nothing can destroy like the tongue and in the same breath nothing can build a person up like the words you speak. If you just think about it, what causes a person to be so angry, to the point that they are a menace to society? What causes a person to be so kind, that they become a Philanthropist and are helping the world?

It is all in the words spoken to us, from the time that we are born till now.

Most of us may not really care what people think about us, however to some degree we do care what they say about us. Words are so powerful and depending on whose mouth they come out of, can speak volumes of your character to others.

When dealing with my boys, I realize that I have to be careful of what I say around them and to them. I remember my oldest son whining before and I said, "Stop whining like a little girl." Man, his face changed so quickly, I could tell that it hurt him. So now I realize that what I say is so powerful, it will affect my relationship with my son. If I keep saying that to him then he is going to respond in a negative way, which will lead to him not wanting to be around me down the road. So, I have to speak life into them both and watch how I say, what I say to them.

The word this morning is very simple; if we just talk to people any kind of way, it can cut so deep that no one can repair his or her heart. On the same note, if we choose to be careful with the words that come out of our mouths, then we can actually help some people heal from past hurt. When words come out of our mouths, it is like shooting a gun, once you pull the trigger, you can't take the bullet back. So let's choose how we say what we say wisely.

Speak life, not death.
God Bless

Sold out

> "However, I consider my life worth nothing to me, if only I may finish the race and complete the task the Lord Jesus has given me—the task of testifying to the gospel of God's grace."- **Acts 20:24**

This scripture is the introduction of one of my favorite Lecrea tracks, off of his "Real Talk" CD. The track is called, "Sold Out" and it is about truly understanding who you are and why you are here. There are a lot of times we get so caught up, trying to get stuff, as if it really defines who we are. There is nothing wrong with having nice things such as a house, car, clothes, or what ever; the problem is, when you allow it to define who you are. When you get so wrapped up in it, you feel almost naked without your stuff.

Here Paul is saying at this point, everything about him is nothing, compared to the assignment that God has given him. He is saying that he is sold out for Christ no matter what, until the end. The interesting thing about Paul is that he had to learn from experience. We all know that Paul, when he was Saul, was a murderer. He had Christians as his target and was relentless in his mission to wipe them out. So there was a time in his life when his agenda was more important, what he wanted was all that mattered. Now, his passion and desire is to just finish what Jesus Christ started, to spread the Gospel all over the world and save souls.

What is it in your life right now today, that after you sit down and think about it, is stopping you from your assignment? Don't feel bad; because we all get off task at some point and time, it is our response to getting off track that matters, once we recognize it. Is it stuff that is stopping you, circumstances, people, is it something that is self-inflicted? Only you know and only you can change it. God gave us all free will to make those kinds of decisions on our own. Take time out of your busy schedule today and spend some time with God, ask Him to help you see what is blocking you from your assignment, if anything. What is it that is stopping you from being "Sold Out" for the Lord?

God Bless

Secure the Covenant

> "Know therefore that the LORD your God is God; he is the faithful God, keeping his covenant of love to a thousand generations of those who love him and keep his commands."
> - **Deuteronomy 7:9**

The first five chapters of the Bible were considered as the Books of the Law. Here the Lord was giving detailed instruction through Moses to the people of Israel. He was laying the foundation for the coming of Christ and establishing the Israelites as His chosen people.

Yet we still have plenty of work to do in order to enlighten others about God's omnipotence and superior power. Many of us know that unequivocally and God has shown us time and time again how faithful He is.

For some reason some people missed the last part of this text where it says that God is going to keep His covenant of love to a thousand generations of those who love Him. I say that because so many people have given up on our youth. As soon as it is discovered that they are disrespectful and out of order, many people lose patience and decide that there is no hope for them. How can God bless for a thousand generations if we let this one slip away? We either don't want to take the time to work with them or we say that we are too busy.

In order for God's vision to bless for generations to come, we have work to do. We owe it to God and ourselves to plant righteous seeds and water them in these two or three generations to come. We have to be relentless with our efforts to save the youth of today. My oldest son said to my wife and me the other day that God is reading a book on our lives and one day He is going to close it. Then, he said, "So we have to get out of this book." My wife and I told him that God is not just reading the book, He is writing it and we want to stay in it as long as we can. We explained to him that when God closes the book, life ends, and of course we went into detail to explain what all of that meant. When we finished, he understood.

It brought joy to my heart to know that the work we are doing at home to save the generations (we are directly responsible for) is working. So I know that if there is hope at my house, there is still hope beyond our four walls. When the Bible says to train up a child in the way that they should go so that when they get older they will not stray, it secures that thought of God's covenant for a thousand generations. Our children still have a lot of growing and learning to do, and yes they will have moments of trying to go against the grain to have their way. However the seed has been planted so it can only grow from here.

Let us do our part to secure God's covenant for generations to come. It is part of our inheritance.

God Bless

Searching

"God looks down from heaven on the entire human race;
He looks to see if anyone is truly wise, if anyone seeks God."
- Psalm 53:2

Believe it or not, we are all born seekers. Many of us are looking for great friends, on whom we can depend and talk to in good times and bad. We are looking for happiness and joy in everything that we do. If we find that our lives aren't yielding those results, we start the journey all over again. There are some who are looking for purpose and meaning. It is not as easy to understand everything that is placed before you and how it relates to your purpose. God has a perfect design and everything that we face draws us closer to understanding the meaning of life. It's difficult for many people to accept and embrace what God has planned for them.

Many are looking for security. I question whether feeling secure and being secure are the same? We think of security as protection against danger or loss. Sometimes security for us is protection from being hurt or endangered criminal activity. In order for us to grow, we at least have to experience hurt or hardship. Not only does adversity open our eyes, it makes us stronger and gives us direction.

More than anything, we are all seeking peace. There may be other things that some of you are seeking; however it is really all a search for God right?

He is the only one I know who can provide all that we are seeking. He is the only one who can provide true understanding of anything that we face. All that is required of us is to have an intimate relationship with Him.

Think about it; when we need to find some information to get understanding, we normally go to Google and type what we are looking for in the search engine which directs us to many resources to find specifically what we need. God has all the answers. The only difference is that He will get you right to what you need versus offering so many options to choose from.

How is your searching going?
God Bless

Restore me

"Restore to me the joy of your salvation and grant me a willing spirit, to sustain me."- **Psalm 51:12**

"Woke up this morning too depressed and shamed to leave my bed/ Can't stand to see my own reflection so I hang my head/ Feel like a disappointment, like the scum of the earth/ I'm so hurt I know you see I can't cover my dirt/ my souls dying hearts weak and I cant even cry/ I'm supposed to run to you but WHY I'm such an evil guy/ The sun's shining but for me it's the darkest of days

Try to pretend it never happened but the guilt remains/ I leave the house it feels like everybody knows I did it/ Feel like they reading my mind and know the sin I committed

Through your blood I'm acquitted but my heart doesn't get it/ Oh God I'm desperate for Help cause I'm grieving your Spirit/ I couldn't sing in the Sunday service, Lord I felt fake and when they started communion I just made an escape /I'm in need of your grace/ feels like you hid your face/ Lord Lead me back to cross and show me my sins erased

I'm so desperate; I can't believe I've sinned against you, Create in me a clean heart (I'm so sorry)

Your mercy is what I need"

These are lyrics from as song entitled "Desperate" by one of my favorite artists, Lecrea. It is basically a record about the sin we commit and how we allow it to consume us. There are many people who are not in Christ and are discouraged from coming to Christ because of sin. They feel that they have done so much dirt that God will never accept them. On the other hand, there are some who are in Christ who are also consumed by sin. They allow it to beat them down so much that they feel that God will never forgive them and this sometimes causes them to drift away from God.

David was in the same situation in this text. He had just committed adultery with Bathsheba and at that time he was in the presence of Nathan. David made it clear that he realized that what he had done was horrible but he wanted to be accountable to God for his actions. The one thing about David is when he did sin against God he didn't waste time going to Him to confess. David had such a great relationship with the Lord that he was very personal and detailed in his conversation with God. We should be the same way as well. In this text he is pleading with God for forgiveness, according to God's unfailing love and great compassion. He asked God to cleanse him of his transgression and pleaded with God not to cast him from His presence or take His Holy Spirit away from him.

Sin has a way of making you feel so low that you begin to disconnect. David had lost his peace of mind and his joy had been taken away by his sin. David wanted to get back to that place of peace, joy, and happiness in God and he knew that the Lord was the only one who could restore him. Also, he asked God to keep him from falling, to keep him in a willing state of mind to accept God's will, and to follow Him and remain faithful to Him no matter what. David was just like Lecrea was in this song: desperate. He knew that he couldn't make it without God's love, grace, and mercy. The truth is that we can't either.

The Bible tells us the God is faithful to forgive and that nothing can separate us from His love. As Christians, we have to know and understand that God wants us to be close to Him no matter what. There is nothing that we will ever do that God hasn't already forgiven us for. He expresses His love and compassion throughout the Bible towards so many to show us that we can receive the same. Don't allow whatever sin is in your life to stop you from being a child of God. Even if you never confess to the person you sinned against, make sure that you take it to God. He will work on that person. After all, God is the only one who can restore you and He will always forgive you. Lecrea ends the song with this line and it applies to us as well, "My sin weighed on me heavy but I am no longer bound. As sure as Christ wear the crown. I know that grace will abound. And even when I feel lost I know in you I am found." Take it to the Lord. There is nothing that He can't handle. He is more than willing to restore you.

God Bless

Renew Your Strength

> "But those who hope in the LORD will renew their strength.
> They will soar on wings like eagles; they will run and not
> grow weary, they will walk and not be faint."- **Isaiah 40:31**

Here is a familiar text that we have heard many times before, but what does it really mean and how do we apply it in our lives? Here, the prophet Isaiah speaks and offers words of encouragement to the Jewish exiles, who are in Babylonian captivity. The kingdom of Judah was independent until Nebuchadnezzar destroyed the city and the temple. Josiah, the king, was killed, leaving them with no leadership. So Judah surrendered to Babylonian leadership.

So we find the Jewish people hopeless because they were in captivity. They were down, feeling that God deserted them and no longer cared about (what they considered as) their miserable lives. God used this opportunity to speak through the prophet Isaiah to reassure them that there was no one greater than He. If you read versus 25 through the end of the chapter, you will see God making it very clear how powerful He really is and how He fulfills His promises. Isaiah's word of prophecy encourages the Jewish people to keep pressing, in spite of their circumstances. They were eventually allowed to go back to Jerusalem to rebuild their temple.

We have all been at a point when we have run out of gas and the vision before us seems grim. We have all at some point felt that God didn't care about our circumstances and that we would be stuck in that situation. Verse 30 basically says that we all experience it, even young folk. However, when we pick up at verse 31 it starts with "but". This one word erases everything before it. So even though we may get tired, all who have hope in the Lord, all who have great expectations in His wonder-working power will become strong again. A renewed strength empowered by God allows you to endure more than you imagined. If we rely on our own strength we will fall and get weary but when our heart and hope is in the Lord, it will allow us to rise above the difficult times. We'll be enabled to believe in deliverance until it happens. Instead of focusing inward, we have to focus outward and especially upward. We have to set our hopes on things heavenly and eternal rather than the temporal. Be careful to look out for unbelief and pride; they will lower your self confidence and take your eyes off of the prize. Have hope in the Lord for every situation all the days of your life and allow the Lord to reveal to you how strong you really are.

God Bless

Remain Confident

> "So do not throw away your confidence; it will be richly rewarded. You need to persevere so that when you have done the will of God, you will receive what he has promised."
> **- Hebrews 10:35-36**

My oldest son just started kindergarten this year. However, it is not his first time being exposed to schoolwork. We started him in preschool at the church and have been working extensively with him at home. Prior to starting school he already knew his ABC's, how to write his name, how to count to 100, and how to identify colors. He had already begun reading as well. It's interesting how his ideas, which are plentiful, aren't always as easy to record on paper. So needless to say, he gets frustrated to the point of tears sometimes because he really wants to get it right the first time. At times, he wants to just quit and so we constantly remind him that he won't get better unless he keeps trying. He knows how to do it; he just has to take his time. Those few words build his confidence and when he exerts more effort, he gets the outcome he wanted. Then, we celebrate with him as a reward for not quitting.

In life things are going to be difficult especially in these days and we will face some things in our lives that have the potential to take us completely out of the game if we let it. There are even times as Christians we see people who are nowhere near trying to follow Christ seeming doing better than we are and we tend to get discouraged. The thought crosses our mind of why am I trying so hard to do right when they don't care and are living better than me. We have all seen this at some point doing our walk. Everything that we do as devoted Christians has a purpose and a promise and God provides both for us. We have to remain confident in the fact that God knows what He is doing and as long as we stay the course what he has for us is for us. The Bible says that if we don't quit then the Lord will reward us but we have to endure until our change comes and never stop believing.

One of my pastor friend's nephew committed suicide last week because of depression. He had a promising future as a star player for the Broncos but his injuries took his mind in a different direction. He began to lose confidence, not only in what he could do, but also in what God could do. He knew the Lord. However, his dire circumstances got the best of him. I have been there before. I wanted to take my life (behind what seemed to be) selfish reasons. For me, there were no doctors around and none of my friends or family knew it; but it was God who saved me. I realized who I really am in Christ and that in order for things to get better I had to fight the good fight and not lose faith and confidence in God. It was difficult doing it alone, but I never lost focus that God will reward those who earnestly seek Him. By the grace of God, some of those promises have been rewarded to me in my having a wife and not one, but two boys! There are people in my life who add so much value to who I am; I will never be able to repay God for that. However, for all that He has done, I am more confident now than ever before. God loves me and wants the best for me. It is the same for you. Unfortunately, Kenny McKinley won't be able to see God's promise for him revealed. Just as my son didn't give up on writing, hopefully you won't give up either. Prayerfully, you will continue to have confidence in knowing that if you can last a little longer, the Lord will bless you for your faithfulness. We all know that weeping may endure for a night but JOY comes in the morning. Don't give up; don't quit. There is more at stake than you realize. The Lord has so much for you do and so much in store for you; our job is to trust what God is doing in our lives and know that he is stretching us to make us stronger. Don't lose confidence; don't lose hope.

God Bless

Press Towards the Mark

"I press on toward the goal to win the prize for which God has called me heavenward in Christ Jesus."- **Philippians 3:14**

Just as the Lord repeats something in the Bible to emphasize it, we will revisit this verse. We have seen it before.

Your goal in life ought to be getting to heaven, where God has already made room for you. That is awesome. There are two things that are definite in our lives: our beginning and our end. What God has given you free will to determine is everything in-between. Sunday at church, Dr. Hartman used an example to help us understand life. He told us to imagine that we were traveling through Colorado and saw a huge mountain. As we drove closer, we realized that there were two mountains, a smaller one in the front and a big one in its shadow. Next, we realized they were not that close because there was a valley in-between the two. We determine, by the grace of God, how we travel through our valley to get to our goal.

When you press you are pushing to with great force to accomplish something. When you press your clothes you have to apply some muscle to knock those wrinkles out. Sometimes when you are going to your car and you press your alarm keypad, you have to press a little harder because the signal is getting weak.

Well, the same is true in our lives. Our connection with God is not always where it needs to be so we find ourselves having to press a little harder. Things in our lives are not always going to go the way that we want them to; it is our pressing that makes all of the difference. We have to P.U.S.H really hard most of the time to get through obstacles. Pray Until Something Happens. Prayer is the most powerful tool we can use when we are in the valley, but it is the least used.

Let us all press or P.U.S.H a lot harder day-to-day toward the goal to win the prize for which God has called each one of us Heavenward in Christ Jesus.

God Bless

Peace

> "And the peace of God, which transcends all understanding,
> will guard your hearts and your minds in Christ Jesus."
> **- Philippians 4:7**

When you consider the condition of the world and all that is going on, peace is truly one thing that a lot of people are searching for. Then to add insult to injury, the current economic situation, with people being laid off, doesn't make it any better. There are even followers of Christ (on different levels in their walk) now searching for peace.

The thought for most people is that if God is so loving, why is He letting this happen? More importantly, why is He letting it happen to me?

Rick Warren has stated in one of his books:

"There will never be peace in the world until there is peace in nations.

There will never be peace in nations until there is peace in communities.

There will never be peace in communities until there is peace in families.

There will never be peace in families until there is peace in individuals.

And there will never be peace in individuals until we invite the Prince of Peace to reign in our hearts.

Jesus is the Prince of Peace."

Non-believers, in their quest for peace have to realize that it is in Christ; eventually they will see they have been looking in the wrong places.

For believers, we have to recognize that we already have peace. We can't allow ourselves to get so caught up in carnal thinking, which pulls us away from what we say that we believe. The bible says in this same verse not to worry but to pray. That is our answer to worrying about our situations. Why? Because when we pray, we will receive the peace of God, which transcends all understanding. It's meaning it is beyond our comprehension. In that though we know that God is in control, and because of that belief we can except and claim peace in the midst of what we are going through. God "got it" and nothing is impossible for Him.

As a result of that belief He says that He will protect our minds and our hearts in Christ Jesus. As long as we think and operate in the SPIRIT, our worrying and doubt will fade.

I have a saying that if you seek your faith; your doubt will starve to death.

Seek your faith in the midst of what is going on around you and God will bless you with His Peace by the power of the Holy Spirit.

God Bless

Pay it Forward

> "That God was reconciling the world to himself in Christ, not counting men's sins against them. And he has committed to us the message of reconciliation. We are therefore Christ's ambassadors, as though God were making his appeal through us. We implore you on Christ's behalf: Be reconciled to God."- **2 Corinthians 5:19-20**

God saw the wickedness in the world and so if there was any chance to save it, He had to do something. He sent His son Jesus Christ to save the world and bring us back into a right relationship with Him. Many of us have been in a relationship, regardless of whether it was with a friend, family member, or a companion and "messed up". The time that there was little or no communication was so rough that you just wanted to get everything right so that your relationship would be back in order. Remember when you had that serious heart-to-heart talk and laid everything on the table just to realize that it wasn't as serious as it seemed? Now your relationship has been restored and seems stronger than before? It works the same way with God.

Here Paul is saying that through our acceptance of Jesus Christ as Lord and Savior, we are now back in good standing with God to the point that He has forgiven us of all of our sins. We have to have a heart-to-heart talk with the Lord and confess our shortcomings and in turn, be forgiven by Him. After having such a life-changing experience with the Lord and having that load lifted off of us, we can now go out and share that same experience with others. Those whom you help to rebuild their relationships with God will experience the same relief that you felt when regaining the relationship (with a loved one) that seemed to be lost forever. You know that when the Lord has you there are no worries. With God you feel liberated and in truth you are. You don't feel limited with your capabilities because you know that with Christ all things are possible. God covers you.

So there is this holy force field around you as you move throughout life. Certain things, unbeknownst to you, were set up to attack you and failed. There is a certain peace about you even in the midst of struggle because your heart and your mind are protected in Christ. You can claim victory in the face of adversity before you even get to the battle because we have victory in Jesus Christ.

Why not share all these riches with someone else? Why not help someone to regain the relationship that matters the most? Many of us have been "fixed up" by a matchmaker before. Now it is your turn.

Help others get the relationship that they have been longing for, the one that matters more than any other.

Someone did it for you; so now it is time to pay it forward.

God Bless

Paul's Prayer

> "I pray that the eyes of your heart may be enlightened in order that you may know the hope to which he has called you, the riches of his glorious inheritance in his holy people,"
> **- Ephesians 1:18**

There are times when my wife and I are talking and she is trying to get me to understand where she is coming from. She tends to get very descriptive, hoping that it will trigger my memory. Instead of saying "forget it", she may go a little deeper in her attempt to turn on the light for me until I say, "Ooh yeah, I remember." She really wants me to have that "aha" moment, expressing that I've finally understood what she was telling me; she wanted me to see it for myself.

Here, Paul is doing the same thing with the Church in Ephesus. He reminded them in a later chapter that they used to be in darkness, but are now in the light. Paul was praying for them to have an "aha" moment. He wanted them to say, "Ok, I see what you are telling me Lord." Paul knows that how a man thinks in his heart will determine how he walks. So his prayer is that they really get a complete understanding of God's grace and His love for them and order their steps in a way that is pleasing to God.

Paul's prayer is not only for the Church at Ephesus; it is also for all who have been brought into the light. As a minister, my sincere hope for everyone that I encounter is that they have a relationship with the Lord. Even more, I want them to love the Lord more than anything and fear Him like I do. I really want people to let the mind that is in Christ Jesus be also in them and everyday strive to please the Lord in all that they do in order to be more like Him. Just like the deer pants for streams of water, so should our souls pant for the Lord.

At the end of the day Paul is saying that his prayer is that, his passion and desire to please and serve God will be contagious. He hopes that being exposed to the light is a small flame that causes us all to be on fire for the Lord. If more people who claim to be in Christ were more Christ-like, the world really would be a better place. Being naughty by nature, or human, is not an excuse because we all have a choice and are accountable for our decisions. God has great plans for us all and it all comes down to our watching our walk. Let us choose to line up with God so that we may completely know the hope to which He has called each of us.

God Bless

Panic Room

"[For the director of music. Of David the servant of the LORD. He sang to the LORD the words of this song when the LORD delivered him from the hand of all his enemies and from the hand of Saul. He said:] I love you, O LORD, my strength. The LORD is my rock, my fortress and my deliverer; my God is my rock, in whom I take refuge. He is my shield and the horn of my salvation, my stronghold."
- **Psalm 18:1-2**

There is this great movie I have seen named "Panic Room," starring Jodie Foster and Forest Whitaker. The film tells a story of a mother and a daughter hiding in a panic room during an invasion by three armed robbers targeting millions of dollars stored in the house.

Jodie Foster's character recently divorced from the owner of a pharmaceutical giant, and her 11-year-old daughter Sarah, who has diabetes, have just purchased a four-story brownstone townhouse on West 94th Street that was previously owned by a disabled, reclusive millionaire. It has a panic room, an isolated room used to protect the owner from an intruder that is protected by a four-inch-thick steel door and an impressive security system, and features a separate phone line.

I lift this up because we all are familiar with panic and anxiety. Panic is a sudden fear that dominates you and disturbs your thinking, affecting you and/or others in a negative way. When we are faced with the possibility of sudden imminent danger, panic is what tends to come upon us and our thinking dictates how we come out of it. The truth is when we face whatever potential danger; we all want a safe and secure place to run. Though that danger presents itself, we are in a place that allows us to feel positive about the outcome. We want to feel like we are protected in our own panic room.

Saul tried to kill David on numerous occasions and it was only because of David's conscious choice to trust God and be obedient to His word, that he felt safe. We all actually have the same opportunity to be protected from danger by the same God who covered David against Saul. The attack may not always be physical; it can be against your character or your beliefs. Whatever the case, we have protection, a mighty fortress that is stronger than Jodie Foster's four-inch-thick steel door and an impressive security system. Psalms 37:28 say that we will be protected forever. It also says that the Lord protects the simple hearted. If we just surrender to the Lord just as David did, we too can say that the Lord is our fortress and our stronghold.

God Bless

Our Place of Safety

"God is our refuge and strength, an ever-present help in trouble."- **Psalm 46:1**

Refuge is a place of safety. This topic makes me think about what we go through to be safe today. Being the man of my home, one of my primary concerns is to provide a safe environment for my family. When that comes to mind, you think about the community you stay in, where you work, where your children go to school, the type of car you drive, and so on. In that same thought, I sometimes concern myself with whether I have I done everything that I can to make sure that my family is safe. The world has so much to offer to make us feel safe and as consumers we often buy in to the latest and greatest "this or that." If they come out with the perfect deadbolt for your door, three months later someone else comes out with a better one and a video to prove it. There were jacks for cars that required us to lock up the steering wheel, now there is Low Jack that allow car thieves to take your vehicle away before being caught in their tracks by a tracking device installed in your vehicle. I have even gone through learning martial arts for a number of reasons. However, safety is still one of the reasons.

We are not wrong for being consumers; we have a strong desire to be safe all of the time and have a sense of peace about it. Everything mentioned above is manmade, so there is a defect somewhere, meaning that it is not perfect or always guaranteed. However I do know a place where you can always feel safe and be confident that you really are safe and that place is in God. God provides safety and strength for us, among so many other things. In Psalms 91, He tells us that we can find rest in His shadow. That is how awesome and powerful God is. When you get to your house and lock the door, a sense of peace overcomes you. The sense of safety is very present because you really let your guard down most of the time. Dorothy from the "Wizard of Oz" said it perfectly when she said, "there is no place like home." I want to submit to you today that the statement is true. The only home where there is complete safety is in God. He really is an ever-present help. So when trouble comes He immediately responds and provides. It is just up to us to be willing to listen and obey.

If you want safety that will never fail, I guarantee that you will find it in the Lord. He will never let you down.

God Bless

Now Faith is

"Now faith is being sure of what we hope for and certain of what we do not see."- **Hebrews 11:1**

Faith is related to trust and belief and is the conviction of the truth of anything. However in scripture, Faith is linked to man's relationship with God and the assurance that He really is our provider, healer, and strength. There are several accounts in the Bible that display faith, why people needed to have faith in God, and what happened as a result of their faith. In every situation God held true to His word. There were many other bystanders who were blessed and became believers as a consequence of someone else's faith.

When I look at the world's present condition, one thing stands out. The righteous will live by faith. The Bible is very clear that without faith it is impossible to please God and after all, isn't that what this Christian walk is all about? It is all about serving God with our whole heart. In the midst of giving our all to Him, we hope to find favor in His sight. I found some staggering statistics about how the middle-class working Americans are being wiped out.

- 83 percent of all U.S. stocks are in the hands of 1 percent of the people.
- 61 percent of Americans "always or usually" live paycheck to paycheck, which was up from 49 percent in 2008 and 43 percent in 2007.
- 66 percent of the income growth between 2001 and 2007 went to the top 1% of all Americans.
- 36 percent of Americans say that they don't contribute anything to retirement savings.
- A staggering 43 percent of Americans have less than $10,000 saved up for retirement.
- 24 percent of American workers say that they have postponed their planned retirement age in the past year.
- Over 1.4 million Americans filed for personal bankruptcy in 2009, which represented a 32 percent increase over 2008.
- Only the top 5 percent of U.S. households have earned enough additional income to match the rise in housing costs since 1975.
- In 1950, the ratio of the average executive's paycheck to the average worker's paycheck was about 30 to 1. Since the year 2000, that ratio has exploded to between 300 to 500 to one.
- Approximately 21 percent of all children in the United States are living below the poverty line in 2010 - the highest rate in 20 years.
- Despite the financial crisis, the number of millionaires in the United States rose a whopping 16 percent to 7.8 million in 2009.

- The top 10 percent of Americans now earn around 50 percent of our national income.

When I read this information on Yahoo, it blew my mind. It also painted a really clear picture of why having Jesus Christ as Lord and Savior is so important. See, with putting all of our faith and hope in God we are saying that we trust Him to protect us in these situations. Only God can protect us from any hurt or danger that comes our way. When we may find ourselves in midst of trouble, it is our ability to be sure of what we hope for and certain that it can and will happen even when we can't see it. Who gives us that assurance? God and God alone.

Have Faith in God, the only one who has the final say.

God Bless

Not Knowing

> "However, as it is written: "What no eye has seen, what no ear has heard, and what no human mind has conceived"— the things God has prepared for those who love him—"
> **- 1 Corinthians 2:9**

If we knew exactly what God had in store for us many people would try to deviate from His plan. Even though we know that with God all things work out for the good of those who love Him, many still wouldn't want to go through what lies ahead of them. Knowing that what we experience will make us stronger; if given the choice many would choose not to do it.

As much scripture as many people read, it still wouldn't push everyone to go through the trials and tests that life brings in order to get to what God has in store. Knowing that the word says that we have victory in Jesus Christ and that no weapon formed against us shall prosper, God knows the plans He has for us. He plans to prosper us and not harm us. I could go on.

It is difficult enough to encourage others to push through the opposition however it is easier when we don't know what he has in store. Not knowing all of God's plans really does build our faith and trust in God. We walk into situations knowing that we have to depend on Him because He is the only one who knows the outcome. More importantly, we also find ourselves being more hopeful and optimistic about our situation because we know that God is not going to hurt us or put more on us than we can bear. Not knowing forces us to develop a strong relationship with God that we otherwise most likely wouldn't do. If given the choice many people would rather be in control themselves than to trust God or anyone else.

That is why God is our shepherd and we are His sheep. He knows what's best for us. I am sure that you have been like me and have asked the Lord to please show you what to do or what is coming so that you can be ready. God is protecting us from that and pushing us to stay ready. The Bible says that one must endure hardship as a good soldier for Jesus Christ and if you know anything about soldiers, especially those at war, they have to stay ready. The best thing about it though is that God is our eyes and ears; He has us covered on all sides, so if we were to fall asleep He would still be on guard. God's plan makes not knowing work so much better and it brings a sense of comfort to us when we find ourselves scared.

Trust in God, never doubt Him, and just believe. He will work it out. His plans are far greater than we can imagine and nothing is impossible with Him. Even though I sometimes struggle because I want to know God's plan ahead of time but, I think that I would do better not knowing and just trusting God. Stay focused and stay the course because God knows the plans He has for each of us. The seasoned saints would say that God is the great physician. Well He hasn't lost a patient and He's not about to start now.

God Bless

Mary's Song

"[Mary's Song] And Mary said: "My soul glorifies the Lord
and my spirit rejoices in God my Savior, for the Mighty
One has done great things for me— holy is his name."
- **Luke 1:46-47, 49**

I will bless the Lord at all times and His praises shall continually be in my mouth. As the deer pants for water so does my soul thirst for you Lord.

> Make a joyful noise unto the Lord, all ye lands.
> Serve the Lord with gladness;
> come before his presence with singing.
> Know ye that the Lord he is God;
> it is he that hath made us, and not we ourselves;
> we are his people, and the sheep of his pasture.
> Enter into his gates with thanksgiving,
> and into his courts with praise;
> be thankful unto him, and bless his name.
> For the Lord is good; his mercy is everlasting;
> and his truth endured to all generations

Today is the day that the Lord has made and we should all rejoice and be glad in it. Despite what you are going through this morning, and regardless of the news you got yesterday, last week, or last month, God is already working it out on your behalf. He says that he knows what you want before you even ask and He will supply your need. The question is: do you trust Him?

Know that the Lord is able. Mary and Elizabeth were having a praise party in this text because of the favor of God. Elizabeth said, "Blessed is she who has believed that what the Lord has said to her will be accomplished!"

They trusted God at His word and believed that what the Lord promised them was already done. So even in the midst of what you are going through, praise Him in advance.

God Bless

Decisions, Decisions

"Father, if you are willing, take this cup from me; yet not my will, but yours be done." -**Luke 22:42**

This was a very trying time in the life of Jesus Christ. Here He was faced with being separated from His Father as a sacrifice for so many others who don't know Him. He is expressing his distress and sorrows because He knew what was coming. Jesus Christ was faced with making a decision on life or death. We all know that He chose death out of obedience to God and to give us the opportunity to have life.

What I find that is so interesting is that Jesus Christ died to save lives long before many had been born so we had no way of knowing Him to even decide to accept Him as our personal Lord and Savior. Regardless to that fact we don't deserve the sacrifice by Jesus Christ, He died so that we can live.

Sitting in church Sunday listening to the pastor, I begin to think about this. What if we had to make a decision like Jesus did? What if we had to choose between life and dying on the cross especially for people that we don't know? Then it hit me. I am more than sure that if any of us had to make that choice more often than not the answer would be to live. I don't know too many people who are willing to die, especially not for anyone else.

So then I pose this question to everyone. If life is our choice over death, then why do so many people choose death daily? There are so many things that we dilute ourselves with that is slowly killing us daily and we freely choose it. We are called to pick up our cross daily yet so many people refuse or the timing is not right for them, their lives have to be in a certain place first.

Jesus had a moment when He thought about all of the suffering that He had to endure for us. The interesting thing that made Him ask for the cup to pass Him was the thought of being separated from God not the pain. We live in a society where things that cause death, is the popular choice and I am not just talking about physical death, we are talking about spiritual death. This is why the Bible says for us to die to our flesh daily because it is in constant battle with the Spirit. You know in the end one of them have to win and the victor is the one that we give power to. Romans 8:6 says, "The mind of a sinful is death, but the mind controlled by the Spirit is life and peace."

Given the decision, what do you choose? Life or death? Jesus Christ chose life for you and me before we were ever thought of and if given the chance He would do it again. "You see, at just the right time, when we were still powerless, Christ died for the ungodly. Very rarely will anyone die for a righteous person, though for a good person someone might possibly dare to die. But God demonstrates his own love for us in this: While we were still sinners, Christ died for us." Romans 5:6-8

The choice is yours. Choose wisely, daily.

God Bless

Love and Faithfulness

"Let love and faithfulness never leave you; bind them around your neck, write them on the tablet of your heart. Then you will win favor and a good name in the sight of God and man." **Proverbs 3:3-4**

The Bibles says that we have faith, hope, and love but the greatest of these is love. If we haven't seen anything else lived out we have seen love just through the sacrifice that Jesus Christ made for us. Here Solomon is reminding us not to let love and faithfulness ever leave us. He places such emphasis on it that he encourages us to bind them or secure them around our neck so we will never forget them. When he uses the expression of writing love and faithfulness on the tablet of our heart, it is because out of the heart flows the issues of life. We are also told to take the word and hide it in our heart so that we won't sin against God.

Love and faithfulness are two very important character qualities that everyone should have. They speak volumes about our attitudes and actions. God is an action-speaks-louder-than-words God and He led by example. A person who truly loves not only feels it, but acts in loyalty and responsibility. Love is something that doesn't go unnoticed. A faithful person believes the truth so much that he works for justice for others as well. Our lives should be more than just thoughts and words because that is not enough. Our lives should really reveal how loving and faithful we really are to God, others, and ourselves.

Showing love and faithfulness shouldn't be about the reward or what you expect to get out of it. It is about creating a standard for yourself and letting others see that you are genuinely that way. It should be about making a good name in the sight of God and man.

Do your actions measure up to your attitude?
God Bless

Light it up

"When Jesus spoke again to the people, he said, "I am the light of the world. Whoever follows me will never walk in darkness, but will have the light of life."- **John 8:12**

When ever I leave my home and I know that we are going to be gone for a while, my first instinct is to turn on the porch light. If I wake up in the middle of the night I find myself looking for light. After we put the boys in THEIR beds, we leave their night lights on.

Just so that you can find your way LaQuinta Inn has a commercial that says," We'll leave the light on for you." Most of our vehicles are so smart now that when they sense that darkness is near, they activate the lights automatically.

We naturally don't desire to be in darkness not because of fear, but just because we can't see or get anything accomplished. We want a clear path so badly that we buy candles and flashlights just in case we get caught off guard by darkness.

It amazes me how we truly don't want to be in darkness. However so many people find it so hard to follow Jesus. He has made it really clear here that He is light and that following Him prevents or counters darkness. Isn't this what we really want anyway?

Don't be afraid of the light. Choose to follow Christ and Light IT UP!

What is it? The World.

God Bless

Lifetime

> "But after he had considered this, an angel of the Lord appeared to him in a dream and said, "Joseph son of David, do not be afraid to take Mary home as your wife, because what is conceived in her is from the Holy Spirit. She will give birth to a son, and you are to give him the name Jesus, because he will save his people from their sins."
> **- Matthew 1:20-21**

A lot of times we take friendships and/or relationships for granted. We often follow the philosophy that a person is in our life for a reason, season, or a lifetime. While this statement is true, many of us really don't take the time to nourish those relationships, regardless of its nature. As a result of not investing the time to nurture those relationships, we really miss the true value of them. All relationships, whether long term or not, give birth to a new outlook and new opportunities that we otherwise would have never been exposed to. You never know what kind of blessing is waiting for you in being kind to a person or taking the time to get to know someone. The Bible says that we should entertain even some strangers, because in doing so we may have entertained angels. Find the value in all of your relationships, even if they are seasonal, because there is a reason that will bless you for a LIFETIME.
    God Bless

Leave Me Alone

"When the devil had finished all this tempting, he left him until an opportune time." **-Luke 4:13 (read 1-13)**

I have found myself repeatedly asking God to get the enemy to leave me alone. Sometimes I get to the point of saying "Look satan enough is enough. I am not falling for that this time." Many, I'm sure have all had this moment. If not, the closer you get to God and the more you try to live right by Him, the more likely you are to have this moment.

I have discovered that the enemy is a trickster as well as a deceiver. There is a show created by actor Ashton Kutcher called Punk'd: a hidden-camera practical, joke television series. Being "punk'd" refers to being the victim of a prank, like the old school television show Candid Camera. Kutcher creates real-life situations for celebrities that appear to have some disastrous ending. After his clueless guest buy into it, he lets them off the hook by unveiling the joke. The more gullible the celebrity the funnier the episode.

The enemy is a practical joker too and has his own version of Punk'd everyday. He looks for an opportunity to catch us slipping and does his best to get the last laugh. In his version, he is the only one laughing unless we discover his plot and spoil it. Though we are aware that the enemy schemes, we just don't always recognize the schemes at first. The Bible says that we have Christ in order that satan might not outwit us. The further we are from Jesus, though the more we become a prime target for the enemy.

In this text we found Jesus being tempted. The Bible says that Jesus was in the wilderness and He was fasting for 40 days; so here we find Jesus at what is considered His weakest point. The enemy always attacks us when we are the weakest, hoping that we will lose faith and hope in the Lord. The word says that for forty days Jesus was tempted by the devil. Here we get three accounts of that temptation. Our focus today is on verse 13, though. It states that after the devil made all of his attempts to trick Jesus into falling, he failed but only left Jesus alone until another opportune time.

Here we have Jesus Christ, the one who has never sinned and will never sin, being tempted. The devil knows more about Jesus Christ than we do so he knows that Jesus is relentless, committed and will never fall yet he is optimistic and willing to continue to try anyway. In 1 Corinthians 1:25 it says, "For the foolishness of God is wiser than human wisdom, and the weakness of God is stronger than human strength." So if the enemy attempted to tempt Jesus at His weakest moment which is our strongest moment, what would make any of us think that the devil wouldn't turn it up all the more with us. The enemy is always trying to create a new episode of Punk'd in our lives daily. He is not going to leave us alone. Instead he is going to take advantage of every opportunity we give him. It is our responsibility to stay close to the Lord and in His word so that we can be prepared for the attack. That is why we have to hide the word in our hearts so that we may not sin against the Lord because we don't all carry our Bibles with us everywhere. My Bible is like American Express; I really don't leave home without it.

The Lord provides all the protection we need from the enemy. We just have to totally submit to Him. He will handle the rest. God will fight for us and expose the enemy every time for who he really is. Jesus Christ is the only one who can turn our situation around and make the joke be on the enemy. Don't get Punk'd; get Jesus Christ and hide behind the Cross.

God Bless

Labor Pains

> "But after he had considered this, an angel of the Lord appeared to him in a dream and said, "Joseph son of David, do not be afraid to take Mary home as your wife, because what is conceived in her is from the Holy Spirit. She will give birth to a son, and you are to give him the name Jesus, because he will save his people from their sins."
> **- Matthew 1:20-21**

Considering what Joseph was facing here in this text; one could understand why he questioned what he should do. Mary, his soon-to-be wife, is pregnant without explanation. I'm sure that if any of us were in that situation we would ponder the same thing.

However, Joseph was in the right frame of mind and had positioned himself to hear from God, instead of being closed-minded. Joseph listened to the angel of the Lord. He trusted what was said and followed through with God's instructions. As a result, he had the pleasure of helping raise the savior of the world. What an awesome position to be in and to have so much favor!

We all have to be willing to be like Joseph sometimes by listening to God. If we humble ourselves more, we can put ourselves in the right position to understand God's instructions, especially when we have such life-changing decisions to make. If you are facing any kind of situation right now, take the time to stop and talk with God. Hear what He has to say. I can guarantee that He can see further in your future than you can and knows the exact steps that you should take to get to a place of peace. God trusted Joseph, who chose to submit to God, with a great responsibility. He willingly humbled himself, listened to the angel, and was blessed with an awesome assignment.

His soon-to-be wife was expecting the savior of the world and didn't even know it.

God is trying to give birth to something greater than you can imagine in you. Will you humble yourself and get in position to receive it?

God Bless

Knowledge Applied

> "For this reason, since the day we heard about you, we have not stopped praying for you. We continually ask God to fill you with the knowledge of his will through all the wisdom and understanding that the Spirit gives,"- **Colossians 1:9**

Paul is the author and he is speaking to the Church at Colosse. He wanted to combat the evil trying to take down the church and show believers that they had everything that they needed in Christ. Even though Paul had never been to Colosse before, he knew that the church existed and religious leaders to include paganism and secular philosophy with Christian doctrine were infiltrating it. So again Paul's mission here was to confront these false teachings and affirm the sufficiency of Christ.

There were people during that time that valued the accumulation of knowledge. They were called Gnostics. Their foundation of what they believe was based on the knowledge that they accumulated on their own. Paul's emphasis was that just having knowledge in itself is empty. If the knowledge is going to be worth anything it must be life changing and cause you to live right. Paul had two prayers for them and for us as well. First, he wants us all to be filled with the knowledge of God's will and understand it spiritually. Second, he wants us to grow in the knowledge of God by bearing fruit in everything that we do.

We all acquire knowledge daily and what we pick up may help us in other areas of our life, but often times it is limited to what we are doing. The only way I can take something that I have learned from my job and apply it to my life is to relate it to the word of God and attach it to a Godly principle. Growing up many of us heard the phrase that "Knowledge is Power". I have since learned that applied knowledge is power and the only way to measure its power is by the change in your life and seeing others lives change as a result of you sharing that applied knowledge. There is no theory known to man that will stand on its own unless it is tested and proven. So far from my research when it comes to this Spiritual walk the only thing that stands strong consistently is the Word of God.

There are a lot of people who believe so many different things and if we are not careful some of what people say will cause you to question what you believe. Some people are so easily influenced that is why it is so important for us to grow in the knowledge of God's will for our lives and gain a full understanding of His word. The Bible says in all of our getting make sure that we get understanding. The only knowledge that we gain that will truly have lasting power is the knowledge of God. Upon us getting an understanding of His word we have to share it with others for it to be affirmed in us and for us to help others grow in that same knowledge. So in essence Paul has called us to be Spiritual tutors. Are you ready for your next session?

God Bless

I Know He loves me

"For God did not send his Son into the world to condemn the world, but to save the world through him."- **John 3:17**

Our confirmation that this text is true is the one verse that precedes it. It is a well-known scripture that paints a picture of true love. Ponder this. Why would God follow through if He didn't love us? Think about what it would take for you to make the same sacrifice. Jesus was very selfless and more than willing to sacrifice Himself so that we could live in Him. Through His unselfish actions we now have the opportunity to live forever with God. Jesus, for a moment, exemplified human feelings with the thought of being separated from God. In Matthew 26:39 Jesus says, "O my Father, if it be possible, let this cup pass from me." Then realizing His purpose He completes His thoughts by saying, "Yet I want your will to be done, not mine."

There are so many places in the Bible where Jesus proves His love for us. However it is so clear in this verse in Matthew. Jesus came to save the world and, more importantly, so that you and I may have eternal life through Him. That is why when the Bible says in Psalms 118:24 that "This is the day that the Lord has made, let us rejoice and be glad in it", we should do just that. The Lord has made a way out-of-no-way for us by making a sacrifice that we would be too selfish to make.

Awake every morning with the full confidence that Jesus came to save the world and He had you in mind when He was nailed to that rough rugged cross.

God Bless

Honor God With Your Body

"You were bought at a price. Therefore honor God with your body."- **1 Corinthians 6:20**

Whenever I go to the store and make a purchase it is for something that I need or that my family needs or wants. Either way it will be used the way we choose for it to be used and that is the expectation. All of us are usually very careful with how we manage our money. When we make a major purchase it is usually well thought out and there is a plan in place on how it will be used. Most of our larger purchases are normally some kind of investment. My wife and I made one of those purchases recently; it will benefit our family. We sacrificed by saving the money for the purchase.

So since we made the investment we are going to do everything that we can to make sure that it works out for our good. At the end of the day, it will serve its purpose and our household will be blessed.

God made a major purchase as well when He gave everything that He had to redeem us back to Himself. The interesting part about it is that God, just like us, already had a plan before He made His major purchase. God wasn't concerned with the risk, because just like the Bible says, eventually every knee will bow before Him and every tongue will confess God. Even though He has a unique plan for all of us, ultimately we are all to serve Him and bring glory to His name with our lives. The scripture is just a reminder that we were purchased at a high price so we have to honor God with our bodies. The text is referring to not being sexually immoral and sinning against our bodies. While that should be a focus, the big picture the Lord put on my heart to paint today is simply this: we have to watch our walk. We were purchased to honor God and we have to make every effort to do just that. Verse 12 says that everything is permissible but everything is not beneficial. So, yes, we have the choice to do whatever we want, but everything we do won't benefit us or bring Glory to God.

Whenever we make a major purchase we always want to make good on our return. The Lord wants the same thing. Consider your purpose today and that God made the purchase for you to fulfill that purpose. Are you honoring God with your body?

God Bless

His Mercy

> "For the Mighty One has done great things for me Holy is His name. His mercy extends to those who fear Him, from generation to generation." - **Luke 1:49-50**

My brother is twelve years older than I am so I had the pleasure of always saying my big brother to people and really meaning it. I really wasn't a troublemaker in school; however if ever I were to start some trouble I always felt like my big brother would handle it. I have seen children, who had older siblings, start picking on other children and creating drama because they knew that their older siblings would defend them even, if they started it. In those days that was security at its finest, knowing that no matter what mess you got yourself into, someone would always bail you out.

Now always having them around, I'm sure became an issue from time to time because a situation could spark and they wouldn't have time to get their help. As a result of not having immediate access to their help, they would always get what the asked for, trouble.

What about now though, now that you are grown, who is going to provide that kind of protection or better? If I called my big brother now because I started some mess he would have a million questions before he would take action, mostly because we are both grown with families. So in essence, there is more to take into consideration.

Here the text is saying to us that God will take the slack for us. His mercy is His protection from consequences that we deserve but don't get. The best part about God is that He is loyal until the end as His word says. So that sense of security that you may have had as a children; can be supplied by God. However you never have to worry if He will be there. The word says as long as we fear Him, which means that we have to be willing to serve Him and submit to His authority, He will extend His mercy to us for generations. So we have the opportunity to set our children's children up to be protected by the Lord.

We spend plenty money on life insurance preparing to make sure that our families will be taken care of when we are gone. How assurance that you and your family will always be protected by the Great I Am? He has a policy with your name on it and the price has already been paid.

God Bless

His Love

"If I speak in the tongues of men and of angels, but have not love, I am only a resounding gong or a clanging cymbal. If I have the gift of prophecy and can fathom all mysteries and all knowledge, and if I have a faith that can move mountains, but have not love, I am nothing. If I give all I possess to the poor and surrender my body to the flames, but have not love, I gain nothing."- **1 Corinthians 13:1-3**

In Mrs. Lynch's 10th grade health class we learned her definition of love. She told us that love is a feeling that you feel when you feel like you have never felt before. I thought it was deep, I can't say I understood it but back then it was deep. I have asked the Lord to help me define love and what I got was that love is a spiritual likeness despite human difference.

Love requires you to give of yourself even when you don't feel it. Love is truly what Jesus did on the cross for us. Here the text is conveying that your status, knowledge, or esteem don't matter, for without love, you are hollow. 1 John 4:6 says, "God is love. Whoever lives in love lives in God, and God in him." You can have everything in the world but if you don't have love you don't have anything at all.

God Bless

Help with the Load

"Carry each other's burdens, and in this way you will fulfill the law of Christ."- **Galatians 6:2**

We live in a world that is so critical of others. The minute that people, especially of status, do something wrong, they find themselves the poster child of wrongdoing. The sad part is that many people adopt that same view without even knowing any information about what happened.

As Christians we shouldn't be so quick to judge others, as a matter of fact the Bible says," Do not judge or you too will be judged."

We should have more concern for our brothers and sisters and be willing to help them carry their heavy loads. That is what burden is referred to here in the text. Everyone wants to be restored when something out of character happens to him or her. The Law of Christ is referred to here in Matthew 22:39 "Love your neighbor as you love yourself." This is the second greatest commandment as stated by Jesus Himself.

Let us have more compassion for our brothers and sisters, especially because Jesus did it for us.

God Bless

Heart's Reflection

"As water reflects a face, so a man's heart reflects the man."
- Proverbs 27:19

As a young child I spent a lot of time in the country visiting my grandparents. I can remember sometimes going fishing as well as going to the lake to go swimming. As I have gotten older one of my friends and I have spent some time fishing out on the water where calmness overcomes us. As I would lean over and look into the water, I'd noticed that the reflection was a perfect image of me. Even when I looked in the water as a child, as I changed position the reflection was still identical, down to the very last detail. Even when I would throw a rock into the water, the ripples would slightly distort my reflection, however once the water would calm nothing about my reflection changed. I couldn't fool the water into showing me something different because it stayed true by showing the real me.

Our text today is reinforcing the same concept. It uses a metaphor comparing a reflection in the water to what's in a man's heart and how it is revealed. The Bible says in Proverbs 4:23: "Above all else, guard your heart, for it is the wellspring of life." It has always been an issue of the heart for all of us. What is in us will be revealed by how we talk to others, how we treat others, and how we feel about ourselves; you can't hide a difference of opinion too long before it comes out. Out of the heart flow the issues of life. So our feelings will always be revealed in some way and paint a true picture of who we really are. If you are not a caring person you can only fake it for so long before the truth is revealed.

This is why it is so important for us to guard our hearts so they won't get contaminated. Think about it. When you get sick, you are not yourself. Once that virus gets in your system, it tries to take over and it causes you to be sluggish and tired. Until you take the proper medicine and get the right amount of rest, people can't see the real you. Our hearts are the same way: If we allow jealousy, envy, or hate in our hearts, they will take over. Consequently, we should daily ask God to create in us pure hearts and renew a steadfast spirit within us according to Psalm 51:10.

We need the Lord's help so that when people see you they get the real you. When people first look at you they see your reflection, but when they listen to your words observe your behavior, they see your heart. When choosing a mate you see the outward appearance but remember that physical attractiveness pales in comparison to ugly ways. That is why the Bible says that beauty is fleeting, what is on the inside truly matters. Proverbs 21:2 says, "All a man's ways seem right to him, but the LORD weighs the heart." If God looks at the heart and we are made in His image, character is more valuable than the superficial. When you look at beautiful pearls, you wouldn't imagine their rough and unattractive origin. If you research pearls, you will find that these jewels are found inside this slimy substance, that on sight you wouldn't think about touching. Our true worth is measured by what we have on the inside, regardless of outward appearances. We have to be careful to guard our hearts so that when people see us they get a true reflection of who we really are. When people look at you, what do they see?

God Bless

He will finish

> "The LORD will fulfill his purpose for me; your love, O LORD, endures forever— do not abandon the works of your hands."- **Psalm 138:8**

Here we find David in the midst of praise to God. Praise is our expression of delight in God Himself, and of love as we consider how great God really is. He is expressing thanksgiving for answered prayers. David had been through a lot in his life and the one thing that remained consistent throughout his experiences is God. God's presence was always felt and His love for David was very evident. After all, God said that David was a man after His own heart. God played a major role in David's life through the good and the bad. David was confident that the Lord would deliver him from those who were against him because of His love. David expressed how even though the Lord is exalted above all, He doesn't judge by human standards. The text says that He looks to the lowly, not the proud, because those who are considered as lowly are humble and shall be exalted. In the same breath; pride comes before destruction, so that is why God doesn't look to the proud. In his humility, David made a simple request; even though he had great confidence in the Lord, he still asked the Lord not to let him down.

We all have plans that we want to manifest in our futures. In order for us to bring them to fruition, we have to include God's plan in our own. We should submit our plans to the Lord and pray that they line up with the Lord's plan for us. We all know that God alone knows what's best for us and He is the only one who can fulfill His purpose in our lives. Our goal should be to have smooth transitions in life and with God that is possible. We have to keep in mind that everything won't always go smoothly; however God loves us so much that He still protects us through the difficult times. Like David says, His love endures forever and we are the works of His hands. We should acknowledge the power of the Lord and make it clear that we know our place by consistently asking God not to abandon us. In doing this, we humble ourselves, submit to God, and show confidence that we are relying on Him alone to get through. Paul says that we should give thanks in all circumstances and we have to take on the Spirit of David and express thanksgiving to God at all times. The song says, "Praise is what I do, even when I'm going through." Our praise aligns us with God and allows us to be lifted out of the worst situations because we are so focused on God. In order for God to fulfill His purpose for us, we must recognize His love for us. He would never leave us or forsake us. We have to trust the direction that He gives us. As long as we are following Him, our hearts desires will be revealed to us and we will be able to succeed.

God Bless

He Will

> "This is the confidence we have in approaching God: that if we ask anything according to his will, he hears us. And if we know that he hears us—whatever we ask—we know that we have what we asked of him." - **1 John 5:14-15**

I sometimes tutor students in mathematics and as we all know this subject is not everyone's favorite. In fact, math can be like learning a foreign language for many, so they lack confidence. Anytime you lack confidence there is a disconnection between you and whatever that is; however the only thing stopping you from being more confident is you. It all comes down to the time you spend getting more familiar with whatever you have the disconnection with.

By the same token, when you know something, confidence is not an issue. When you are really sure about anything you will stand on it and be willing to put everything you own on that because you are so sure. Think about the last time someone tried to prove you wrong about something that you were so sure about. Then, think about the energy and the emotion involved with proving your point until the end. Most people will get so emotional that it is upsetting if the other person doesn't understand. There are times that some people are even willing to fight just to prove that they are right; they are very passionate.

When you think about your relationship with God which of the two categories are you in? God's desire is for us to be completely sure and confident in Him. We should be in a place where nothing will change your mind or perspective on who God is and what He will do. There are, however, a number of people who are not too sure about their relationships with God so they are very hesitant to go to God with their requests or prayers. If they go to God, there is still uncertainty that anything will happen as a result of their actions. Having that kind of disconnection with God puts us in a dangerous place. We are very vulnerable at that point and the enemy sees us as prime targets to seek and attempt to destroy. If you have ever gone to God for anything He has provided what you asked, even if not in the way you wanted. God is not like Burger King where you get things "your way right away." He operates in His time and He is always on time. God supplies us with what we need when He feels that we need it. It is up to us to believe that He is always operating on our behalf with our best interest in mind.

Just as the text says, we have to be confident, sure that when we ask God anything according to His will that He hears us. Not only does He hear us, He will also provide for us according to His will. If we lack confidence in God, we don't recognize when He actually provides what we need. Draw closer to the Lord today; spend more time with Him and know for yourself that without a shadow of a doubt that you can count on Him always.

God Bless

He Already Made a Way

"However, as it is written: "No eye has seen, no ear has heard, no mind has conceived what God has prepared for those who love him"- **1 Corinthians 2:9**

When it comes to people that we don't know, we tend to handle them from a distance with extreme caution. This behavior is mostly accredited to not feeling safe around them because we don't know them or what they are capable of. What we see and hear in the media has helped to shape this mindset. There is nothing wrong with being cautious and protecting you at all.

When we feel like we know a persons motives and who they are, we tend to open up a little bit and invite them to a closer view of whom we really are. Some people develop relationship with us and it is simply to get something out of us, not that the relationship is not genuine. The truth of the matter is, that some of us do the same thing knowing that there is only so much that this person can help us acquire. That could be more knowledge and understanding about something or just relationship to gain favor from someone in position to help us get ahead.

Either way, in these relationships, we tend to go all out sometimes and have no limits to what we will do or allow, just getting what we think they can help provide. In time we find out that there are certain conditions that we have to abide by in this relationship to get to our goal and if we violate anything then we are back to square one.

It is interesting to me though, how we have the Holy Bible as a guide, so we know Jesus' purpose; we know what God wants to do for us. Truthfully, if we just read the word, we get a view of the end result before we ever start our journey with the Lord. We know that He wants to work *everything* out for our good; we *can* do *all things* in Christ Jesus. God wants to mature us so that we are *lacking nothing*, yet we won't go all out for Him.

The scripture here says, "We have not seen or heard what the Lord has prepared for us who Love Him." Meaning, God has already made a way for our success beforehand; before we were born into the world He already had everything planned out for us specifically. No matter how great our mind is, there is nothing that we can imagine that will add up to the vision that the Lord has for our lives. How is it that so many people trust man, who can only operate in the power that the Lord gives them, more than they trust God?

God Bless

Guard the Truth

> "What you heard from me, keep as the pattern of sound teaching, with faith and love in Christ Jesus. Guard the good deposit that was entrusted to you—guard it with the help of the Holy Spirit who lives in us."- **2 Timothy 1:13-14**

Paul was giving Timothy some very important instructions before he released him with major responsibilities in ministry. He was telling young Timothy to be confident in what he knew and seal it by his faith and love in Jesus Christ. What Paul says here is that there was a pattern of sound teaching. This meant that Timothy went through a process where he received the word of God from someone who has very sound doctrine. It included several conversations about his life in Christ and what he should do and how he should live. Timothy staying mindful of his teachings will allow him to also be a great leader and live a life worthy of being imitated. Throughout Timothy's preparation, he has been on a continuous learning curve with the word. When you receive the word, it is not just for you to keep to yourself, we should be like Jeremiah, weary of holding it in.

Paul makes it clear that God has made a major deposit in Timothy and the truth is He has done the same for us. We all have to guard that deposit that God entrusted us with, and we have to guard it with our lives. The comfort in this is that we don't have to worry about doing it by ourselves because the Holy Spirit is going to help us. As a matter of fact, the Holy Spirit is a deposit from the Lord guaranteeing our inheritance. We are sealed in Him until the day of redemption, so that help is with us always.

I pray that you all are at a Bible based church getting fed the infallible word of God. I encourage you like Paul, to continue your journey of drawing closer to God and hide His word in your hearts, so that you won't sin against Him. Know that you do have help and the help is in the Power of the Holy Spirit who dwells in all of us.

God Bless

God's Plan vs. Your Plan

"Many are the plans in a man's heart, but it is the Lord's purpose that prevails." - **Proverbs 19:21**

Anyone who has a pulse makes plans for their life. Some take longer than others to decide to do it, however at some point everyone makes a plan. This doesn't mean that you have put much thought into the plan. For some they have a plan A through Z.

The true disappointment comes when your plan doesn't succeed. After you have made every effort to make it work and the outcome still is not what you envisioned. For some at this point, they want to give up and just call it quits. Disappointment has the ability to really knock the wind out of you. Get you off course.

Your relationship with God is very important when you draw this conclusion. Knowing the word of God will give you hope even when your plan is not working. God always has your best interest at heart. He is always looking out for you.

When Flour started layoffs, my plan was to do everything I could to keep a job so that I could take care of my family. I wanted to either stay under the radar or find a job locally because moving out of the city or state was out of the question. I received a call for a job interview but it required me to go three hours away and then I discovered that the job was three hours away as well. My first thought was, that is not apart of the plan so I'm not doing it. In a matter of five minutes, my emotions were all over the place because this news deviated from my plan.

The Holy Spirit spoke to me through my wife and I trusted God and His plan. As many of you know the Lord worked it out for me to work for that company but it was because I trusted God and His plan. Since the Lord's vision is always larger than life, I work about 10 minutes from my house.

When God's plan work out it is always what's best for you.

God Bless

God's Grace

"Who has saved us and called us to a holy life—not because of anything we have done but because of his own purpose and grace. This grace was given us in Christ Jesus before the beginning of time,"- **2 Timothy 1:9**

Paul cries out in Romans
"Oh, what a miserable person I am! Who will free me from this life that is dominated by sin and death?"

This is the cry of a believer who wants to shake sin and start fresh with a clean heart.

I bring this up because even in Paul's situation when he was Saul, he did what most people would see as some very unforgivable things. However God had a purpose for his life and at the appointed time he was called to do what God had set aside for him to do. God saved Saul and changed his name to Paul, giving him a new identity and an opportunity to start over.

We too are sinners, saved by grace through faith in Christ Jesus our Lord and Savior by the Power of the Holy Spirit. If God handled us according to our sin, just imagine where we would be right now. The awesome thing is He saved us too and we can plainly see that it had nothing to do with us or anything that we have done. We don't deserve what God is doing for us, however His grace allows it. We too should have a strong desire to shake sin off and start anew.

Grace is the free gift from God to receive His mercy and favor with no prerequisite besides willingness to follow, trust, and love him. Sometimes that is not revealed until after we go through some hardships. What GOD asked of us is free. However, what God has done for us cost Him everything and there is no way that we can repay Him. We deserve the penalty of our actions, the consequences of our pre-meditated thoughts; we deserve death, but God said, "No I'll take that for you and allow you the option to choose to follow me." He doesn't want us to try to pay Him back. That's grace.

In saying that GOD loves us so much that before we were a sparkle in our parent's eye or even a thought, God granted us grace and he designed a purposeful life uniquely for each of us. Often times we can't see what God is up to, so we have to be confident that He has already worked it out for us. Because of His grace, we can fulfill God's purpose in our lives.

Shake off your past sins; God has already made allowances for you to live a purposeful life. Embrace what God has done for you. The things you have learned and experienced are all a part of God's plan. The journey is the most important thing; the destination is a reward.

God Bless

Give Your All

> "Hear, O Israel: The LORD our God, the LORD is one. Love the LORD your God with all your heart and with all your soul and with all your strength."- **Deuteronomy 6:4-5**

This text comes from what's called the Pentateuch, the Torah, and The Laws of Moses. Torah is Hebrew for teaching or instructions and this verse is from the book giving specific instructions to Israel on obeying God and following the law. Prior to verses four and five, verses one through three explain that they are about to be taught the commands and decrees to cross into the land flowing with milk and honey. The author was very clear that these commands and decrees needed to be taught to their children and their children's children so that they may fear the Lord and have long lives.

The author; presumed to be Moses, is very specific about their being careful to be obedient so that they can receive God's promise of entering into the land flowing with milk and honey with prosperity. This verse picks up, making it very clear again for them to listen carefully to what is being said. The Lord is one, meaning He is the only God; He is God and God alone. Verse five is pretty straight to the point. We can attach ourselves to other people, for example. When you first meet someone that you really like, if you tell the truth about it you give everything you have to showing them that you care and want to be with them. It can get to the point that there isn't anything that you won't do for them. You would spend your last so that they could have, you would sacrifice your time and miss appointments, take off from work, and stand your friends up. We tend to look at them as if they can do no wrong in our eyes. If I am the only one who has done this before, shame on you. The funny part about this is that you are doing it because you really want to and not because you will benefit from it.

If we could learn to love God that way and give that kind of treatment and consideration consistently to God, just imagine how much closer to Him we would be. The thing that most people miss is that if you can't love the Lord with all that is in you, how could you possibly love anyone else that way? Give God your all and receive all that He has in store for you.

God Bless

Give Freely, Praise Freely

"Yours, O LORD, is the greatness and the power and the glory and the majesty and the splendor, for everything in heaven and earth is yours. Yours, O LORD, is the kingdom; you are exalted as head over all."- **1 Chronicles 29:11**

Originally my thought was to highlight that everything belongs to God. We wake up daily wanting to know about certain things for sure, like how our day is going to go or if we will be successful at what we are doing that day. The truth is we don't have to guess at who is in control. The earth is the Lord's and the fullness that dwells therein.

Then I read verses one through twenty and realized why David praised the Lord the way he did. David was a leader and he did just that; he led. He gave all of his resources for the building of the Lord's temple, which was his son Solomon's task. As a result of David giving all of his resources, his people did the same thing. The Bible says that they gave freely and wholeheartedly to the Lord to consecrate themselves for the building of His temple.

Consequently, their being so willing to help with Solomon's task made them open to experience true praise. They didn't view the task as Solomon's and feel that he was on his own. They gave freely as well, knowing that everything belongs to God anyway. It was by His grace that they had it to give.

The opportunity comes daily for us to give what the Lord gave us. "Our money, singleness, marriage, talent, and time were all loaned to us to show the world that Christ is Divine" (Don't Waste Your Life by: Lecrea). He goes on to say in that song that Christ is for him all the time because our whole world is built around Him. He's the Life in our Line. So everything we have, including our lives, belongs to the Lord and we should be willing to give freely and wholeheartedly to the Kingdom of God. In our giving we will move into a spiritual place that will allow us to praise God like David did. We will be in positions to lead the way for others to follow. So, let us remember the words of Lecrea and more importantly let us remember why David was praising the way he was. Let David's actions move you to action and prayerfully your actions will start a movement amongst the people of the world.

God Bless

Get a Better Reception

"Very early in the morning, while it was still dark, Jesus got up, left the house and went off to a solitary place, where he prayed." -**Mark 1:35**

When considering communicating with God, there is not a lot that needs to be considered. No matter where we are or where we go, we can always take time out to talk to God. The awesome part about it is that He is always available.

What we should take in to consideration is following the model of Christ. A lot of time when we are talking to the Lord it is almost like speaking to someone in passing. We are on our way to work or school, getting the children dressed, brushing our teeth, or just getting into the bed and falling asleep while praying.

Jesus got up early in the morning while everything was still quiet and everybody was still asleep. Jesus found it so important that He went where He could not be disturbed or distracted in order to talk with the Lord. I know that my days are very busy, however I recognize the need to follow this model. It makes your day go a lot smoother and puts you in a place of peace before everything gets started.

It's funny how when we are having a conversation on our cell phones we tend to find the best place for the best reception because we want to hear everything and, more importantly, to be heard. Sometimes it gets so serious that folks will pull off of the side of the road to talk so that they can concentrate on the conversation.

Don't you think that God deserves more attention than everybody else? I mean what if we found it important enough to pull on the side of the road to talk to God? Think about how many people wouldn't have accidents or get cursed out for driving crazy. What if we found it so important, that we designated a time to go off to a quiet place to get the best reception with our communication with God? How much better would your day be?

Wow! I really have some work to do because I too can be too casual with my conversation with God. Make the commitment today. I am.

God Bless

Fruit of the Spirit

"But the fruit of the Spirit is love, joy, peace, patience, kindness, goodness, faithfulness, gentleness and self-control. Against such things there is no law." - **Galatians 5:22-23**

When I was younger I would always visit my grandparents in the country. In my grandmother's front yard was a big pear tree, from which she would get an endless supply to make her most famous pear preservative. It amazed me at such a young age to learn that fruit came from a tree. I also observed that the tree only produced pears and not apples or oranges. It was the tree's nature.

When we become a new creation through Jesus Christ we too take on a new nature. That new nature also produces fruit that are listed in our text for today. If you look closely, you will recognize that the fruit of the Spirit is not what you do; it is what you are. These descriptions are all about your character and not your activity. Your character is an account of your qualities; it defines who you are.

It is possible for some of these characteristics to be stronger in you than others. However, the goal is to be strong in them all. The key is that you have to believe that Christ can become all of these things in you. When we accept Jesus Christ as Lord and Savior we are asking Him to come in and take control of our lives. The only way to answer the question if you have really become a Christian is if you have surrendered your life to Christ, and have trusted God to be in control.

In order for you to become stronger in your walk and make these characteristics stand out, stop trying so hard to be in control. It is understandable that it is difficult to do because we become so accustomed to doing it. As Christians, we have to make a simple decision everyday to give Christ the control. When we release the power and give it to Jesus, His nature produces the fruit of the Spirit in us. Just like when we plant a fruit tree we can't control how fast it grows. We plant that tree and we trust that it will go through its natural process and grow. We sit back and allow nature to do its thing. We don't have to struggle so hard to be like Jesus in order for these characteristics to be produced in us; we just have to let Jesus Christ be Himself in us.

Which of these characteristics can others see in you today? Which one would you love to grow stronger in? In order for the fruit of the Spirit to manifest in our lives we have to let go and let God.

God Bless

Fearfully and Wonderfully Made

> "For you created my inmost being; you knit me together in my mother's womb. I praise you because I am fearfully and wonderfully made; your works are wonderful, I know that full well."- **Psalm 139:13-14**

When I was younger I used to put model cars together and it was so much fun. The detail of the work and connecting every piece one at a time until completion was so gratifying. It brought me joy because of the time I put into making the car and seeing the finished product was the great reward. Looking at the car after it was done, after picturing everything in my mind down to the innermost details, (even what the eye couldn't see) was so amazing. Once you put in the time detailing it becomes a masterpiece to you and you want to preserve it as long as possible. Its value has increased with you because you shaped it and molded it.

God sees us the same way. He took His time shaping and molding each one of us to a unique finish. The awesome part about it is that we are all originals, one-of-a-kind creations. Anybody who knows art knows that the less prints you have of a masterpiece, the more value it carries. Look at how valuable you are to God. There is no one like you and no matter how hard anyone tries; there will never be another you. So in God's eyes we are priceless.

We have to have the same view as the psalmists. They came to the understanding of how valuable they were and we have to do the same. God took His time crafting us and He made us so valuable that no one could afford the price tag but He. He didn't have to pay the full cost, but He did because we mean the world to Him.

Don't let anyone steal your value or make you feel worthless. If others try to devalue you, let them know that God made you unique. You are a blood-bought original, a one-of-a-kind.

God Bless

Expecting

"For I know the plans I have for you," declares the LORD, "plans to prosper you and not to harm you, plans to give you hope and a future. Then you will call upon me and come and pray to me, and I will listen to you. You will seek me and find me when you seek me with all your heart."
- **Jeremiah 29:11-13**

The first part of this text was covered before so now we have to bring it on home. As stated before, in this text, where we pick it up, God confirms for us that He knows what He is doing. So you don't have to question Him or doubt His love for us. When you face a challenge He is right there, having already worked it out on your behalf. God's plan is for you to achieve greatness in all that you do and nothing less.

The challenge for us is to believe the Lord at His word and not allow doubt to get us off track. Doubt leads to paralyzing fear that stops your progress. Once you embrace God's plan for your life, you can pick up at verse 12. That is what the word "Then" signifies after you accept God's promise. You will then be ready to call upon the Lord with confidence that He will answer. You will be open to growing an intimate relationship with Him in prayer and when He speaks you will listen. Listening to God will require you to be still and patient.

When you seek for the Lord you won't just do it half way. You have to do it with all that is within you and have the expectation that you will find Him. My little sister had her first child and throughout her pregnancy, everyday she was excited about the day she would see her son. During the course of her pregnancy she put all of her heart and soul into staying healthy and eating right and doing everything that she could to protect the life within her and to ensure that once her journey was over, she would see little Baron. There were several very difficult days, during which she had to go to the emergency room. She never stopped believing or expecting to see his face. On February 22, 2010 she met the second love of her life and now life as she knew it will never be the same.

When you seek the Lord you have to do it with the same passion as a mother who is expecting her child. You have to expect the Lord to meet you right where you are every time you seek Him and you have to do it with all of your heart.

When you seek the Lord now knowing His plans for you, do you expect to see Him?

God Bless

Eternal Security

"He who dwells in the shelter of the Most High will rest in the shadow of the Almighty."- **Psalm 91:1**

We all want to feel secure or protected and those with families want to do everything to make sure that their families are protected. It is estimated that 72% of Americans feel that they can cut their risk of being burglarized by protecting their home with alarm systems. So there are a lot of people who really want to feel safe. What about eternal security for your soul?

The Bible says hear that those who take up permanent residence in the covering of God will rest in the shadow of the Almighty God. First, it has to be a choice to submit your life to God to be used by Him for a greater Holy purpose. Once you decide that is what you are going to do, you are subjected to being covered by God or in other words protected by the Most High God. The emphasis here on Most High, I believe, is to confirm that there is no one greater that God; so when you are under His protection you are truly covered.

The text goes on to say that you will rest in the shadow. "Will," suggests that it is inevitable, incapable of being avoided. Who wouldn't want to go to a place where one can't avoid getting rest, a place where one can have peace of mind about being covered? Here is a place where one doesn't have to worry about anything, because the Peace of God rules in the heart.

When we look at the shadow of the Almighty we have to define shadow. A shadow is a reverse projection of the object blocking the light. Since God is light, when you are resting in His shadow and your enemy approaches, guess what he sees? He sees God before he sees you because it is God's reflection of light protecting you. When your alarm system sounds at your house the first thing that activates is the light because the enemy hates light. God is so awesome and powerful that His shadow has wonderworking power. Everywhere that you go, His light covers you.

So while 72% percent of people say that their homes need protection, I am saying that 100% need God's protection. No one will look out for you like God. When you call Him He is sure to answer and His response time can't be beat. No one has a guarantee like the Lord and He can back up is word with a host of testimonies. So if you are looking for protection from the enemy, and want to provide eternal security for you and your family, don't call ADT; call on GOD. With God you're not only in good company, the one who is always there protects you.

God Bless

Don't Go Astray

"Do not those who plot evil go astray? But those who plan what is good find love and faithfulness."- **Proverbs 14:22**

Considering the history of the world we know that there are a lot of evil people, a number of them who bluntly execute their evil plans and are not ashamed to let others know that they did it. Of course these folks will be dealt with accordingly.

What about those who plot or conceive evil plans but get someone else to carry them out? What about those people who plan harmful things or who carry out sinful and wicked acts towards you? These people are moving away from what is desirable by God. They are off the right path. The truth is they will be dealt with according to the word. The Bible says in 2 Thessalonians 1:6 "God is fair. He will pay back trouble to those who give you trouble."

The purpose today is not to focus on those who do evil but to help us all know that God is paying attention and when He says that He will be with us always, He really means it. Most importantly, we can't do evil for evil. As tempting as it may be to plot to get even with someone, we have to remember that the Bible says that vengeance is the Lord's, not ours, and it is He who will handle those who oppress you.

We want to put ourselves in positions to always receive God's love, faithfulness, and mercy. We have sinned enough coming into the world and will have moments when sin will continue to take place in our lives. What we don't want to do is to have premeditated plots of wickedness that we carry out or get someone else to help us carry out. Trust God and know that he will fight your battles for you. He is the only one I know who has never lost fight. Folks don't even see it coming when He hits them and even if they do, they can't move fast enough. There is nowhere that they can hide.

Join me as I do my best to resist even having sinful thoughts towards others, let alone carrying them out. Let us trust that God can handle our heavy and lightweight. Anything that someone does to you is small compared to what God has in store for you. Heed the words in a book I have looked at before that reads, "Don't sweat the small stuff, it is only small stuff."

God Bless

Don't fool yourself.

> "Do not be deceived: God cannot be mocked. A man reaps what he sows. The one who sows to please his sinful nature, from that nature will reap destruction; the one who sows to please the Spirit, from the Spirit will reap eternal life."
> **- Galatians 6:7-8**

When I read this verse it says so much to me, especially when reading verses 1-6 and 9-10 along with it. There are some people apparently who believe that they can fool God and that God can be deceived. Here Apostle Paul is setting the record straight by saying, "Hey, don't fool yourself."

We have all at some time in our lives been caught up in sin. Though not proud of it, however, we allowed whatever it was to manifest. Once realized, our response to sin is so essential because it lays a foundation for the days ahead. If we continue to ignore the tugging of the Holy Spirit, of course we are feeding that negative spirit and just as the Bible says, it will lead to destruction. We can find ourselves losing so much because of the sin that we commit. The sad part is that we often don't see it until it is done.

On the flipside, doing our best to please God in all things yields nourishing fruit and propels us to eternal life in Christ. The verses before 7 & 8 are clear in saying that we can't always do this alone. Those of us who are spiritual when we see our friends or family caught up in sin; give them tough love. Our job is to do our best to restore them being careful not to get caught up ourselves.

This is not going to be an easy task depending on the individual because he or she has to receive your tough love after accepting where he or she is, not forgetting that you are not perfect either. Do your best to stay focused on God's plan for your life and no matter the temptation, just know that if you just stay focused and never give up, you will reap a harvest. Even if you have been caught up by the power of the Holy Spirit, that situation can turn around and work out for your good.

God Bless

Don't fall for it.

> "No temptation has seized you except what is common to man. And God is faithful; he will not let you be tempted beyond what you can bear. But when you are tempted, he will also provide a way out so that you can stand up under it."- **1 Corinthians 10:13**

It is so amazing how the word of God is so relevant and timeless. As we continue our journey through life, time and our weakness determine the temptations we face. The truth of the matter is that everyone will be tempted by something. Even those who feel so connected to God will be tempted by something. What is important is your response to the temptation.

Recognize that many of us fall or have fallen for at least one thing that we have been tempted by. For many there was a valuable lesson learned as well. However for some, the same temptation comes and they keep falling for it over and over. Many want to blame God; but the word is clear that God will not tempt you. Almost everyone wants to say "the devil made me do it" and I say that you are giving that dude too much credit.

The enemy doesn't have that much power. As a matter of fact, he is powerless until we supply him power by moving away from God with our thoughts or our actions. The enemy is an opportunist and he will take advantage of an opportunity given the chance. If we second-guess ourselves, especially in an area we are weak in, he will come in and try to seduce you so that you will cross that boundary in front of you. Once you cross over he becomes motivated and turns up the heat.

The word is very clear here we will all be tempted, however God is forever faithful and always with us. When temptation comes and keeps calling your name, God says that He has already MADE A WAY of ESCAPE for you in that situation. Here is another time we know that God is so powerful and He really loves us because He sees the traps before we get to them and has His hand out to lead us away from a potentially dangerous situation.

Based on this word, we can no longer blame anybody for the temptation we fall for. I say this because we have the power to choose what we will and won't do. So if you fall for temptation it is because you choose to do it, not because someone made you do it. We have to take ownership of our actions and make better decisions with this precious thing God calls life.

If you fall for the temptation God still provides a way out if you choose to escape. Please don't fall for temptation and then decide to go all out since you are in the sin. Run to the light to expose that dark force coming against you and it will flee.

Here is another word for you to from James 4:17, "He who knows the good he ought to do and doesn't do it, sins."

In other words, you are accountable for what you know.

You have now been empowered; what are you going to do about it?

God Bless

Don't Crucify Them

"Above all, love each other deeply, because love covers over a multitude of sins." **1 Peter 4:8**

What makes love so special? To start, it is what motivated our Heavenly Father to send His one and only Son to die for us. Detrick Haddon has a song that goes," You ain't got nothing if you don't have love." He goes on to say," Without true love you're on a road going nowhere." So love really is as powerful as the word of God says it is.

Here, we are told that above everything else we should love one another. As Christians, that is one thing that we should have in common. The contrast to that though is when someone offends us, most of us do everything but show love. As children of God we should be able to forgive and do our best to forget whatever the offense is. Instead of forgiving, so many are quick to wrongfully expose our brothers and sisters without thinking because of the hurt that we feel. The hurt blinds us from focusing on the love of God within us. Truthfully, when someone offends me my impulse is to throw them under the bus. However, I have grown to not react so impulsively anymore. Instead, I really think it through and ask God to reveal the opportunity in this inconvenience for Him to get Glory. I still address the individual; however I do so in a loving way. Keep in mind that someone who is in Christ should understand. For those who are not in Christ, this process may be a little more difficult. However your approach should still be the same. You never know that if you show love (to someone who has never been loved) you may gain him or her for Christ's sake.

The truth is no matter how we handle it God is still going to handle it with love. He sent Jesus to be the example for us and so He expects us to follow the model of Christ. He forgave and told us that He would forgive us if we forgive others.

So don't crucify those who offend you instead begin to practice showing them the love of Christ.

God Bless

Don't be Foolish

"A fool has no delight in understanding but only in revealing his personal opinions and himself." -**Proverbs 18:2**

Have you ever shed light on a situation and the person you were talking with was more interested in your finishing what you were saying so that he or she could talk? Have you ever been talking with someone about something you were going through and he or she turned it around and made it about them and never helped you with your problem?

God has blessed us all with wisdom and the ability to gain more wisdom and knowledge about His word and life. You name it. One scripture though, makes it really clear. Proverbs 4:7 says," Wisdom is the principal thing; therefore get wisdom: and with all your getting get understanding."

So many people miss that simple principle. Understanding is simply getting a mental grasp on something, comprehending it. Instead so many people always consider themselves resident experts on all things about life. The truth is that they are just showing a lack of understanding by just giving their personal opinions.

Don't get me wrong. Your personal opinion may be valid. However, it may not be relevant to the situation at the time, so that is where getting understanding comes in. When I have a conversation with someone about something that I am dealing with, I don't always want to hear a long soliloquy about him or her if it is not relevant and leading me to a solution. Ultimately what the result is that many people are not good listeners or so caught up in themselves that other people really don't matter.

Take the time out to listen when someone comes to you about a situation and make sure that you really soak it all in, even if you have to ask questions to make sure that you understand what they are talking about. I will say this. In your response to them, if you lead with the word, you can't go wrong. This applies to any situation, not just when someone is going through something.

I used to stand around and listen to the fellas talking about sports and without knowing anything about what they are saying. I would sometimes throw something in the conversation just to be a part of it and when I did, the conversation paused for a moment. In that silent moment I realized how foolish I was for saying something that wasn't relevant. Now I get a better understanding before I make a fool of myself.

God Bless

Do you know the Father and does He know you?

> "[The Children of Abraham] To the Jews who had believed him, Jesus said, "If you hold to my teaching, you are really my disciples. Then you will know the truth, and the truth will set you free."- **John 8:31-32**

As I read this morning's verse, a few thoughts come to mind. First, there are so many people today who claim to be in Christ, and to have such a great relationship with Him. Yet when the Father looks at you, can He really tell that you are with Him? Are those just words that come out of people's mouths or can we tell you value Jesus by the way you represent His name? Most importantly, can God tell that you are His disciple? Here, some of God's chosen people were kind of suspect to Jesus, which is part of the reason that in verse 31-41 Jesus said that they were children of the devil. If we are in Christ, folks should be able to tell that we are. There shouldn't be much room for questioning our faith and our walk with the Lord. It doesn't mean that you have to walk around all day quoting scripture, however the scripture should live through you and others should be able to tell. Everyone should know, including you; that your identity is found in Christ.

You should also be able to recognize God, not so much in the physical sense, just in your spirit. You should know when you are in His presence and when you hear Him speaking to you. Think about it. No matter where you are, for those who have children for example, when they hear your voice they know that it is you. When I call my house and my wife puts me on speaker phone my oldest son says," What's up daddy?" and the Baby always says, "Hey!" or "Daddy!" They do that because they recognize my voice. The awesome revelation in them knowing my voice is the fact that they spend a lot of time with their father. If anyone is not sure that they hear the Lord when he speaks, it would probably mean we are not spending enough time with Him. I even have those moments sometimes when I ask God, "Is that you?"

Let us hold true the teaching of God so that we will know Him like He wants us to and there will be no question that we are His children. In doing so just like the scripture says we will know the truth, which is in Jesus Christ, and the truth will set us free. We will be recognized as the sons (meaning mankind) of God and not slaves to our sin.

God Bless

Do you Know Where You're Going to?

"But our citizenship is in heaven. And we eagerly await a
Savior from there, the Lord Jesus Christ,"- **Philippians 3:20**

"Theme From Mahogany", a song made very famous by Diana Ross in 1976 asks very important questions.

Do you know where you're going to?
Do you like the things that life is showing you?
Where are you going to? Do you know?
Do you get what you're hoping for?
When you look behind you there's no open door
What are you hoping for?
Do you know?

Do you know where you are going? Do you like the things that life is showing you? If not, what are you doing about it and if so, are you secure in your thought?

Paul makes it very clear here that our minds should be locked in as Heaven being our goal. Citizenship means that you are a citizen of a particular community and here it is in Heaven amongst those who believe and follow Christ. He says that all of us, who have matured, who have persevered, should share the same view. Living for Christ is not an easy task, which is why Paul says that he presses towards the goal. To press implies that there is an opposite force pushing back or applying pressure. The truth is that the enemy wants to knock us off track to prevent our accomplishing our goal, so we have to be ready to press everyday towards the goal. Just as Paul stated, there are many who live as enemies against the cross and they will do whatever they can to get us to join them. I had a conversation this weekend with a friend who has done so much research that he is starting to believe that the only true Bible is one written in the 1800's. In his mind, any version printed after that has been tainted and manipulated and it is unreliable, consequently.

The word of God is the word of God and no matter how many interpretations come out they do not take away its power. The central theme of the Bible is Jesus Christ and that is not going to change. Just like I told him, the true believers in Jesus Christ will study to show themselves approved unto God, rightly dividing the word of truth. So we have to go into the word, study for ourselves, and not just take someone else's word for it. That is all apart of that pressing process. The bottom line is this: The Lord has set aside for us some Holy Real estate and there is not a devil in hell or on earth that is going to cause me to foreclose on my property. I am a child of the Most High God and my destination is Heaven because that is where I belong and the only place that I will fit in. I am convinced of it and am willing to do what it takes to obtain what God has wanting for me. I am a citizen of Heaven and I will be ready when Jesus Christ comes to pick me up.

The only way to be sure about your future is to go out and create it. Do you know where you're going?

God Bless

Do You Believe

"So do not fear, for I am with you; do not be dismayed, for I am your God. I will strengthen you and help you; I will uphold you with my righteous right hand."- **Isaiah 41:10**

Assurance brings about a peace that many may not understand. Here God is speaking to Israel, giving him a command and a promise. See, Israel is Jacob's new God-given name. When you have an encounter with God, there is no way you can avoid being changed. In earlier text God was saying that Jacob was different from all the others because they were like a distant land. However, God pulled Israel from the far corners and brought him close.

If you read the whole text from verses 1 -10, you will see that God uses both the names Jacob and Israel. God didn't want us to lose focus that the conniving deceiver didn't go anywhere. He still exists, however he has encountered the Lord, so his life has changed. In all of us who have accepted Christ, we are all ex-something. Just because we are now in Christ doesn't change our past and the truth of the matter is if we allow ourselves to fall asleep on our assignment, we can create the opportunity to fall back down that slippery slope. So in essence, this is God's way of saying not to get it twisted; don't fool yourself into believing that you are perfect and infallible.

The command here is, "Don't worry about anything. God's got you." To worry or have fear is a paralyzing sin. When we serve the one True God who created all and He says don't fear we need to be obedient to His word. We can trust His word. In the same breath this is a promise as well. God is saying, "With all that you have been through, you sinner, since you have allowed me control over your life, you don't have to worry because I am with you." God even makes it personal by saying that He is your God. God is powerful so His strength and glory make Him able to help us but it is His love for us that makes Him want to help us.

Why would anyone not want to trust God? Even when He doesn't microwave your blessing, meaning give it to you right away, He still comes through in the end. It is after many give up on Him and start complaining, that God still comes through. People are so funny because when you allow yourself to believe in someone and they don't come through when you want them to, you quit on them. It is like they only get one chance and that is it. How many chances has God given you after you let Him down? Yet He still trusts you and provides for you?

God says not to fear for He IS with you. How many of you believe that God is really going to be with you through it all?

I do!

God bless

Do Not Love the World

"Do not love the world or anything in the world. If anyone loves the world, the love of the Father is not in him. For everything in the world—the cravings of sinful man, the lust of his eyes and the boasting of what he has and does—comes not from the Father but from the world."- **1 John 2:15-16**

There are so many opportunities for us to get so caught up in worldly ways, when God's vision is to set us aside for a greater purpose. Even the thought of trying to accumulate stuff to justify your status is really out of order because your stuff doesn't determine who you are.

When I was younger, I had a number of friends who would always go and steal just to get what they wanted. If they weren't stealing, they were selling drugs. Even when I got older, many of my friends smoked and drank almost everyday.

I decided not to follow their lead and to be the odd man out. As a matter of fact, it was exciting and challenging to be different from everybody else. What's so remarkable is that my decision worked out in my favor because to this day I have never drunk, smoked or been to jail. I have never even been suspended from school. Little did I know, I was practicing God's order and making it a lifestyle before I really got serious about following Christ.

This world in which we live and even the skin we are in, are temporary. We have to do the best with it while we have it. Not following the worldly ways and standards makes it a lot easier to clean this house that we live in as well as make a statement that God is our Lord and that it is in Him we live and move. Don't get caught up in worldly ways. They are detrimental to your future.

God Bless

Diligent

"God is not unjust; he will not forget your work and the love you have shown him as you have helped his people and continue to help them."- **Hebrews 6:10**

Have you ever wondered if God was paying attention to all of your good works?

We know He sees and knows everything as well. There is no reason to get discouraged when you think that God has forgotten about you. God is fair not unjust. He never forgets or overlooks our hard work for the kingdom.

Just because you may not be receiving the rewards of which you feel worthy, doesn't mean that God doesn't see your efforts of love and service.

The Bible tells us, "Being confident of this very thing, that he who hath begun a good work in you will perfect it until the day of Jesus Christ." What God has started will be finished so He is modeling for us how we should live our lives. We are to remain diligent in our service to God until the end, just like an athlete who trains hard and performs well with the thought that there is a great reward that lies ahead. They also keep training and working hard to avoid getting lazy, which would slow their progress.

God wants us to serve just like Christ and to remain diligent, knowing that there is a great reward coming. The ideal situation is to serve so much that it becomes a way of life, versus doing it to receive a reward. We want our motives to be pure when we are serving.

So remain diligent in your service, knowing that God will not forget the work and love you have shown Him as you continue to help His people.

God Bless

Dethrone the King of Sin

> "But now you must rid yourselves of all such things as these: anger, rage, malice, slander, and filthy language from your lips. Do not lie to each other, since you have taken off your old self with its practices and have put on the new self, which is being renewed in knowledge in the image of its Creator."
> **Colossians 3:8-10**

Paul made an interesting statement when he said in Romans 7:21, "So I find this law at work: When I want to do good, evil is right there with me." He had basically come to the realization that even though he was in Christ he still couldn't escape his flesh. This is another good example of the Bible revealing to us that we have two natures. We have our sinful nature (which is most commonly known as human nature) and of course, we have the Holy Spirit who dwells within us.

Many times people will find themselves doing something that they know they shouldn't do, using the excuse sometimes that they are only human. I often tell people and the Bible is very clear that being human is not an excuse anymore. Once you surrender to Jesus Christ, you shouldn't want to live your life the same way and the truth is the Lord is not going to just let Christians get by with living according to a sinful nature. Your human nature didn't die when you accepted Jesus Christ as Lord and Savior. You just crowned a new King within you. Romans 6, talks about how sin must no longer rule in your body; so in essence before Jesus Christ your sinful nature was in charge. But now sin should have no power to control you except for when you choose to become a slave to it again. Accepting Jesus meant that we made a conscious decision to become a slave to righteousness. So we belong to our choices.

Our text today makes us accountable for making the necessary changes to rid ourselves of voluntary enslavement by our sinful nature. It is true that change does not always happen overnight however if people are really serious about their conversions; there are some things that should not be a major struggle. It is interesting how people will pull the Jesus chord when trying to check you on something that they want you to correct because they feel that you are wrong. However in that same thought they will turn around and destroy your character and say and do things that make you wonder if they are really saved. In this text in verse 7 it says that you used to walk in those ways when you lived your old life but now you have to get rid of those things.

We have to be more accountable for our actions and realize that we really do belong to our choices. If you are really sold out there should be some evidence, a noticeable change in your life. Don't lie to yourself, to others, and more importantly to God just for the sake of it. No it means that you choose to be Christ-like in all that you do. You won't be perfect and that is clear. However we should always at least strive to be better. For me, becoming more like Christ comes off as if I have become passive and I try to avoid conflict. The truth is if I allow that my old self to rise up, most people would prefer my passive side. It's not about you or what people think about you; it is more about your being a reflection of the SON.

God Bless

Depth of His wisdom

> "[Doxology] Oh, the depth of the riches of the wisdom and knowledge of God! How unsearchable his judgments, and his paths beyond tracing out!"- **Romans 11:33**

Doxology is a short hymn of praise usually sung to close out the service. Here we have the Apostle Paul talking mostly to the Gentiles and then to the Jews as well. There were some Jews who rejected Christ and at the time hated the Gentiles. They hated Paul more for being the one who ministered to the Gentiles. The Jews rejecting Christ opened the door for Paul's ministry and created an opportunity for jealousy among the Jews and the return of unbelievers back to Christ. Despite their differences, in the end around verse 31, Jew and Gentiles were converted by the mercy of God, which led Paul to sing praises starting at verse 33. He says that God's wisdom and knowledge are so valuable and so deep that there is no way for us to completely understand it. No matter how hard we try, we will never be able to keep up with the Lord and how He moves things in our favor.

As I sit today thinking about how life is and what I want versus what I see, I realize that God is always at work. He doesn't disregard my desires. He knows what's best and He releases things in my life to get me closer to what I desire, little by little. However, it is only if it is His will. I realize that God knows what is best for my family and me and we accept that and move according to His will. As a result of my understanding that God's knowledge and wisdom is beyond my mind's reach, I don't want to limit God. So instead I will move according to His word because I know He knows what's best for me. Paul said it best in verse 29: "for God's gifts and his call are irrevocable". There is nothing that we can do to change what the Lord has already set in motion and He has given us everything we need to fulfill His vision in our lives.

So instead of our trying to give the Lord direction, let us submit to His authority and live according to His will. Even though Romans 11 has a different context, this verse is still relative to us today. The Jews thought that things should have been different and for some reason they thought that they could stop what Paul was doing. However in the end they learned that God is in control of all outcomes. Since God knows what's best for us and His wisdom is beyond our reach, let us allow God to be God and not put Him in a box. We too should sing His praise in the end because He really does know what's best for us and He is always moving on our behalf, even when we don't know He is.

God Bless

Dead to Sin

> "We were therefore buried with him through baptism into
> death in order that, just as Christ was raised from the dead
> through the glory of the Father, we too may live a new life."
> - **Romans 6:4**

We often hear that we must close one chapter before we can move on to another one. It is always good to have some closure to whatever you are moving from because it allows you to clearly move on without anything holding you back. It is also our experience that sometimes (specifically in relationships) we don't always close chapters before we try to move on to a new one. From personal experience, I know that life as we know it becomes so much more difficult when we do this. It is more difficult to focus on what's new in your life if you are still dealing with the past and it is truly hard to fully commit when part of you is still in the past. The best example I can give of finality is a funeral. Once the casket closes, the body is committed, it is lowered, and the dirt is dropped; that chapter is closed.

Here Paul is helping us to understand salvation, and baptism, by painting a picture of how dying to sin really looks. When we go through baptism it is symbolic of what should have already happened in our hearts. Just as Jesus Christ was buried and raised to new life, we also have to participate in that burial. We are not buried in a physical sense, but in our heart and mind we have to die to sin so that we can be raised to walk in new life with Jesus Christ. So we have to bury our sins and the past that caused us to sin in order to fully commit to a new life lived through and by the power of the Holy Spirit. So, the water baptism is considered a watery grave.

It is going to be very difficult to walk in the newness of Jesus Christ if we are still holding on to the past. If you bless the past, it will set you free, free to live as God intended. There comes a time in everyone's life that a decision to move on from the past has to happen so that you can fully give yourself away to God's purpose in your life. It took a few life-threatening situations to get my attention and force me to ultimately decide that enough was enough. I didn't realize that I needed to have a funeral for my past and my sins in order to bring some closure to that part of my life. If I had been in tune with God I would have made it a big ceremony. Instead it was a quiet, intimate closed casket ceremony because I neither wanted to see or deal with the past anymore nor expose anyone else to it.

The spark for me to have this closure was realizing the will of God for my life. When I realized His will and accepted it, I entered my period of sanctification naturally and without any setbacks. Are you willing to make the arrangements for your sins? Have you arrived at that moment in your life when you realize that if you keep doing what you are doing, yet expecting a different result, you are going to go insane? Have you thought about the fact that God can't bless you with this new thing for your life until you open your hands to let the past go? God can't put something new in your hands if they are full of your past because you are still holding on. Make today your day of declaration. Trade in your old life for the one that God really has in store for you and never look back. Like Kirk Franklin, you have to declare today that "This Is It!!"

The choice is yours and time is not on your side. It is time to do the committal for you're past ashes to ashes and dust to dust.

God Bless

Cut it off

> "If your hand causes you to stumble, cut it off. It is better for you to enter life maimed than with two hands to go into hell, where the fire never goes out." -**Mark 9:43**

There are many things that I am sure that I can live without. However for me I can't imagine what it would be like to have to adjust and living life without a limb. I know people who have adjusted really well and live normal lives without many restrictions at all. I am sure, though, that if they had their way they would not have to adjust.

Here Jesus is not speaking in a literal sense of cutting off your hand; He is, however, making a clear point of how serious He is about how we live our lives. As Christians we have so much potential that we must do whatever it takes by God's standards to fulfill. The thing that causes us all to fall is sin and here Jesus is saying that anything that causes us to sin we need to cut it off or cut it out of our lives. We have to abandon our worldly attachments, friendships, and anything else that leads us to a life of sin. Perhaps you always find yourself doing something that you shouldn't be doing with particular friends or groups. You have to find the strength to avoid them or just separate yourself, at least until you get stronger spiritually and can go back and become a positive influence.

Everybody has a weakness and we all know what that is; the hard part for us is choosing to let it go. When Jesus says, "cut it off" He wants us to understand the stakes we are facing. It is far better to attain eternal life without enjoying the pleasures of sin than to enjoy life with no regard for what you are doing and be lost. At some point we have to be real with ourselves and recognize how valuable life really is. Playing with sin is like playing Russian roulette; you take a chance of losing your life every time you pull the trigger.

Some may feel like they are in too deep to come out and the Lord says that He is faithful and just to forgive you and cleanse you from all unrighteousness. All it takes for you to be cleansed is the willingness. Believe that God will do what He says he will do. In order for any of us to enjoy a little heaven on earth we have to be willing to avoid sin and remove temptation at all costs. You want to put yourself in a safe position for when you go before the judgment seat of Christ; He is willing to stand up for you Himself. No one wants to burn forever. I know I don't. As a matter of fact, I don't like the heat that much to even get close enough to it to get burned.

It may be a difficult process to separate yourself from whomever or whatever can cause you to fall, but you have to do it. Eternity is determined by every step you take and every choice you make. The devil is relentless in his pursuit so you have to be relentless in yours.

God Bless

Customer Service

"So in everything, do to others what you would have them
do to you, for this sums up the Law and the Prophets."
- **Matthew 7:12**

When I go to a restaurant I always pay attention to the customer service, from the time we walk through the door until the time that we leave. Of course, I pay the most attention to the servers. In their minds, if they give us great customer service, we will give them a great tip. In my mind, the better the customer service, the more likely I am to come back and recommend someone get the same experience.

Our walk with the Lord is really the same. The only difference is that we are always being watched. Now it is true that if we serve someone well, there is a great reward. Who doesn't want to be rewarded greatly by the Lord?

However, our main focus should be satisfied customers who desire to always come back. As Christians, the way that we treat people can be the deciding factor in whether that person wants to consider Christ as their Lord and Savior or run in the opposite direction quickly. We are on the front lines and everything that we do represents the kingdom and the Lord. So just like the golden rule says do unto others as you would have them do unto you, stand true with this verse. The more we serve Christ in excellence by serving others the better chance they may want to meet Christ for themselves and serve the Lord as well.

If people see that you really enjoy serving God, there is a better chance that they will be drawn to the cross. Ultimately, whether you are up or down, once it is all said and done, we all want great customer service. We all want others to treat us well in everything so if we give great customer service we will have a better chance of receiving it.

God Bless

Cover Me

> "Therefore confess your sins to each other and pray for each other so that you may be healed. The prayer of a righteous man is powerful and effective." -**James 5:16**

There is a song by a ministry named 21:03 entitled "Cover Me." Some of the lyrics read:

Remember to cover me
that I might go in peace
Remember to keep me lifted
that I might go in spirit
Keep my name on your lips
When you pray remember this:
I need you
to cover me.

I don't know anyone who doesn't need prayer. There may be some who think that it is a cliché but when you hear the words "prayer changes things", it is for real. For me prayer is the only way to keep from losing it, especially when (being) challenged. If I can't talk to the Lord, everything will fall apart.

Prayer is one of the most powerful tools that God have given us, yet it is the least likely used. There was a poll in the Reader's Digest to which one hundred fifty people from several countries responded. Only fifty-five percent of polled Americans reported that they pray often. So roughly about eighty-three people said that they pray often; out of one hundred fifty people. That would be an awesome percentage if it reflected the entire population. But it doesn't.

James tells us that we should have someone that we trust to confide in knowing that they are going to pray for you and not start rumors. Everybody needs at least one somebody to tell everything to with confidence that person will cover him or her in prayer. I have a friend who faced a life threatening illness several years ago. He told me when he found out and we prayed consistently for a year. When he returned to the doctor this life threatening illness that had no cure also had no signs in his body. The Power of Prayer. Look at the young man from USC, Stanford Johnson, who was doing weight training and he apparently lost control of the bar and it landed on his neck. He had to go immediately to surgery and it was presumed that he wouldn't be able to play ball again. However by the grace of God and many people praying for him, he not only recovered, but is a candidate for the NFL Draft this year.

We can't deny the power of prayer. Let us not take for granted the privilege of prayer and the importance of having someone in your corner to pray with you and for you. Prayer is just a conversation with God and you don't have to be a Bible scholar to do it. Some also have the misconception that there is a time limit to prayer and it isn't. We have God's ear, His undivided attention so why not take advantage of it. Honestly I don't think there is a person reading this who would say that prayer doesn't work. You have prayed or someone has prayed for you and you saw for yourself God move in your life. If you haven't seen God moving yet then just keep breathing and paying attention He is not done with you yet. Prayer is a privilege so use it often. Please remember when you are praying that I need you to cover me.

God Bless

Copycat

> "Be imitators of God, therefore, as dearly loved children and live a life of love, just as Christ loved us and gave himself up for us as a fragrant offering and sacrifice to God."
> **- Ephesians 5:1-2**

As a father, by my boys I am closely watched. They are very observant, so I know that they catch everything. My behavior is like a tutorial for them. I am teaching them even when I think they're not watching. The funny thing is our younger son does everything his older brother does. Just last night I shared with our oldest to be mindful of what he teaches his little brother, an impressionable boy who mimics his older brother.

Children are great imitators and they are so open and unrestricted; they will do exactly what they see without missing a step and sometimes they may add a little bit to it. So in essence parental figures have to be careful of their daily activities because they never know who is watching and imitating them.

God gave us the perfect example to follow in Jesus Christ and here Paul starts off telling us to be imitators of God. The only way to imitate God is to follow the leader who is Jesus Christ. Go back and read Ch. 4. One thing stated in the fourth chapter is that we were taught to, "put off our old self, which is being corrupted by its deceitful desires; to be made new in the attitude of your minds; and to put on the new self, created to be like God in true righteousness and holiness."

In order to be imitators of God through Christ we have to be willing to let some things go and that starts with an attitude adjustment. Once you make the decision to be better, it lines up with what is already in your heart and allows change to take place. It is just as simple as my children imitating everything I do. They see it and they decide to do exactly what they see and eventually it becomes a part of who they are.

Our youngest child understands that when someone does something for him, he should say 'Thank You' and when the food is ready the first thing he should do is stop what he is doing, put his hands together, and say "God".

It is a choice that grows into a lifestyle. I encourage you to read Ephesians Ch.4 and you can make your own decision to imitate God.

God Bless

Confident in Christ

"Then Caleb silenced the people before Moses and said, "We should go up and take possession of the land, for we can certainly do it." -**Numbers 13:20**

Many of us face giants in our lives daily and we all deal with them differently. The key to overcome what you are dealing with is how you look at it. Your mindset plays a big role.

We have said before that as man thinks, so is he.

Here we have the Israelites with an assignment from the Lord. He told Moses to send men to spy on Canaan, the land flowing with milk and honey. Moses sent out twelve men and they came back with a report. All but two men saw how big the men there were and the size of the wall around the city and they were fearful. So they were defeated before they started. However Caleb said to go and posses the land because he was sure that they could do it. Caleb had facts because he had visited the land himself. He trusted God because God promised them the land anyway; it was theirs for the taking. He also had the right attitude. He believed that they could do it. All it takes is a mustard seed of faith to move mountains. How many times have you faced a challenge in your life and you went in defeated before you started?

We have to learn to do the same thing that Caleb did: look at the facts, trust God, and never stop believing. In the crowd of unbelievers Caleb wasn't afraid to stand out and be different. He stood on what he believed and no one could change his mind. He knew that there was something inside him that was much stronger than what he was dealing with. We have to approach life and the challenges that come the same way.

Don't count yourself out before you start. Trust that if God is for you then He really is more than the world against you. Take a stand like Caleb and watch the Lord work with what you bring to the table.

God Bless

Comfort

"Praise be to the God and Father of our Lord Jesus Christ, the Father of compassion and the God of all comfort, who comforts us in all our troubles, so that we can comfort those in any trouble with the comfort we ourselves have received from God."- **2 Corinthians 1:3-4**

When Jeremiah heard from the Lord in Jeremiah Ch.1 and God told him that he was a prophet for the nations; Jeremiah was scared. He said, "I can't do this. I am only a child." When those words came out the Lord comforted Him.

When Joshua had to take on the leadership role after Moses died, God knew what Joshua was feeling uncertain about because he too was young. Joshua found peace in God's word and was comforted.

Webster's Dictionary states that, comfort means "to give strength and hope to; to ease the grief or trouble of." So in essence it is to bring cheer as well as consolation.

I know for me, being a preacher/teacher of God's word, I find my self-giving comfort to others a lot even when they don't ask for it. The joy comes when I see their spirits rise and their tones and countenances change. I can see them coming back together. What I have come to realize is that all it takes is a word even if you don't totally understand the situation. Also it doesn't take a long time to plant that seed of hope. It all depends on how confident you are in yourself to speak life into someone else. You don't have to be a Bible scholar to comfort someone because just like this text says, God does it for us all the time. All we have to do is speak from our own personal experience and something that small can change someone's life.

I do encourage those who are still growing in God to be prepared because there are some you may see as more spiritually mature than you, who needs comforting as well. The comforter needs comforting too. I have moments when I need someone to give me a word to help me get over the hump. Just because I know and study the word everyday doesn't mean that I have all the answers and can comfort myself all the time. It is true that the Lord speaks to me and just thinking about His word uplifts me. However, we sometimes need someone who can help affirm what we may already know.

I believe that many of us are in positions to encourage ourselves through the power of the Holy Spirit. Let us not take for granted the opportunity to speak life into someone else. Just know that you are a child of God and there is nothing that you can't do. The Bible says that we can do all things through Christ who strengthens us. Speak life in to someone today.

God Bless

Clear Your Conscience

"So I strive always to keep my conscience clear before God and man." -**Acts 24:16**

I am not sure about you but it is difficult for me to function daily if I don't have a clear conscience. I believe that if you don't free your mind you are just carrying around a lot of extra baggage that you don't need and all it does is weigh you down.

Your conscience is connected to your high moral character and really, the God in you. It tells you what He expects of you and it helps to keep you in line with His will. It is the eye that looks out either towards God or towards what it regards as the highest, so your conscience records differently in different people. If I am in tune with God, my conscience will always introduce God's perfect will and indicate what I should do. The question here is if I will obey. Will you obey in the same situation?

We all have to make a great effort to keep our conscience so sensitive that we walk without offense. We should all always be so in tune with God that we are always seeking to fulfill that good, acceptable, perfect will of God by the renewing of our minds daily. In other words, we have to get into the habit of always having a good conscience. God pours into us daily so we have more than enough "word power" to stay in line with His will. It all comes down to our choosing to obey when He puts that choice before us.

God Bless

Celebrate Jesus

> "Later, knowing that all was now completed, and so that the Scripture would be fulfilled, Jesus said, "I am thirsty." A jar of wine vinegar was there, so they soaked a sponge in it, put the sponge on a stalk of the hyssop plant, and lifted it to Jesus' lips. When he had received the drink, Jesus said, "It is finished." With that, he bowed his head and gave up his spirit." -**John 19:28-30**

The death of Jesus was a defining moment in all our lives. I remember watching the "Passion of Christ" and how it made me feel. It really made it clear all that Christ went through in order for us to have the opportunity to live life more abundantly. To physically see some of what really happened truly drove the point home for me on how much God really loves us.

When we look at the text today it is the defining moment of Jesus' presence amongst man, a moment when Jesus is on the Cross and has gone through all that He was destined to experience. So the text picks up by saying that all was completed. This is signifying that Jesus had fulfilled His purpose on earth and the battle with the enemy was over. Jesus' mission to come and take on the sins of the world had been completed so He could return to the Father. His suffering was over and the scripture, fulfilled.

Jesus asking for a drink further confirmed that He did in fact have a human quality about Him. It confirms that He was fully God and fully man because it is a human quality to thirst, especially for they who possess streams of living water from which we can all drink and thirst no more.

As we move closer to Easter let us reflect on the life of Jesus Christ and why He really came and more importantly, why He died. The one thing that we can stand on is the word of God and when Jesus says that it is finished, just know that it is. Jesus gave up His Spirit and now we all have the Holy Spirit with us. We are never alone. So not only did He give all of Himself for us to live, He is living within us all to help us stay on track.

Let us celebrate the true reason for Easter - the life, death, burial and resurrection of Jesus Christ.

God Bless

Be the Example

> "Fathers, do not exasperate your children; instead, bring them up in the training and instruction of the Lord."
> **- Ephesian 6:4**

Today, most households are lead by single mothers, and those households have very loving, caring, influential mothers. So we as men have a big task in front of us. We have to be the examples for our children, whether they are our biological or societal children, and they are watching us. We have to teach our young men how to be men and our young ladies how to be treated by a man so that they won't stray when they get older. We can't afford to irritate, agitate, or cause our children to be enraged because that will push them further away from us and from following God's command.

Our children can only be what they see. So it is our job to give them a view that is pleasing to God. It amazes me how many times I hear people talking about our young people and how they aren't doing anything with their lives. The question is: what are you doing to add value to their lives? The biggest task before us is to learn how to communicate with our youth today. That is the only barrier that we have to get over because they desire structure and leadership. If you have youth in your home, that is where lifelong values should be taught. Take the time to sit down and talk with them on a regular basis, so that you can open the lines of communications. You will be exposed to more than you knew existed in their world. If there aren't any youth in your home, make it a point to be a mentor or just talk to young people and speak life into their lives. The only way to secure our future is to go out and create it. So help create a new reality for our young people instead of talking about them. Talking down on them only creates several degrees of separation between their generation and yours, when we need to draw them closer in order to save them.

Who are you training up in the ways of the Lord?
God Bless

Be Still

"Be still, and know that I am God; I will be exalted among the nations, I will be exalted in the earth." - **Psalm 46: 9-11**

The Assyrian Empire waged an attack on Zion and this time they met their match. Of course this outcome is to be expected when God is in control. The text here is highlighting how God is our refuge, our shelter, and our strength, especially when we need Him most.

God displays some of his power in this text. He speaks about ceasing wars and destroying weapons.

Whether going through a rough time or not, we have to allow God to remain in control instead of trying to fight ourselves. God has the power to bring whatever we are battling to an immediate halt and He can destroy opposition so that it never rises again.

With God, after a victory, there is a period of peace. In order for us to experience God's peace we can't worry about the obstacles we face. We have to be still and know that He is God.

When you were young, if you had a big brother or sister, you should relate to this. If someone at school or around the house was bothering you, because of your older sibling you didn't have much fear. You knew that he or she would handle the problem for you. Even if you were the oldest child, you played that role. Either way, there was a sense of security because there was protection for you if you needed it. Not only did you believe in that protection, you were confident that it was fail proof.

Can you trust God even more? Can you truly be still even at the peak of your frustration and know that He is GOD?

God Bless

Be on Guard

"No one knows about that day or hour, not even the angels
in heaven, nor the Son, but only the Father. Be on guard!
Be alert! You do not know when that time will come."
- Mark 13:32-33

When I first entered college for the summer I got a job with TSA at the Houston Hobby Airport. We were trained to be on the lookout for certain items as people passed through our check station racing off to catch their planes. There were some who would work the X-ray machine, the metal detectors, and the hand wands. There would even be a person placed at the end of the X-ray machine looking as if he was helping passengers to gather their belongings, but he was really there to make sure people didn't run off. Our jobs were extremely important since we played a vital role in ensuring passenger safety and overseeing airport security.

I wasn't always expecting to find anything suspicious; however we still had to be prepared in case someone caught us off guard and jeopardized the safety of everyone in the airport. That $5 an hour seemed pretty insignificant until early one morning, when a gentleman came through and I saw a gun in his bag. My job, all of a sudden, demanded more of a risk than it paid. Had I taken my job for granted by focusing on the fact that I was underpaid, I would have overlooked the gunman's weapon. However, the importance of saving lives superseded my uncontrollable work circumstances.

If we knew that Jesus was coming and the world was ending in a month, what would you do?

A lot of people would be scrambling trying to get their lives right and helping others as well, in an attempt to secure a spot in glory. Otherwise so many people just coast through life with no sense of urgency. We don't know the time when the Lord is coming back, so why take the chance and act like we have plenty of time? We really don't know. Just as we airport security guards stayed on guard, we should adopt the same approach when working for God. Everyday we should be doing our best to save others and ourselves. The enemy is always looking for ways to get things past our Spiritual detectors to take us out. If we are doing our best to live according to the Word of God, there is a natural defense supplied by God to protect us from the enemy. So our best bet is to stay alert, be on guard, and (when the Lord comes back) avoid getting caught sleeping on the job.

God Bless

Be Light

> "You are the light of the world. A city on a hill cannot be hidden. In the same way, let your light shine before men, that they may see your good deeds and praise your Father in heaven."- **Matthew 5:14, 16**

When I was younger, I used to play outside and for most of my friends the indicator to get in the house was illuminated streetlights. In the Cuney Homes, (the projects) there were these big floodlights that one could see from far away. When they came on, they lit up everything; there was no area that was full of darkness.

The awesome thing about light is that it illuminates and can be seen from miles and miles away. The phrase "Light at the end of the tunnel" represents hope. It is saying that even when you are going through, as long as you see light, you are in good shape.

God has called us to be a beacon light for the world to see everywhere that we go. We should be just like that city on the hill the Bible is talking about; there is no way that anybody can miss it because it stands out. So when we enter a room- be it at work, at home, at school, or in public- you should be light. Church should be the only place where nobody outshines others, since all should be shinning. It is important for others to see Christ in you just as those Hebrew boys; they were light and caused others to desire that same power.

The revelation about the streetlight is that it is only really needed in darkness. It has a sensor on it so that when darkness seems to try to take over, it automatically, boldly comes on and shines brightly until darkness disappears.

Be light in a world full of darkness.

God Bless

Be Holy

> "Therefore, prepare your minds for action; be self-controlled; set your hope fully on the grace to be given you when Jesus Christ is revealed."- **1 Peter 1:13**

The word *therefore* in its original sense means "as a result of", so that leaves one to question the cause. Well, in the twelve verses before our text, the story is told. It talks about how we have new birth into the living hope through the resurrection of Jesus Christ and how we have been graced with an inheritance that will never perish, spoil, or fade. It will be kept in heaven for us.

It's so assuring to know that our salvation guarantees our inheritance. However, there is a condition to this. It says that while we are here, our faith, which will perish from time to time and refined by fire, we will be tested. We will have to suffer many trials.

Not all trials will be life threatening. They could be mental laps resulting from financial hardship or the loss of a loved one. All these trials are opportunities to prove our sincerity, genuineness and faith. The Bible says that we are filled with an inexpressible and glorious joy.

So our text tells us that since we will have to suffer many trials in order to receive our inheritance, we must prepare our minds for action. The only way to stay level-headed and patient in adversity is to be self-controlled. If we keep in the forefront of our minds that what we are going through is for a greater reward, knowing that our goal is Heaven, we will put ourselves in a better position to receive the Glory of God and the grace given to us through Jesus Christ.

If going to heaven truly is your goal, this verse should be lived through you daily. The enemy is relentless and aware of God's plan for us, so he will do everything to get us off track. Prepare your minds for action and be self-controlled.

God Bless

Be Encouraged

"We ought always to thank God for you, brothers, and rightly so, because your faith is growing more and more, and the love every one of you has for each other is increasing."
- 2 Thessalonians 1:3

You know the bible says that one must endure hardship as a good soldier for the Lord Jesus Christ. Considering the time we live in right now, all of us have had to endure more than we thought we could bare in some area of our lives. So in essence God, has been shaping us to be good soldiers for Him.

In this text Paul, Timothy, and Silas are encouraging the Thessalonians because of the persecution that they have been enduring. During their persecution, we are able to see their perseverance and faith increase and strengthen. So Paul wanted to take the time to encourage them along the journey so they wouldn't give up.

Today I want to encourage you as well. No matter where you are in life, you have overcome far more than you once thought you could. You have had more victories in your life than failures. Know that destruction is, in essence, a form of creation. So when you are going through a rough stage, know that God is shaping you for something much bigger than you. Just like diamonds, we have to go through extreme heat to be purified and polished. I am reminded that the bible says that we should not get weary in well doing, because we WILL reap a harvest if we don't give up. Know that God is true to His word and all things really do work for the good of those who love Him. In all things, we are more than conquerors.

God Bless

A Gentle Word

"A gentle answer turns away wrath, but a harsh word stirs up anger."- **Proverbs 15:1**

This morning I jumped out of bed and slowly made my way to the kitchen to see what time it was. As I was returning to the room at a faster pace and with a heavy sigh, my wife asked me, "What's wrong?" My reply was, "Its 6:06." I was running late and the alarm clock, which was on her side of the bed, sounded without my hearing it. What is important here is how I responded to her question. In a calm, quiet voice I replied instead of doing so angrily. I have to be at work at 6:30. When I got in the truck my prayer to the Lord was, "if being late to work is the worst of my morning, thank you God because it could be worse." I thanked God for my wife, my children, and my life because I had a clear mind. I surly could have gotten up and blamed my wife for not awakening me. However, I just viewed it as the Lord allowing me a little more time to get some well-deserved rest.

When I arrived to work the new security guard stopped me to record all my information. I was already ten minutes late. As I lowered the window I asked, "Do you need anything else from me?" I gave him the information and then he asked, "Where is your sticker?" I pointed to it and said calmly, "It's right here in front of me." That scenario could have been very different had I answered him in a rude manner.

The point is that the word is true because my gentle answers turn away wrath and anger. The truth is that neither of the scenarios needed to end in wrath or anger because it wasn't worth it. However, the enemy is always a busy opportunist. These two situations could have turned out really badly and the enemy was anticipating my giving him power to start working. Well enemy, "You're a liar and the truth ain't in you." We can't always be so quick to cut someone up just because we have justified a reason to do so. Every situation doesn't warrant that kind of response and we all should get into the habit of not being so quick to give a harsh response, even if in our minds we feel that it is deserved. That one response can dictate the course of your day and you will be responsible for it. Allow the Lord to work through you by watching *what* you say and *how* you say it. Remember that the enemy is waiting for the opportunity to throw fiery darts and handle you like a puppet.

Think about what you are going to say and how you are going to say it before you open your mouth. Even if you feel the person doesn't deserve it give him grace anyway. After all, the Bible says that we should season our words with grace. A gentle answer really does turn away wrath.

God Bless

A Cloud of Witnesses

> "Therefore, since we are surrounded by such a great cloud of witnesses, let us throw off everything that hinders and the sin that so easily entangles, and let us run with perseverance the race marked out for us."- **Hebrews 12:1**

Oftentimes we find that people will grab a scripture and run with it without doing at least a little bit of reading. As stated once before, "therefore" indicates that something happened and as a result a resolve follows.

Hebrews 11 speaks volumes about those who have come long before us and lived by faith. It says plainly that all of these folk talked about how they never got to enjoy what they had faith in. They just saw it and welcomed it from a distance.

Today, most people will have faith (in something) that only last a few days before they start questioning God. In fact we have many examples in the Bible of those who were relentless with their faith, some believing than more than ten, twenty, or thirty years.

Here we are encouraged, and as a result of those who have come before us, we now have a great cloud of several witnesses as examples. Though they may not have had the opportunity to enjoy what they believed in God for, they trusted God until death.

So for us, by removing all the distractions and our wrongdoings consciously, we can focus on what God has for us and believe that we will receive it. We know that what they believed in did come to pass. We can possibly will ourselves into a position to enjoy what we have been trusting God for. It is going to be a race to the finish; however how many people do you know who get into a race not expecting to win?

God Bless

A Child-like Faith

"I tell you the truth; anyone who will not receive the kingdom of God like a little child will never enter it."
- Luke 18:17

As we have gotten older, we have made trusting and having faith in God more complicated. Some of us want to over-analyze to explain everything. When it seems that things aren't going our way, some of us lose faith and hope in whatever that is.

My oldest son is so persistent that it is unreal. He may ask me a question on Monday and I might respond, "No, not today." His response is, "You want me to wait?" I'll say, "Yes another day." Still expecting to receive what he asked for, he will remind me either every day or every other day that he wants an answer. He has faith that he can get what he is asking for and he knows that if he is persistent, it will eventually come to pass, even if it is a week or two later.

The text today is simply helping us to understand that we have to have a child-like faith, especially when it comes to trusting God and having faith in Him and His power.

What are you believing God for in your life? Are you willing to persevere and hold on until your change comes?

God Bless

You Will Live

"Jesus said to her, "I am the resurrection and the life. The
one who believes in me will live, even though they die;"
- John 11:25

When God created us He said that our lives were predestined to be like Christ. He went on to say in Romans 8:30 "And those He predestined, He also called; those He called, He also justified; those He justified, He also glorified." So when the Lord says that He knows the plans that He has for us, He really means it. Verse thirty really walks out our entire life from inception. Then He goes on to say that we are not guilty because Jesus Christ paid a high price for us. He stepped up in the courtroom and took our place and accepted our penalty and paid for it with His blood.

This is all based on those who believe. It's God's hope that we all choose to believe in Him, choose to accept Christ as Lord and Savior, and follow Him. Jesus is the only one who has the power to give us eternal life, the life that we have to look forward to once we pass away. Jesus was talking to Martha, assuring her that He had the power over life and death. We all know how the story ends. The key component here, though, is Jesus Christ and believing in His power.

We have all been called to take up our cross and follow Jesus Christ. The life that we live today is truly a prerequisite to how we will spend eternity. Are you following the plans that God has laid out for your life? If today were your last day, would you be ready? Jesus Christ is the only one who has the power to give you life and give it more abundantly, according to John. Are you living a life that is worthy of His sacrifice?

God Bless

You Have Seen and You Have Heard

"You have seen many things, but have paid no attention; your ears are open, but you hear nothing." -**Isaiah 42:20**

My boys are four years apart, one being 5 almost 6 and the youngest, two. Since my oldest could understand I have been grooming him to the ways of the Lord and the house. Growing to be a mighty man of God, there are certain things that he has to learn. I am his father so I have to teach him. There are certain areas in his life that he picked up quickly like respect, and manners. However, there are certain things that he seems to have selective memory of and we find ourselves having to repeatedly revisit those areas.

It is so interesting how he can find himself in trouble behind the same things. Once I get on his case and correct him my last question is "do you understand?" His reply is always "Yes sir." Yet a day or two later, (sometimes a few hours later) he will engage in the same misbehavior. My youngest is learning quickly though. There are some things he won't repeat because of watching his brother. I know that my oldest is only five so he has a ways to go. I don't want him to grow up too fast, however he should learn some things the first time.

Many of us are the same way with God and then we question why we are still in the same position. It is because we have seen many things and have heard many things, however our actions show something all together different. It is like the Lord has never disciplined us for our actions or maybe we are like my son; sometimes we decide to do our own things anyway. You would think that we would have learned the first time, but that is not always the case.

The Israelites were saved from being enslaved, yet many times they still followed their own minds and as a result, wondered in the dessert. Many saw the Promised Land but never made it. Judas walked with Jesus. He saw miracles and witnessed lives being changed. He saw the sick getting healed, the blind recovering their vision, and the dead rising back to life, yet he still sold Jesus out. As a result, Judas went crazy and hung himself.

There is nothing good that comes out of turning a blind eye and a deaf ear to the Lord. The Bible says in James 4:17," **Anyone, then, who knows the good he ought to do and doesn't do it, sins.**" So really, once you are exposed to the truth, you are accountable to heed it. I understand that it is going to take patience for my son to finally get it and we have to continue to build our relationship. Right now it is difficult for him to understand that I can be the greatest daddy and disciplinarian at the same time. I also understand that he is only five, so what is our excuse?

God speaks to us through His word as often as we read it. He speaks to us through prayer and others as well. The question is whether we will hear His voice? Why is it so hard to hear His voice? Are we just making it hard? You too have seen many things and your ears are open; will you take heed to the word or will you be a repeat offender?

Blessed are your eyes because they see and your ears because they hear, so let he who has ears hear.

God Bless

You have kept me

"I will never forget your precepts, for by them you have preserved my life."- **Psalm 119:93**

Look back over your life and think about that one thing that happened that changed you, that one unforgettable lesson that you learned the hard way. I can remember two such incidents that tied together. While in college, for homecoming, one of my friends decided that he was going to be obedient to the theme "Set Your Homecoming Out" and he got so drunk. The next day when we got up for breakfast this dude was still lying in the grass where we left him and I thought about how dumb that was. The other incident involved another one of my friends. His grandmother used to drink and smoke everyday, especially on weekends. Well it got to her and one day we were at the hospital visiting her and I saw her in her bed gasping for air, struggling to breathe because of her desire to drink and smoke. Those incidents helped me to decide to never drink or smoke, period. There were other situations as well but I can proudly say that I have never ever had a drink or smoke and I don't plan to start now. There are memorable, life-changing moments in our lives that will shift our lives in a positive direction.

Paul will never forget that day that he met Jesus on the road to Damascus. After that encounter his life did a complete 180 and he never looked back. The text today is saying that we should never forget God's commands. God has instructed us to do something in our life and many end up learning the hard way. However, after we learned that hard lesson we never wanted to endure it again.

For some reason though, there are some people who either just don't care or don't value life much because they keep going down that same road over and over. They have retraced their steps so many times, it seems they are in an inescapable cycle. God does everything for a reason and most of His commands are conditional. He is straight up about some things and there is only one way for you to respond. That's it. Either way, if God is the only one, who can preserve you, protect you, and keep you in perfect unaltered condition, how could you ever forget what He's done for you? By now, the whole world should have heard the gospel regardless to if they believe or not. But, you know better and those who you keep in close company should know better too.

Don't allow the enemy's plot to blind you and cause you to bump your head on "crazy." We play with our friends all the time but God is not the one. If Jesus hasn't done anything else for you, He gave up His life for you. He paid a price that none of us is willing to pay. So don't allow yourself to get caught off guard. Don't ever forget how great God is and what He has done for you. Can you imagine life if Jesus would have changed His mind? What if God would have said, "forget those folks; they are not worth my one and only son?" Where would we be?

God, I will never forget your precepts because by them you have kept me. Thank you.

God Bless

You Are Not Forgotten

"Are not five sparrows sold for two pennies? Yet, not one of them is forgotten by God. Indeed, the very hairs of your head are all numbered. Don't be afraid; you are worth more than many sparrows."- **Luke 12:6-7**

Last part of the summer I left for our third mission trip, excited about getting to our destination. When I arrived, to my surprise, we were lodging in a comfortable cabin nestled deep in the woods. From our balcony door there was a clear view of the lake. There was no television in the room and the bed looked like my grandmother put it together herself so I knew would be some great sleep. For a minute I thought we had decided to vacation and get away from everybody because it was so peaceful and quite.

To my surprise, early Friday morning I passed out and before lunch I passed out again. Soon after my body went down in the dumps, I had a horrible sore throat, fever, and aching body. There was no emergency care close by, especially not at that time, but we did have a camp nurse. Here we are a little over a week later and I am just starting to feel better.

The revelation that I got from that experience was that the Lord allowed me to make it safely and then allowed my body to have a little break-down so that I could get some well-needed rest. What I thought was going to be a couple of days turned into eight; God is big on His numbers, huh? I believe God allowed this to happen because he values me obviously more than I do. He knows me down to the hairs on my head and He knew that I wouldn't slow down like I needed to rest. The truth of the matter is that He knows you as well.

Our true value is God's estimate of our worth, not our peers'. We are judged, evaluated, and categorized by others according to how we perform, what we achieve, and how we look. God doesn't care about any of that. He cares for us just like He does all of His creatures because we all belong to him. With confidence know that God cares so much for us that we don't have to fear life. For a moment last weekend I started to panic because I felt like I was going to die. It wasn't until I calmed down did I realize that God is still in control; He is still on the throne, especially in my life so there was no need for me to fear. Instead I trusted God and listened to what He was saying to me. I had a brief moment that I felt well and the Lord allowed me to participate in baptizing a little over fifty young people. I believe that He was showing me that even in my weakness He could still get glory.

Jesus is speaking in this text so these words are straight from His mouth. God is not a man that He would tell a lie so we can stand on His word and be confident that we are standing on a solid foundation. Don't doubt God or His love for you. He has and still will go to any extreme to show you how much he still loves you.

To God is the Glory for my health, my life, my family, and for you.

God Bless

You are Feared

"If you, O LORD, kept a record of sins, O Lord, who could stand? But with you there is forgiveness; therefore you are feared." -**Psalm 130:3-4**

Seemingly frustrated and stressed with a feeling of being on their last leg, the psalmist cries out in confession of their sin. In the same breath they also acknowledge that what they are dealing with they can't deal with alone. They exalt the Lord and proclaim His willingness to forgive. Here the psalmist is saying to God that they know they have done wrong; they have taken this thing called life and they have jacked it up. They have allowed things to get out of control and now the have come to the actuality that if God really kept a record of our sins and held them against us like people do they would be in a world of trouble. The truth of the matter is God has an account of everything that we have done, however He wipes our slates clean and gives fresh starts. Imagine driving in your car and it is raining like cats and dogs; your windshield is so loaded you can hardly see the road. Your natural response is to turn the windshield wipers on to wipe away what is stopping you from clearly reaching your destination. God does the same for us when we sin because Jesus Christ bled we are cleansed from all our sins. God turns on the holy windshield wipers to remove our sins so that we can continue to move closer to Him. Can't you see how hard a windshield wiper works? It has three speeds to it; however it only takes God one time to wipe the slate clean. So when you are driving in the rain, imagine every time the windshield wiper cleans your window that is God cleaning your sins away. We just have to humble ourselves and confess to the Lord that we are sinful, yet working hard on sinning less. He is more than willing to forgive us and cleanse us.

The main reason that stops most people from confessing to God is that they don't believe that He will forgive them or they are scared. Just know that God already knows anyway so you might as well have the conversation with Him, just like most parents know when their children have done something wrong, so they wait for their child to come to them with it. Quite naturally whenever you do something wrong there is a certain level of fear of the consequences that you may face. When my son does something that he knows he shouldn't have done and I ask him about it, his voice immediately changes and he is very slow to respond to my questions. There are times he has tears in his eyes because he fears that I have had it and his worst fear is about to come true. We have all been there before at some time in our lives and what the text is trying to help us with today is that we are in the perfect position when that happens. The Bible says that the fear of the Lord is the beginning of knowledge. So when we fear the Lord we recognize that He is in control of our lives and we totally submit to His will. It should be natural for you to fear having to face the Lord when you do something that you know you shouldn't do. So many of us are better off than what we know. As a matter of fact, fear of the Lord has kept me out of a lot of a lot of trouble and it keeps me from being out of order as much as I can control it. The reason is because I don't want to deal with the potential consequences from the Lord and I don't want to add one more thing for the Lord to talk to me about on the Day of Judgment; there is already enough stuff on His list. The Bible says that we will have to give an account of every careless word we have spoken. So God has a list however He has already forgiven for the sin.

If the Lord were to keep a record of our sins like people do, none of us would be here. He would have wiped the Earth clean a long time ago. Thank God for His grace and His mercy. Just know that when some situation comes up in your life and you find yourself saying things like, "Jesus Christ, Lord have mercy, or Father help me," you are crying out to God for help. Just know that He is faithful and just to forgive our sins and He is more than willing to cleanse us and make us whole again. What can wash away our sins? Nothing but the blood of Jesus.

God Bless

Wrestle Not

> "For our struggle is not against flesh and blood, but against the rulers, against the authorities, against the powers of this dark world and against the spiritual forces of evil in the heavenly realms. Therefore put on the full armor of God, so that when the day of evil comes, you may be able to stand your ground, and after you have done everything, to stand."
> **- Ephesians 6:12-13**

I don't know too many people who really enjoy conflict. I really would rather not have conflict at all; however it always tends to creep up in our lives. Even though I have been trained well in conflict resolution, for some reason I can't even escape it myself sometimes.

All it takes is for people to say the right thing at the wrong time or have certain looks on their faces. You misinterpret its meaning and before we know it, it is on. Most of the time you may not even have a problem with that person. You could be bothered by something else and they come along and get the heat from something that they had no dealings in.

One of the key components to misunderstandings is third-party conflict. This component has started wars whose causes we are still trying to figure out. It is the catalyst behind many of your arguments and fights. Third-party conflict is simply this; it is when some unknown force that is always actively at work sparks a misunderstanding. So in essence, most of our fights or battles are from some instigator who steps in, drops a bad seed, steps out, and watches the war begin. The interesting part is that we always give the wrong person the credit for being that unknown third party.

We tend to always blame the person we are at odds with when in actuality it is just like the scripture says; it is a spiritual thing. I am not saying that the devil made you do it. However, we tend to always leave room for him to take advantage of the opportunity. We all know that his mission is to kill, steal, and destroy by any means necessary. If you sit back and think about the times that you have had a fight with someone consider the real reason behind your getting into it? What is the root cause? Most of the time it has nothing to do with that person. He or she just happened to come along and say or do something that you took out on them or vice versa.

The only way to combat that is to see things with our spiritual eyes. This verse says to put on the full armor of God so that you will be able to stand in the evil day. If we look at the world through God's eyes, our perspectives change. If we continue to allow ourselves to be puppets in the enemy's show, when we really have to face challenges. We won't make it. God has equipped all of us with the power to resist falling for these powers of evil forces. He has given us the ability to really see it for what its worth. We just have to get out of our own way and not fool ourselves by thinking we are being aggressive to protect ourselves or take control of the situation.

Trust God in every situation and know that He has you covered on all sides. No one can see what's coming like God. In fact, He knows long before we do. Put on the full armor of God because He knows how to protect us against what we can't see. Let us really think about the source of our misunderstandings before we get so involved in it trying to do it your own way versus letting God handle it.

God Bless

Worry Less, Pray More

> "Do not be anxious about anything, but in everything,
> by prayer and petition, with thanksgiving, present your
> requests to God. And the peace of God, which transcends
> all understanding, will guard your hearts and your minds in
> Christ Jesus."- **Philippians 4:6-7**

Whenever we embark on something new in our lives there is often a sense of uncertainty, at least at first. For some, it is a little stronger. Worry and doubt begin to take over. We have already discovered that doubt has the potential to paralyze you, stopping you from walking out the steps that God has already ordered for your life.

Here Paul is so adamant about his though that he repeats the same thing three times three different ways. The theme of what Paul is telling us in the text is to worry less and pray more. He starts by saying don't be anxious about anything, which simply means not to worry. He quickly follows it with the word, signifying that worrying is irrelevant and that instead we should use prayer in everything.

To worry is natural. However, when you pray about it, you take those doubtful thoughts captive and submit them to God. The question here is, why do you pray? The answer is to get God's attention so that His power will be activated in your life upon your request, recognizing that He is sovereign. When Paul uses the words "petition" and "making your request", he is referring again to prayer. So in essence, Paul is saying that instead of worrying about anything we should pray, pray, and pray more.

The key to prayer though is believing that God will move on your behalf. Just know that when you find yourself in constant prayer that God will give you his peace that no one will understand, not even you. You will find yourself in a very troublesome situation, but when you pray you will feel that everything will be all right, even though at the moment it doesn't appear to be.

The awesome part about it is that God says that He will protect your heart and your mind in Christ Jesus. The only thing that keeps me from losing it sometimes is this scripture, particularly the fact that God is protecting my heart and my mind not only from the enemy, but also from me. We need the Lord to help us to have peace of mind because that is the part of us that gives birth to our thoughts. We all need protection from our thoughts. Additionally, out of the heart flow the issues of life. So, once again, God is really needed to direct us in that area of our lives.

Remember. In every situation, worry less and pray more and trust that God will do the rest.

God Bless

Work Hard Don't be Lazy

"Work hard and become a leader; be lazy and become a slave." -**Proverbs 12:24**

The only way to be sure about your future is to go out and create it. It has been said that there are a few types of people in the world: the haves and the have not. The difference is decided by the amount of work put in. Your commitment to work hard at whatever you are doing or not, determines whether you are a producer or a consumer. I have always said that anything worth having is worth fighting for.

The Bible makes it very plain today. It simply says that if you work hard, you will become a trailblazing leader and if you are lazy you will be a slave to your circumstances. Those who are diligent at creating opportunity for themselves have a certain level of control over their destiny. They will prosper. Lazy people will at some point be defeated by life and all that comes along with it and will be forced to serve others.

Laziness or hard work carries over in every area of your life. Spiritually we have to work hard at perfecting our faith. Living the Christian life is not easy because we face so many challenges. The truth is whether we are in Christ or not we face many challenges. However, it is only in Christ that we can truly experience victory. Those who choose to work hard at their relationship with God eventually become slaves to righteousness. They exercise self-control and become steadfast and unmovable in what they believe. The stronger you become in your faith, the closer you get to the Lord, which leads to victory in your rough times. No one in Christ can afford to have a lazy spirit because it puts you in a position to become complacent. You begin to settle for less and before you know it, you are a victim of your circumstances. Ultimately, this leads to you being a slave to your sinful nature. It is hard to fight your way out of a corner when you have never thrown a punch.

We are all creatures of habit; once we get used to doing something, it becomes second nature to us. It doesn't mean that those who are lazy will always be lazy and vice versa. There is hope for the lazy if they desire to be better. The hard workers have to protect themselves from laziness by staying focused on the results. There is always something driving hard workers. They seek to accomplish a goal or overcome a tough circumstance; they are always inspired by something to do better and be better. Allow the promises of God to be your muse. Knowing that you can get a little bit of heaven on Earth is more than enough to keep you pushing to see how the Lord is going to show up and show out in your situation. God promised we can have eternal life and that is enough for me to work hard on lining my life up with His will so that I can receive His promise.

Are you a worker or a slacker, a producer, or a consumer? Really, the choice is yours.

God Bless

Words Go a Long Way

"A man finds joy in giving an apt reply— and how good is a timely word!"- **Proverbs 15:23**

Anytime most people open their mouths they want to sound intelligent. Some people find themselves trying hard to say something so profound or deep at the right moment. What is important here is that you have a willingness to have effective communication. A lot of times people think that communication is all about one person saying something and the other person attentively listening. Well, effective communication requires that you give a response, after first acknowledging what you heard.

There are so many people who sometimes (you may not even know) may start a conversation with you. If it is a stranger, we don't always feel obligated to respond. We sometimes miss what that person is really trying to say to us and it may take a little conversation to get it out. There are times when people are going through and just want anybody to listen, even a stranger. I've seen it too many times on the news: someone went to talk with someone who didn't make time. Something tragic happened as a result.

When I taught high school mathematics students would come by my room all the time. At times I may have been teaching a lesson and someone would knock on the door needing to talk. I created time to listen and respond to the students and in turn they begin to trust me more. There was a time when one of our popular students went missing. Her body was found in the bayou. The students were devastated and the administration with all of their big degrees couldn't get the school to stabilize. These students were all over the place, grief-stricken by the news. The administration heard of my relationship with the student body, found a substitute to take over my class, and found a room big enough for everybody. Those students wouldn't talk to or respond to anybody but me, just because I had taken the time out of my day to listen to them and respond.

It is not always about what you say or how you say it; it is just your willingness to participate. What you say doesn't always have to be so profound because sometimes the simplest words are so timely. You can tell when someone wants to really talk versus someone being messy. I encourage you to be willing to take the time out to listen and respond to others; you never know what kind of impact you may have on them. I wish I had the opportunity to have taken a moment to speak to Shemora Porter; I could have said something simple, but timely, that could have possibly saved her life.

God Bless

Wisdom

> "But the wisdom that comes from heaven is first of all pure; then peace-loving, considerate, submissive, full of mercy and good fruit, impartial and sincere. Peacemakers who sow in peace raise a harvest of righteousness."- **James 3:17-18**

Some people may think that having wisdom is to know it all. That's not true. Wisdom is having discernment or insight, the ability to effectively and efficiently apply perceptions and knowledge to produce the desired results. Wisdom often requires control of one's emotional reactions so that one's principles, reason, and knowledge prevail to determine one's actions.

It is very easy to react or just act period to any and all situations. However, it takes a little bit more to do it with wisdom. Wisdom will cause you to pause and think thoroughly before you move, being careful to pay close attention to what you do and say. Applying wisdom in every situation gives you a better chance of achieving your desired outcome as well. Using wisdom allows you to make the best use of your knowledge.

If you don't have control over your emotions, it will be difficult to use wisdom because there is a tug of war going on inside of you. It is as simple as if your managers say something to you out of the way; you know that you should still respect them because of their positions; however, because you are mad and can't control yourself, your response gets you in a world of trouble. In that type of situation, wisdom would not have been applied effectively. I have discovered that if I respond in love, that changes the outcome of the situation, even if there is emotion burning on the inside of me. My response changes how I feel about it and often changes the predictable outcome to lean more in my favor.

We sometimes are quick to respond with that smart remark that pops into our heads or the one that usually rolls off our tongues before we know it. However, wisdom is learning how to control ourselves in those situations and choosing to respond differently. I applied wisdom in a meeting yesterday involving spending money and even though I wanted to respond one way, my response instead was very sincere and full of peace. Thus, results were favorable.

Apply this scripture in your life today; I guarantee that an opportunity will present itself and change the outcome. Remember, the Bible did say that you reap what you sow.

God Bless

Will You Be Waiting

> "So Christ was sacrificed once to take away the sins of many people; and he will appear a second time, not to bear sin, but to bring salvation to those who are waiting for him."
> **- Hebrews 9:28**

Where will you be when Christ comes back? When I ask this question I am not just talking about where you will be physically; I mean spiritually and mentally. Many of us are going through life expecting Christ to come back so we are doing our best to get our lives in order. However, there are still some who feel that they have time so they are trying to "live their lives" before they really get focused on living for Christ. Let's face it; there are a lot of people who feel like living their lives for Christ bring about too many restrictions and rules that they aren't willing to bend on right now. I have to be honest. I have been able to do things I have always wanted to do in Christ. You are not limited by Christ's standards to live your life; you are limited by your own interpretation of Christ's standards.

Jesus got really serious about being about His father's business at the age of 12 and He never looked back, which says that there is no age barrier to living for Christ. I would be willing to say that 99.9 percent of you hit 12 a few years ago, so in realizing that it is time to put ourselves into position. Jesus made the ultimate sacrifice for us at the age of 33. He was so majestic and perfect that it took sacrificing Himself for us one time to become a ransom to set us free from our sins, so still at a young age He was serious. His purpose wasn't to keep repeating this act over and over again every time we sin, like we find ourselves sometimes apologizing for the same thing many times. That is why the word says that when He comes back, it is not to bear sin because He has taken care of that already. He is coming to bring freedom from eternal damnation; He is coming to bring eternal life to those who are lined up in position to receive it. Everyday that we awake, the world is deteriorating more and more, so why would we choose risking living forever with God.

Please realize that the second coming could be tomorrow if God so chooses and the question is where you will be if that happens. Will you be in the position where God can clearly see that you are imperfect but ready? Does He see you working hard now seriously to overcome your strong holds and humanly ways so that you can live for Him? Will it be clear that your life brings God glory? The scripture says that when He comes He is bringing salvation to those who are waiting for Him, which would suggest that living for Christ is a way of life. We can't behave like we do when company drops by hiding clothes in the closet and pushing stuff under the bed. Our house has to be clean and in order, not because company is coming, but because that is the way we should keep our houses all the time.

Will your house be in order? Will you be in position waiting for Him when He returns? The choice is yours.

God Bless

Who is calling you?

"She has sent out her maidens, she cries out from the highest places of the city, Whoever is simple, let him turn in here! As for him who lacks understanding, she says to him, Come; eat of my bread, and drink of the wine I have mixed. For she sits at the door of her house, on a seat by the highest places of the city, to call to those who pass by, who go straight on their way. Whoever is simple, let him turn in here; and as for him who lacks understanding, she says to him, stolen water is sweet, and bread eaten in secret is pleasant." **Proverbs 9:3-5, 14-17**

Normally when the phone rings you already have it fixed in your mind if you want to talk, depending on who's calling, what you think they want, whether you want to be bothered, or if its a call that you have been waiting on. Technology has spoiled us so much now that we have Caller ID, so we know who it is before we answer. It is so advanced that you can check the id on your television screen. This text today helps us focus on who is calling. My brother in Christ, Kristoffer Lands shared this with me:

Check the caller ID! Both wisdom and folly are calling you, both inviting you to come on in. Don't be so quick to answer the phone; you run the danger of being a victim to some foolish whim or desire. Moving or acting without the direction of the Holy Spirit indicates that we never checked the caller id. Sometimes we do things and make decisions without thinking. Beware of the 3A's: anxiety, anger & avarice (Extreme greed for wealth or material things); they will each cause you to answer or act too quickly.

Set your Ringer! Wisdom prepares ahead of time. Building the house, setting the foundation, and so on take preparation. Today we are able to know regular calls on our phone by putting a unique ringer on wanted or special calls, calls that we NEED TO TAKE. In the course of a day you don't want to pull the phone out and look at the screen all the time. Instead you need be able to hear the ringer and know that your call is coming. The challenge is, however, to set the ringer you had to have SAVED the call. Have you heard the call of wisdom? Have you saved the call? HOW? By reading and meditating on the word. Pray before your day gets going. This readies you now in the thick of things to hear the voice of wisdom when you would normally have given into folly.

Answer the Call! Humble yourself to God and His word. Admit that you don't know, even if you think you might. The Lord's ways are above ours and His thoughts are not our own. Who knows how He might use you or the situation you are going through? Some of us are repeating old tests simply because we have not learned the lesson that the Lord has been attempting to show us. Stop, hear the call, open yourself to direction and redirection, and place yourself in the way of many WISE counselors. Wisdom is calling. You've tried listening to folly. Won't you answer the call of wisdom? Make sure that the phone is on the hook so that when wisdom calls it won't get a busy signal.

God Bless
Thank you Kris Lands

Who Do You Say I Am

"But what about you?" he asked. "Who do you say I am?" Simon Peter answered, "You are the Christ, the Son of the living God."- **Matthew 16:15-16**

Jesus Christ asked the disciples who the people say that he is. Without thinking about it they rattle off the responses. This sparked a few thoughts in my mind. I looked at their responses as they were both being true to Jesus and giving Him a true account of what was being said in a joking manner like they couldn't believe the responses. Or when they heard the responses they wondered themselves if He was really who He said He was.

This comes up because there have been countless encounters with the Pharisees and Jesus and His disciples in which the Pharisees challenged Jesus. Instead of doing the obvious, Jesus retreats and tells the disciples not to tell people about His miracles and refuses to show signs of His power to the religious leaders. At this point of course some of the disciples couldn't understand why Jesus wouldn't just let them have it. They had been first hand witnesses to what Jesus Christ was capable of. So without saying, this led to frustration for the disciples because they were thinking "if He just shows them who He really is, surely the people will believe." The disciples also questioned why He kept retreating? This says to me that even though the disciples were with Jesus everyday and saw Him deliver people and all of the many miracles and signs and wonders, they still obviously weren't sure. Within their hearts and minds there was stillroom for doubt. Here Jesus' question could have been, "if you know me like you say you do then how could there be any doubt?" Either way, He senses that there was some doubt and so Jesus set it up by asking the question, "Who do others say that I am?" The funny part is everybody had a response until the spotlight turned on him or her. When Jesus asked the disciples who they say that He is you notice only one confident person answered the question.

I really want to deal with the fact that Jesus had the power to expose Himself to the others, yet used restraint for a reason. It is called meekness and many of us need it. Being meek means power under control. I will save that for another day though. Today we will deal with acting like we know Him. No one likes fake people. Equally important, is seeing the true value of the person that you call friend. We tend to just go through the motions sometimes and assume that the people around us are genuine but we don't always take the time to really develop strong relationships with them. In developing these relationships, you have to pay attention not only to what they say, but also what they do. People often reveal their true selves by their actions, not always solely on what they say. Check the company that you keep and see if they really know you. Turn the spotlight on them every now and then to make sure that the folks around you can give a true account of whom you are.

When it comes to Jesus Christ, we all need to be prepared to answer His question at any moment. People may hear you mention His name or say how good God is. But do you really know Him? When someone asks you who Jesus Christ is to you, what is your response? Do you have to think about it or do you rattle off a response like Simon Peter? Once Simon gave His response, Jesus changed His name and blessed him tremendously. He didn't do it because of who Peter was but because he knew who Jesus was to him and he wasn't ashamed to tell it. Jesus has done so much for you, but do you really know Him? There are going to be several occasions that he will need you to come to bat for Him in front of your peers. Will you have His back? Who do you say Jesus is?

God Bless

Who Can I Run To?

"I love the LORD, for he heard my voice; he heard my cry for mercy. Because he turned his ear to me, I will call on him as long as I live."- **Psalm 116:1-2**

There is a popular R& B singing group from the 90's, Xscape, who wrote a song titled "Who Can I Run To." When I read the text this morning, that song came to mind. Some of the lyrics are as follows:

"As I stand here contemplating,
On the right thing to decide.
Will I take the wrong direction,
All my life, where will I go,
What lies ahead of me?
Who can I run to,
To share this empty space?
Who can I run to,
When I need love?"

Here these young ladies are in search of true love and want someone to count on. Above all it appears as if they want someone that they can trust and who loves them as much as they would love. The interesting part is one of those young ladies was married two weeks ago. So from 1995, when they wrote that song, she is just finding that love 15 years later.

My question is, "do we really have to wait that long and do we really know who we are looking for?" Psalm 146:3 says not to put your trust in man who can't save and it goes on to say that those who put their hope in God are blessed. I am much like the psalmist. I love the Lord because He truly is always right there. No matter what I need or when I call, He is always available. The Lord is always honest with me and He knows me so well that He knows what I need. So if I ask for something that I don't need He says *no* and I understand that His *no* means *no* for now, not forever. I may not be ready for what I am asking for so he is protecting me from myself. There is nothing to try to figure out with God because He genuinely loves me and He feels the same about you. We live in a seeing-is-believing type of society and even though we weren't there, we know that God sacrificed His one and only Son to show us how much He loves us. Even when I make horrible decisions I can count on the Lord to still be right there with the truth showing me the right way to go. I don't have to worry about half the country in the middle of my business. No one understands what it takes to maintain a relationship like the Lord and there is no one who is more loyal and committed.

So when Xscape asks the question, "Who can I run to?" The answer is Jesus Christ. He is the only one who will give us guidance and direction. He will have compassion for us and show us unconditional love. He is always fair and firm. So as long as I live I will trust in the Lord. I know that He is ready to answer me before I call so I too will call on Him.

God Bless

Which Side Are You On?

> "I have been crucified with Christ and I no longer live, but Christ lives in me. The life I live in the body, I live by faith in the Son of God, who loved me and gave himself for me."
> - **Galatians 2:20**

In the heat of battle soldiers really rely on each other. There is no room for anyone who is undecided or unsure if they are in or out. It has been sited in professional sports where there are key players on a team who want to be traded to another team so they half way play up to their potential because of their strong desire to play with someone else. It can also be disappointing when a family member whom you are really close to turns a back on you because of being influenced by someone else.

Paul is pretty upset here in this text and it started with Peter. If you read all of chapter 2 you will see how Paul and Barnabus met with Peter, James, and John. They came to a common place. The same God, who gave grace to Paul to be entrusted with the Gentiles, is the same God who gives grace to Peter to be entrusted with the Jews. Peter, James, and John gave Paul and Barnubas the right hand of fellowship. The right hand of fellowship is like a peace offering saying that you are considered family; you can break bread together because you are accepted and are well respected for what you are doing.

When you get to verse eleven all of a sudden it seems that Peter had a memory lapse. Peter was sitting and eating with the Gentiles but when men from James came (believed to be non-Christian Jews) on the scene Peter began to draw back and separate himself. The picture here is painted that these men from James were like Jewish nationalists, kind of like the mob and it is believed that their presence made Peter fear being seen having fellowship with the Gentiles. The reason is because earlier on there were extreme penalties for Jews who shared any kind of time with Gentiles and Peter thought his fellowship with the Gentiles would cause some harm to his home church. This was a contradiction since Peter was supposed to be so extreme in his faith in Christ. This is also the same reason Paul was so upset and to add insult to injury Peter had such a strong influence Barnabus was led astray as well and he was the Pastor of Jews and Gentiles.

Paul went on to exclaim that if he was to rebuild his old ways and go back to what he used to follow before Christ, he too would be a lawbreaker. He made the point that because he chose to be sold out for Christ he is not going to turn his back on what he believes. The word clearly states that we are justified in Christ; in other words we are declared not guilty. We are free in Jesus. So our text today allows us to see how convicted and convinced Paul really is when it comes to his relationship with Jesus.

He says that not only was Jesus crucified; he has died to his old self with Christ and now Jesus lives in him. He now lives his life by faith in Jesus Christ who he knows loves him and has done everything for him. No outside influence is going to change that because if he allows himself to doubt the power of God in anyway, then Christ died for nothing.

We face that same challenge everyday: to live for Christ believing in the power of His resurrection or allowing someone or something to cause us to doubt. Jesus wants to know if we are in or out. We can't straddle the fence; we have to make up our minds and stick to them. Which side are you on?

God Bless

We Must Accept One Another

"Accept one another, then, just as Christ accepted you, in order to bring praise to God."- **Romans 15:7**

Those who know me know that I haven't always been the tallest guy, especially when I was younger. I can fit in now as far as height is concerned but it hasn't always been that way. Most of my friends growing up were almost always five to six inches taller so I guess I always visualized being taller by hanging out with the taller people. Anyway when it came to playing neighborhood sports I was sometimes the last to get chosen because of my size. Once they realized how fast I was, things changed. I wasn't accepted because I wasn't like everyone else. There was something about me that was distinctively different so it caused people to shy away from teaming up with me.

As I grew taller, so did everyone else, however they began to accept me as being able to play an equal role and in that experience the value of having me apart begin to shine. I believe that the combination of self-confidence and acceptance can bring the best out of a person. Just think about it, you get the opposite effect when you isolate and reject someone.

As Christians we are expected to accept one another no matter how different we are. Really it is our differences that make the whole complete when we all really come together. Everyone brings value. We are supposed to follow the example of Christ anyway, so why wouldn't we accept others?

Look back over your life and tell me at what point were you perfect. Even though we have been liars, cheaters, thieves, and fornicators the list can go on however, Jesus Christ still accepted us as we were. The awesome part about Jesus Christ is that His love for us covers a multitude of sin. No matter how dirty we are the Lord is more than willing to wash us as white as snow if we are willing. He looks at all of us the same way and accepts those whom we may reject, which means we are still all a part of the same family.

Everything that we do should bring glory to God. Any friend of Christ should be a friend of ours. We should draw people to ourselves and allow them access to our hearts. I didn't say give them an all access pass but show kindness to others to help draw the best out of them for the glory of God. One of my youth told me about a year ago that he is really atheist and the only reason he let me baptize him was an obligation to please his mother. Well instead of pushing him away I drew him closer to me, knowing that God would handle the rest. The Lord is slowly breaking those barriers thanks to our brutal honesty with each other. He is God's child regardless of his perception of reality and everyone that we deal with on a daily basis is God's child as well; some of them are cleverly disguised as something else but still belong to the Lord. Let us be cautious with others, being willing to draw them towards you so that the light can shine on them too. You may help them discover some hidden value that just needed exposure. In doing so, they experience growth. God will still get the glory.

God Bless

We Have Authority Over the Enemy

> "I have given you authority to trample on snakes and scorpions and to overcome all the power of the enemy; nothing will harm you." **-Luke 10:19**

As a little boy growing up in the projects I saw a lot of things. Being exposed to that type of environment causes you to grow up fast and it toughens you so that you can protect yourself. I was always the smallest guy so all of my friends would always want to wrestle with or pick on me. For us it was like a neighborhood code where the older boys would rough up the younger ones to make them tough in case somebody outside of our neighborhood would bother us. So at a young age I felt empowered to deal with anybody who was against me.

As you can imagine the projects weren't always the cleanest place to live due to over crowdedness. No matter how much you'd clean your house, some critter from someone else's house would always find its way to you. Being young, I always saw those critters as a threat to our environment so I would always get pleasure in stomping on the enemy. I remember running into a snake one day, though, in country and the situation was a little different. It was in the chicken shed and my grandfather grabbed a garden tool and killed it. From that day forward I felt prepared to protect myself in a similar situation.

In this text God is giving us authority over our enemy; in other words He is saying that he has empowered us to be victorious. The author uses the snake and scorpion in his example because these two creatures are true threats to anybody, given the circumstances. One bite from the snake or one sting by the scorpion has a high probability to end your life. So the author says that God has given us authority to trample or tread on the snake and scorpion, which means God will preserve us from that danger. Like Daniel in the Lion's den, those lions were a very present threat to Daniel, but God preserved and protected him.

So here God is saying that He will protect us from malicious people who threaten our lives. He will always give us power to overcome satan. God will empower us to be victorious over all of the enemy's power and schemes, showing that He has divine power. He affirms that we don't have to fear our enemy. Just like when I was younger, growing up in the projects was no longer a fearful thing because I felt empowered and seeing my grandfather conquer the snake eased all my doubts. I realize now that the only people who feared the projects were those who never lived there. Just like the older guys in the hood protected me and empowered me God has done the same for all of us, but on a much larger scale.

No one can make a promise that nothing will harm you but God, who can back it up. Here is another reason we should trust God in all we do. His guarantee is one that you can be sure of.

God Bless

We Have All Sinned

"For all have sinned and fall short of the glory of God, and are justified freely by his grace through the redemption that came by Christ Jesus."- **Romans 3:23-24**

Many people see you a certain kind of way based on how you carry yourself. No matter where you are, there is always someone watching you. We consciously want to make sure that we put our best foot forward. The truth is that we don't always have it together and things aren't always what they seem from the outside looking in.

I have had the privilege to be exposed to many people and by the grace of God, humbly speaking; I am an open, caring, and understanding guy. I tend to listen well and when needed the Lord gives me some great advice to give to others while encouraging myself. From the outside, people see this calm, not-easily-moved brother who seems to have it all together. The truth of the matter is that I don't always have it all together. Spiritually, the Lord has brought me to a place to accept my imperfections and shortcomings, even though there were times I wanted to live up to other people's expectation of me.

There are many people who are trying so hard to cover up where they are and what they are going through and it is taking more energy to try to come across as a person with no issues. People who do this will eventually realize how exhausted they are trying to appear as someone that they are not. We all have to embrace that we are not perfect and have sinned at some point in our lives. We have to make a conscious effort to push ourselves away from our weaknesses, for that aids in our ability to sin easily. We have to surround ourselves with positive people whom we can be accountable to; we really have to learn to forgive ourselves and push to be better.

In the same breath, we have to realize that everybody has a past and that no one is perfect. We can't condemn people, knowing that when we fall short we don't want to be judged. If Christ says that there is no condemnation, what gives everyday people the right to try to change that? At times, the way we treat others is a direct reflection of our own secret insecurities.

I expose myself to others so they can relate to me and grow with me. However, I am careful whom I expose myself to because everyone is not spiritually mature enough to handle sensitive information. Being transparent liberates me and puts me in a position to be helped through my challenges. I don't have to try to hide my feelings and possibly put myself in more danger. In the movie *The Mask*, actor Jim Carey became someone that he wasn't every time he put the mask on. It got to a point that he didn't want to remove it because his identity was defined by other's perceptions. He soon realized that he still had to deal with that dude underneath the mask and that running only worsened the problem.

We should all take off the masks and be who God called us to be. We are giving ourselves and others the death penalty because of our sin and God says that we are not guilty by His Grace through Jesus Christ. We have all sinned and will sin again; but thank God that we are covered and he already paid the price for our freedom. Our job is to recognize our shortcomings and be mindful that we are not without sin; however we should do everything we can to sin less.

God Bless

Stop Playing

"Come now, let us settle the matter," says the LORD.
"Though your sins are like scarlet, they shall be as white as snow; though they are red as crimson, they shall be like wool."- **Isaiah 1:18**

I have heard the phrase before, that history repeats itself and I have lived long enough to witness it as well. I was born in the 70's, when folks were still wearing bellbottom jeans and rocking afros. Once we got into the late 90's, even after 2000; people are throwing 70's parties and the afro has come back in style. I can't say if that is a good thing or a bad thing, but it is back. The world is constantly revolving so change is evident. However, there is one pattern that exists that you would think we would have the upper hand on by now.

In this text, we have the Prophet Isaiah expressing words from the Lord, concerning the vision of Judah and Jerusalem. He discussed how children were given to corruption and so many people had turned their backs on the Lord. He talked about how the city was once full of righteousness, but now it is full of murderers and how the leaders were rebels and they loved bribes and chased gifts. During that time, they didn't defend the case of the fatherless nor the widow.

When I read the 1st chapter, it sounded a lot like the world today. There is so much corruption and hypocrisy; it is almost like those same things that Isaiah was addressing. The warning that the Lord gave them was if they were willing and obedient, then they would eat the good things of the land; but if they resist and rebel, the sword would devour them.

So, verse 18 finds the Lord saying lets sit down and see if we can settle this issue. He says that even though they are filthy with sin, He can cleans them and make them as white as snow, he can give them all a fresh start. He was saying that they had so much blood on their hands; that they needed to be cleansed. This is so on time for all of us, because we are seeing some of the same things that they saw and we are dealing with the same sin. It had gotten so bad for them; that God said that their sacrifices were a burden to Him and when they opened their hands to pray, He hid His eyes. When they actually prayed He said that He wasn't listening.

God is not interested in our sacrifice or our religious routines; He wants us broken and contrite trusting only in Jesus Christ. The word says that He wants us to clean ourselves up, do right, and seek justice. If we are obedient, then we will bless others, and ourselves if not then we will be devoured. It sounds to me that our future is in our hands. Every decision that we make counts; every consideration that goes against God's plan for our lives is a set back, that can be avoided by us choosing to simply say yes. Yes to His will and His way. God is bottom line, when it comes to negotiating. He doesn't bend at all, don't count on Him changing His mind or compromising. He says that it is going to be His way or your way, just be prepared to deal with the consequences if you choose your way. His way is not always easy, but we can bear it with the Lord. I would much rather have the Lord with me, rather than not have Him and cry out to Him and He is not listening.

It is time to stop playing church and be the Church.

God Bless

Watch What You Say

"The unfolding of your words gives light; it gives understanding to the simple."- **Psalm 119:130**

What you say and how you say it really matters. Sometimes, what we really feel just rolls off our tongues and before we know it, heads turn. I have often said too many people that the most dangerous weapon in the world is the human tongue. When you open your mouth, you can speak life into someone and give them the needed boost to make it, or you can tear them down to the point that they stop wanting to live.

Most people, when communicating, don't always think about what they are going to say before they say it so what is truth to them unintentionally comes out. Sometimes, their words cut like a knife or destroy like a nuclear bomb. The text today says that your words give light really to who you are. Everybody has days when they may have had a rough time; so the way we communicate may be a little rough. It doesn't make it right. However, it does happen. In your day-to-day communication our goal should be staying mindful of whom we are talking to and how we say what we say. The Bible says that we will have to make an account for every word that comes out of our mouths so we are accountable. We have to speak the truth but how we say it counts.

I often think about what I am going to say to a person to prevent having any regrets. I understand one important fact: Everyone may not be ready to hear what you have to say, so timing is very important. People when caught off guard might misunderstand you. We could also be misrepresented by others. As a result, we run the risk of jeopardizing our relationships by being honest. One student (whom I've tutored), was crushed by his father, who told him that he wasn't college material. He wasn't ready to handle that information, which was communicated the wrong way. I explained that his father was really challenging him to do better because he knew that his son was not living up to his full potential. I also emphasized that if his grades and study habits did not improve, his father would not fund his college education.

There is a line from an old R&B song that goes, "You better be careful what you say to me, because it might turn around on you." This young man, as a result of his father's words, thought that his dad didn't believe in him and created some distance between them.

What you say and how you say it may be more important than you think. A snappy response or an unconscious smart or angry reply may present a false representation of who you really are. Words are the least pervasion of the truth so lets be careful how we use them.

God Bless

Walk in Light

"But if we walk in the light, as he is in the light, we have fellowship with one another, and the blood of Jesus, his Son, purifies us from all sin."- **1 John 1:7**

As unfair as it is, we are often classified by others based on the company that we keep. Most people are products of their environments but those environments don't determine the rest of our lives. That statement means that God has provided an opportunity for us to choose.

There are friends and family who live their lives a certain way. Some are in the dark and have no desire to come into the light anytime soon and some straddle the fence. While others are in the light and they either are all in trying to help others get out of darkness or truthfully some part of them still struggle with their own selfish desires to be in darkness sometimes. The truth of the matter is God said in Revelations 3:16 that we can't be lukewarm because if so He will spit us out of His mouth. No one should want to put a bad taste in God's mouth. Let's be honest we don't want anyone around us who is cool with you one day and on something different the next day. No one really likes what we call wishy-washy people. We would rather they be true to who they are and we can decide if we want to be around them.

Here in this text the word is telling us that we have a choice to make. We can choose to be in darkness or in light. If we say that we are walking with the Lord there should be some evidence to support it other wise the Bible says that we are liars and the truth is not in us. God is light and there is no darkness in Him at all so for us to be in relationship with Him we have to be in light as well. The decision to be in light is not hard it is following through with the decision that we make difficult. The reason we make it difficult is all in our mind. Most people think that being in Christ is boring and many feel like they are alone. When the truth is there is more to do in the light than in darkness and you don't have to figure out how to cover it up when its all said and done. One statement I have heard over and over again and it is what happens in the dark will soon come to the light and this is so true. So if what you are doing is going to be exposed to the light anyway why not just start in the light and be done with it. Of course being in the light is living a life that honors God.

God also says that the blood of Jesus will purify us from all of our sins. Watch this. When we drink water, we make sure that it is filtered first because we want it to be as pure as possible. We do this because we don't want anything in our systems that could possibly sicken us. Some guy came to our house and tested our water to show us how filthy it was and we spent a lot of money on a water treatment system to purify it. So why live a filthy lifestyle? Jesus is the test. Compare our lives to His and on our best days we are still filthy rags. I have said it before and I will say it again: a half clean room is still dirty; it has to be all or nothing.

It is possible to be in darkness and you are fully committed to Christ. In that scenario you have a purpose for being in darkness and that is to shed light on others to pull them out of darkness. The only way that will work though is to be cover by the Lord and you have to be strong in your faith for that mission. Just like Paul went to Arabia for three years to spend time with the Lord so that when he came back to his old environment it wouldn't have the same affect on him. So we have to go through something like sin detox to really be ready to be light amongst darkness. Only you and the Lord can determine when you are ready for that however your desire to be in relationship with the Lord should be reflected in the way you live your life. Nothing good ever comes out of darkness so choose light always.

God Bless

Wait quietly

"My soul finds rest in God alone; my salvation comes from him."- **Psalm 62:1**

The New Living Translation reads, "I wait quietly before God, for my victory comes from him." As I look back over all my victories, I realize that God's fingerprints were all over them. In many of those occasions I may have pushed as hard as I could to get things done and I may have fought as long as I could, but it wasn't until God moved that anything happened. At that point I begin to realize that only in God's timing will anything happen.

Surely He gives us the leeway to have some control over our destiny. The Lord gives us the opportunities to go out and create futures for ourselves. However, in the end He still has to bless them to be fruitful. So in a society that feels that the world should be a huge Burger King (where you have everything "Your way right away"). I have learned that patience is a virtue not treasured by many. David says to us here that he waits before God, which suggests that he recognizes God's authority and is constantly in God's presence. To wait before God, means that he had to be in front of God. Also, David said that he waited quietly; so if he did this quietly, on a consistent basis I would imagine that he could find rest. Too many of us try to tell God how to bless us or how we want things done instead of trusting Him, because He already knows. The funny part is that many people don't spend the time developing their relationships with God like they should, yet always expect God to come through. We have the audacity to get mad if He doesn't when we want Him to. I have found many people who murmur and complain because life is taking too long to bring about change. David says that we should wait for the Lord quietly; Isaiah says that those who wait for the Lord will renew their strength. David even says in Psalm 37:34 "Wait for the LORD and keep his way. He will exalt you to inherit the land; when the wicked are cut off, you will see it."

Knowing that our victory is in the Lord and only through Him will we receive it, I am more than willing to find rest in God and God alone. If a sure victory only requires that you do your part, spend time with God and wait quietly; isn't it worth it to wait for God? After all, God is the only one I know who is truly undefeated against the enemy. His track record precedes Him. I don't know about you but I am going with the sure thing and if that requires that I wait quietly, I won't say a mumbling word. Lord, please have your way.

God Bless

Wait for the Lord

"Wait for the LORD; be strong and take heart and wait for the LORD."- **Psalm 27:14**

David touched on a thought that has to be addressed. When you read all of Psalm 27 it really makes the picture clear. There is one thing for those people who feel that they have done so much wrong that there is no way that the Lord will come to their aid. By the way that is not true because the Lord loves you and He is at His best when you need Him most. However, what David is talking about in this text is different.

I have learned a while ago that patience is a virtue that is not treasured by many. A lot of times when our back is up against the wall and it looks like there is no way out some tend to go through a series of emotions. Panic, fear, doubt are just a few of these emotional journeys that some people often go through in their time of need or when they are under attack. David's approach is to do what you can and then wait on the Lord.

David gives us the blueprints on how to handle an attack from the enemy. First, he recognizes that God is in control. Just that point alone will stop you from trying to be in control and help you realize that your issue is bigger than you. David had faith in the Lord and the Bible says that without faith it is impossible to please Him. So he made it clear to the Lord that he believed in Him even in the midst of his situation.

David had confidence in the Lord and expressed it when he said that he was sure he would see the goodness of the Lord in the land of the living. In other words, he believed that while he was living he would see the evidence of God working in his life. David had assurance as well. He knew that his faith was sealed and that he was sealed by the Holy Spirit in the Lord and without a doubt the Lord would come through just as He had before.

David helps us understand that we really have to be strong and stand firm on what we know and believe. There has to be something in you in order for the Holy Spirit to have something to work with. Every time that the Lord has come through for you should give you the same confidence that David had especially in the face of your enemy? We have to move to a place where we really believe what we are saying and reading about God and His word. We also have to take the necessary steps to apply God's word in our life at all times, not just in cases of emergency. We tend to treat God like the little red lever closed in glass that says break in case of emergency. If we never try Him before we feel like we really need Him, then how will we ever be confident that He will come through? God's word always calls us to action so that His power and His Glory will manifest in our lives and cause us to believe that with God all things really are possible.

So we have to take David's lead on this applying the same mindset and that will allow us to be able to wait on the Lord.

God Bless

Use Sober Judgment

> "For by the grace given me I say to every one of you: Do not think of yourself more highly than you ought, but rather think of yourself with sober judgment, in accordance with the measure of faith God has given you."- **Romans 12:3**

No one knows you better than you except God. You know your boundaries and capabilities, what motivates you as well as your insecurities, if any. On the same note you know all of the victories you have had as well as the struggles. You know the journey you have been on and when you allowed the Lord to have control over your life. When you sit back and think about all God has done for you and everything that should have happened but it didn't, should cause you to see life differently. Even when you think about all of the blessings in your life and all of the ways made out of no way, it should be the foundation of humility in your life.

Here we have Paul speaking to us from his own experience with God. He starts out by recognizing that if it weren't for God's grace he wouldn't be. Not only that he makes it clear that God gave it to him so he recognizes that he didn't deserve grace but God still gave it anyway. He goes on to say be real with yourself when doing an assessment of yourself. Don't give yourself more credit than you should; there is a thin line between being confidence and conceited. When you are conceited you have unrealistic expectations of yourself. We are all gifted and God has given us gifts that are specific to us to use to fulfill our role in the body of Christ. When we begin to operate outside of our capabilities it produces frustration, disappointment, discouragement, and ultimately failure or defeat.

It is important for us all to operate in the area of our gifts. If someone around you gets really sick and you are not a doctor, what do you do? You call one because you don't want to mess anything up. I once took a job that required me to drive a stick shift car. Well at the time I didn't know how to drive one. However, I felt that I was smart enough to figure it out. Needless to say that was a very long day and not much positive came out of it all because I thought more highly of myself than I should have. I knew that I didn't know what I was doing but I went for it anyway and I almost destroyed that car. Part of my job was to drive people to their doctor's appointments so I really went too far but the grace of God kept me.

Based on the measure of faith that God has given us, we know our limitations. Make sure that before you move on something you do a true assessment of what you are capable of doing and be real with yourself. If whatever it is is truly outside of your capabilities, make sure that you do the right thing. When we operate within our gifts, we please God and we are a benefit to the kingdom. However, when we try to operate outside of our gifts, we leave a lot of room for failure and we misrepresent the kingdom of God.

God Bless

Two Covenants

"He has made us competent as ministers of a new covenant— not of the letter but of the Spirit; for the letter kills, but the Spirit gives life."- **2 Corinthians 3:6**

In my college days I had a relationship with the Lord mostly because my parents and grandparents kept me in church. I gave my life to the Lord. In my mind back then that meant to be baptized and confess with my mouth and believe in my heart that Jesus Christ lived, died, and rose again for me. I knew that I had to go to church and read the Bible enough to qualify as a Christian. I did my best to abide by my general understanding of what I had read and heard from the preacher and felt that I was really strong in my environment.

I used my inner strength to avoid drinking and drugs, even in a college atmosphere. To this day I still have never experimented with drugs, nor have I had a drink of alcohol (not even beer or a wine cooler). Even though I was truly convicted, I still missed the mark on fornication, but in my mind I was an all around good person who knew that I could make up for what I had done. It wasn't until I had the incident with the truck falling on my chest, the narcolepsy, and homeless living with friends that I realized that I was just going through the motions with God. I was leaning on my own strength trying to make it into Heaven, not realizing that God having total control was the key for me to truly get it. I wasn't living a totally surrendered lifestyle; I had halfway committed because part of me still wanted to be in control. As a result I found myself falling out of His will constantly.

Here Paul is comparing two covenants or two agreements. We have a choice to have life in the new covenant or end up breathing to death under the old covenant. Paul says that with the new covenant is life giving, but the old covenant kills. A new covenant lifestyle is lived by the power of the Holy Spirit, who is the life-giver. This covenant gives life because it starts on the inside and works its way out. It works internally to produce change in our hearts and minds, causing us to respond to life in a godly manner. Paul describes this change in Ephesians 4:24 as "...the new self, which in the likeness of God has been created in righteousness and holiness of the truth." God gives us righteousness and promises to make us holy men and women. It is his doing, not ours, and this is what I was lacking in my college days and many people lack even today.

The old covenant is life lived in the power of self to be everything that we think that God wants us to be by our own power. The results here referred to the letter kills because it forces us to be obedient, but doesn't give us the internal power to obey. The nature of this covenant is trusting in self to please God by doing His will. We set ourselves up for failure taking this route. Sadly enough, this is the place where many people are because they don't want to release total control to the spirit. Paul's life was devoted to keeping every aspect of the written law of the Old Testament until his encounter with Jesus on the Damascus road. At that point he spent years trying to line himself up with God to really learn what it means to live out of God's grace rather than his own self-effort. I went through a few life-changing situations that opened my eyes and turned me to being sold out for God. Sadly many people have to go through something life-altering to make up their minds to release all control to God.

My prayer is that the light turns on for all of us and we stay committed to a new covenant lifestyle. There is no way that by our own strength, can we stay on track with God's plans for our lives. The Bible says that our lives were predestined by God so if He has the plans, let Him lead. God doesn't need our help, just our willingness to surrender totally to Him. Think about when an event is sold out. That means there is no more room for anyone else to enter, so we should all be sold out for God. Let us put our life on autopilot and allow the Lord to take the wheel. Now is the time to sit back and enjoy the ride, knowing that the one in control has a direct route to your set destination.

God Bless

True Leadership

"But I will stay on at Ephesus until Pentecost, because a great door for effective work has opened to me, and there are many who oppose me." -**1 Corinthians 16:8-9**

There were many great leaders in the Bible that we can learn from as well as many great leaders in our past. It is unfortunate that, in my opinion, we don't have many known great leaders today. Most of the leaders today are people like you and I who are leading our households the best that we can. I pray that the Lord continue to give us wisdom and guidance as we press on.

Leadership can be some difficult shoes to fill and requires a special person who is not afraid to fail and more than willing to push through the opposition at all cost. We can learn something from the Apostle Paul in this particular text today. Paul was a recognized leader by God and there is a law of leadership that says if you're going to be used by God to help change a situation, expect opposition. It is Newton's third law which says that for every action there is an equal and opposite reaction. This is something that Paul knew too well, considering that most of his letters were written while he was in jail.

Dr. Mark Hartman preached on this Sunday and he raised a great point. He was talking about Nehemiah, saying that we must recognize that opposition can help improve our plan. It did for Nehemiah in that story and Paul points it out in the text today. Opposition creates a great opportunity to reveal what we are made of. As a great leader you have to lead from your heart and when you put your all into something, you are relentless. Considering leading from your heart indicates that change takes place inside of you first. That helps to adjust your vision. Once you see yourself victorious before you start, you improve your plan. This happens because you now really have a purpose for what you are doing and you want to feel the victory that you envisioned.

In order for Paul to accomplish all of his goals, there was no way for him to do it alone. One of his strongest understudies was Timothy and he poured so much into Timothy, it was like he was everywhere that Timothy was. This highlights the point that the plan you are trying to accomplish can't just be yours. There has to be a team effort. As a leader, you have to share your dream, and vision with others in a way that they embrace it as if it were their own. Once that happens you work together to accomplish the task. When you take the opportunity to work together, you will find that you can get more accomplished in a shorter amount of time.

This is a valuable lesson that we learn from Paul and it can be applied in every aspect of our lives. We can apply this at work, at home, in business, and at church. If you think about it, this information can be used parents to pull villages together to help raise their children. There are many things we can learn from true leadership. We can take what we learn and apply to our lives. One of the key points here is leading from the heart because when we do this we really give our all. Considering that we are all leaders being used by God in some capacity, we should expect opposition. Instead of thinking negatively, we can see it as an opportunity. Accept your role, be empowered, lead with your heart, and expect great things as a result of your leadership.

God Bless

The Word Stands Forever

> "For, "All men are like grass, and all their glory is like the flowers of the field; the grass withers and the flowers fall, but the word of the Lord stands forever." And this is the word that was preached to you."- **1 Peter 1:24-25**

When I think about the analogy of men being like the grass and their glory like the flowers of the field, I think about what it takes to keep the grass green and the flowers alive. Lawn care is one of the biggest businesses around and there is so much work to be done that the market won't be saturated for a while. You have to water your grass on a regular basis. Some people take the time out to go and stand outside for at least an hour, waving at the neighbors while they water. Some go to Home Depot and buy the little sprinklers that connect to water hoses and they may go through two or three different kinds before they find the one that works. Then there are those who are like my neighbor, who spent the entire summer digging up his yard and running piping underground. I assisted him, making sure that everything was measured out and lined up. It is a long process when you want it done right. He is just about finished putting the system in now, with winter coming in soon he will be prepared for the spring.

Flowers are the same way. They need special attention on a regular basis in order to survive. Either way, both of them require so much and they never last the entire year. You always find yourself having to start over at some point. Depending on people is really the same way; you can only count on them for so long, some longer than others. With the flowers and the grass, seasons change that bring new challenges. People may have a new season everyday. It just depends on how life happens. You may have someone on your side one day and you may look at them funny and before you know it you are on your own. The bible says for us not to put our trust in man because he can't save. This is true.

Christians in the work place are so interesting to me. Some of them give you this great presentation to let you know that they are a believer too but once they get pressure from the powers that be their Christianity is either out the door or hidden for a minute. I have run into a few who are very consistent, but not many. Make it a point to be as consistent as you can, no matter where you are.

The main point here is that there is nothing or anyone that you can depend on from start to finish like the word of God, which has withstood the test of time. If you want to measure the integrity of a man, measure him against the word. If you need an answer to any issue, the only thing that is going to remain true is the word. You can depend on it when you are up or down or even sideways. The word won't cut any corners for you. It will correct you and put you in your place in love and encourage you along your way, even to the point of giving you a little praise for doing the right thing. Just like the text says (and I know it is true because I have tried it) the word of the Lord stands forever.

Many people think that they need coffee to make it through the day, only to find out that they will crash later if they stop drinking it. What you really need is the word of God to help you make it through the day. You will crash eventually if you don't have a constant supply.

God Bless

The Word Cuts

> "For the word of God is living and active. Sharper than any double-edged sword, it penetrates even to dividing soul and spirit, joints and marrow; it judges the thoughts and attitudes of the heart."- **Hebrews 4:12**

The New Living Translation puts it this way, "For the word of God is full of living power. It is sharper than the sharpest knife, cutting deep into our innermost thoughts and desires. It exposes us for what we really are." What gives the word of God living power in our lives? It is like a seed that is planted; once the soil receives it there is a connection and growth takes place provided that it is good soil. The word of God is the same way once we receive it and understand it; the word is planted in our hearts it depends on the nature of our hearts on the amount of power that word has. Either way it has power once it is planted and the strength of its power is to expose.

Think about it. If you plant a seed it exposes the soil it is planted in, just like in the parable about the different soils in Matthew. Planting seeds will reveal whether your soil is dry and hard or if it is good soil that will produce fruit. That parable was about the heart that God's word falls on and it exposed the different types of people who receive the word. The word of God cuts the hearts of sinners with conviction and it defeats the enemy. We can say that the word of God is a discerner that penetrates our innermost being and deals with the spiritual aspect of man as well as man's life, irrespective of his spiritual experiences. That is the source of the metaphor of dividing soul and spirit to joint and marrow.

The word of God is so powerful that the enemy tries his best to snatch it from you before it gets in your heart. He does this because he knows what the word is capable of and ultimately it destroys all of his plans. The enemy knows that if he can intercept God's word, we want be exposed to the light, the truth. He understands that anything that is exposed to light becomes light and once the truth is revealed. Then, there is no hope for him. So the word of God has the power to judge, divide, or separate truth from what is not truth. It is just like a surgeon knows how to go in and spot a potential danger attacking your body and cut it out to improve your chances of survival. So when the Bible says that we must hide God's word in our heart so that we won't sin against Him, it is very critical that we do that or we give way to the enemy to invade our hearts.

The big message here is once anything gets exposed, change should take place. Anytime you find yourself in the presence of God, you should experience some kind of change because being in His presence puts you in a position where you have no choice. The word of God is powerful. It does expose you for who you really are. Not only does it expose you to yourself but it will expose you to others as well. Our goal daily should be to be more Christ-like, which requires us to be on a constant cycle of change. I understand that man fears what he doesn't know and not many people like change. However, if you are a child of the most high God, you might as well get used to change because His presence alone causes change all the time.

Recognize the power of the word of God and know its capacity. Just know that if your heart is broken God is the only one who can fix it and the repair starts with allowing the Word of God to penetrate the wounded area. I am prepared for a heart transplant and that Jesus Christ died so that He could be my donor; and he has done the same for you. Don't resist the word because it exposes you; embrace it because it will make you better.

God Bless

The Truth in Love

"If your brother sins against you, go and show him his fault, just between the two of you. If he listens to you, you have won your brother over."- **Matthew 18:15**

There is an interesting choice of words used in this text. Overall, the Lord is giving us steps in this parable about conflict resolution and how the goal is to gain them for Christ. Often times when a conflict arises, especially when someone sins against you, someone becomes defensive. The scenario mostly never starts with the two parties talking with each other, but instead there is often a lot of murmuring going on with others who have nothing to do with the issue. Sometimes we are hurt and we just hold it in for years, which can easily give birth to other issues.

Very seldom do we go to the other person in love to talk it out and get some kind of understanding and resolution. The times that we do go in this manner, something is said or done that may cause us to lose it anyway and then we leave asking what the use is. I can say "we" because I have been there before.

The first thing noted in the text is if your brother sins against you go tell him but keep it just between the two of you. We are all considered brothers and sisters in Christ even if we don't always act like it and this text is referring to the whole body, not just brothers. Either way, just know that this situation is a private matter between you and the other person. Whatever the sin, it is not for you to go and immediately start telling others without trying to deal with the person you have the issue with. The Bible says that if you have a problem with your brother, you should go quickly, not to everyone else but to him. If you check your attitude and delivery of the evidence when you go to him you may stand a greater chance of gaining him in the end. The hardest thing to do will be not to wear your feelings on your shoulders, so praying will be really important here and going in the right Spirit.

Next, if that person doesn't hear what you are saying, you should get a couple of witnesses to go with you so that they can give an account of everything discussed and hold you both accountable. These witnesses are not there to help you gang up on the other person but instead to lend an ear and impart wisdom. This should be someone who has great integrity and is careful not to choose sides. It should also be someone that the person you have an issue with sees as a person they trust and are willing to talk to. You want someone who will listen objectively to the issue.

The scripture goes on to say that if those two approaches don't work, go to the church (not to present before the congregation) in private, still in hopes to resolve the issue and still gain the other. If that doesn't work, you know how to handle them at that point; the Bible says treat them like a tax collector. We still have to deal with them. It just comes down to how we deal with them.

In most cases for most of us, our situations may never involve the church. However, this text still gives light to how we can handle any conflict that we have because of sin. I have had to apply this in my life with a friend or two and it wasn't the easiest process. In one case I lost my brother for a while and he eventually came around because I continued to show him love. My goal was still to gain him even though he was upset with me for telling him the truth in love. We all have to be really careful how we handle conflict, especially when you feel that someone has sinned against you. Always remember that the goal is to still gain them by showing them the love of God and having them to repent. We are not the judge. God is and we don't have a Heaven or a Hell to put anybody in. If you have a friend, though, and this situation applies to you, ask yourself what allowed you to be friends with that person in the first place. The other question is that friendship worth fighting for and for Christ's sake, yes it is. If they don't want to meet you half way pray for them and keep moving. Show them love when the opportunity presents itself and that is all that you can do. God will do the rest.

God Bless

The Time is now

"Teach the older men to be temperate, worthy of respect, self-controlled, and sound in faith, in love and in endurance."
- **Titus 2:2**

As a father of two boys, I am struck by this text. Considering that my father and I didn't have the best relationship when I was growing up it has been difficult for me to get a true picture of what the man of the house is supposed to look like. So for my boys I knew that I had to get it together quickly or I would be training them the wrong way. There were older men that I paid attention to and I learned from even without their knowledge. I am the man I am today by the grace of God and the influence of a collection of men that I had the pleasure of being around, including my father.

The text here is saying that aged men should have the following characteristics. They should be mindful of what they allow themselves to be exposed to working hard not to over indulge in the excess of their sinful desires. This man invests his time wisely and he discerns which things are of greater value and importance. He strays away from impulsive decisions and erratic behavior like he participated in so often when he was younger; he knows that self-control is the key. They should carry themselves in such a way that brings them honor. He should live his life in a way that is worthy of special respect. He should have the kind of faith that doesn't waiver in the face of adversity, the type of faith that will endure to the end.

When I look at the world, I realize that we are in trouble because we don't have many men who posses half of these traits. There aren't many men to look up to or to model ourselves after; there aren't many leaders stepping up to the plate. I am by far not perfect by any means. I acknowledged that I was failing by not spending time with my oldest son. I once believed that providing for a household was a man's most important duty; but there is more to it. At one point I wasn't having much fun time with my boys, until I saw my oldest have fun with another man, I quickly learned what I needed to do. I work long hours and I only get 30 minutes for lunch but every chance I get I try to go home for lunch, even if just for a few minutes to interact with them. We pray at night and I make it a point to try to catch my oldest in the morning before school so that we can pray over his day. There are many other things we are doing. I am still trying to master my weaknesses. I refuse to make excuses for not fulfilling God's expectations of me because of lack of good example.

This is really a call for men to rise to the occasion. It is funny the effort we will put in to get a higher position just to have to work more even though we are getting paid more. It is even crazier the way some will step all over whoever just to get ahead while leaving their family behind. Brothers, think about where you are and how your children perceive you. If you don't have children I guarantee that someone's child is watching you. The Bible says that when I was I child I thought like a child, acted like a child, and reasoned like a child, but now that I am grown I put childish things away. Think about that the next time you go to all the parties and get so wasted you can hardly make it home. Think about that when you ignore your family because you feel like you really need some you time not realizing that they need you too. Sisters, encourage the brothers especially those who are trying. It's hard out here trying to maintain and still keep peace and joy at home. If your man is far from what is described here in the text, pray without ceasing.

If we don't have more men to step up to the plate and posses these qualities, our future is in a world of trouble. Just read the news now because we are heading there fast and guess who is leading the way?

Are you up for the challenge?

God Bless

The Righteousness of God

"God made him who had no sin to be sin for us, so that
in him we might become the righteousness of God."
- **2 Corinthians 5:21**

After this weekend this scripture really captures the true essence of what God have been sharing with me and through me. I spoke at a local high school one Friday, where we discussed how your destiny is tied to the company that you keep. The Lord used me again on the following Saturday for one of the most beautiful weddings I have ever been a part of. This couple is so awesome and their vows captured what God really means about love. Then on Sunday morning the Lord shared through me a lesson on music and culture. The picture that was painted was that God has done too much for us to allow the media to (one) portray Christians in such a negative light and (two) to sway the mindset of our young people in an attempt to brainwash them into being less than what God has called them to be.

In all of these messages it all comes back to sacrifice. Not sacrifice in its original meaning but metaphorically speaking as in the giving up of oneself as a selfless good deed for others. I am convinced that there are some people in the world who don't truly understand the sacrifice that God made to save the world. So many people are turning John 3:16 in a cliché, totally disregarding the true price that had to be paid for our lives. We are a sinful people and because of God's love for us He made the ultimate sacrifice of giving of himself so that we can live for him. In this same chapter it says that because of God's sacrifice, we are new creations; we have been reconciled back to God and are now Christ's ambassadors as if God is now making His appeal through us.

We, as children of God, have to make a stand for what is right and desire to be in right standing with God. The awesome part is that God gave His all through Jesus Christ and somehow He still has more to give. My co-worker just left my office telling me that she has to have surgery. We have never discussed that I am a preacher; however she sees something in me because she has been giving me opportunities to minister to her. Today was the day. She says that she may have lymphoma in the neck, which is a form of cancer. I can't begin to go through her story that she shared but she has been through a lot. The doctors told her that they would perform the procedures free. This is significant because she is a contract worker; she has no insurance. So, of course you can see God's fingerprints all over her situation.

The interesting part is that she and I never talk about anything except work. When I am at work I would rather wait to see if someone sees God in me, than tell them I am a preacher. Today the Lord has once again reminded me that I am His ambassador and He wants me in right standing with Him. I could have chosen to be quiet or wished her well. Instead, I chose to stand for Christ and encourage her.

We all get this same kind of opportunity daily and yet some don't take advantage of it, perhaps because they don't want people to know they are Christian. Again, God has done too much for us not to stand for Him and He desires for us to be closer to Him daily. Let us think about the sacrifice Jesus made for us and let us make a commitment to sacrifice for Him, regardless of how it makes us look. God desires a closer relationship with us. We never know how he is going to use us. He didn't just do it for me; Jesus paid it all for all so that we might become the righteousness of God.

God Bless

The Right to Remain Silent

"If you keep your mouth shut, you will stay out of trouble."
- **Proverbs 21:23**

We all have the right to remain silent. However, most people hardly ever take advantage of that right. The majority of our trouble results from or revolves around indiscrete speech.

We hide behind clichés like, "I'm just keeping it real", or, "It needed to be said" or we will say what we really mean and respond with, "I'm just playing."

Our words are like bullets; once we pull the trigger we can't get it back. Immediate damage is done and depending on where it hits our human target; life as we presently know it (with that person) could end. It really doesn't matter if we say it privately or publically, words still travel. Ill-spoken words can be intentionally spoken, but are usually spoken out of ignorance. They are usually insensitive and thoughtless. Some people are so selfish to the point that they just have to be heard, never considering how they affect other people.

Some advise the easily offended not to listen to their inappropriate words. Getting off of their soapboxes, would eliminate the need to tune them out. Everyone is entitled to their opinions; however, we all don't have to always be exposed to most people's insensitive approach to expressing themselves. The enemy always encourages our speaking our minds and not caring who hears. He enjoys our talking too much; that leads to yelling, bickering, fighting, and so on because it puts us in a position not to be able to hear the voice of truth. We don't have a right to say what we want to say the way we want to say it because the Bible tells us to always season our words with grace. I slip sometimes myself. Though difficult, I self-correct when I realize that I have uttered something that the Bible forbids. There is a way to say what we feel without taking folks out with your words; we just have to process our thoughts before speaking respectfully.

We argue and continue to argue when we don't think we have been heard.

You have the right to remain silent! Anything you say
will be weighed against your character.

Kristoffer Lands, a very dear friend of mine, shared this with me:

Search for the value in what you are hearing.
Intently listen! Challenge yourself to hear what is being said to you.
Leave behind your preconceived opinions or ideas and listen; you might learn something new.
Expect the best!

Never speak when you are emotional. Cool down, count to 100, and decide if something still needs to be said.

Test your talk! Are you about to say the right thing, the right way, for the right reason? Are you expecting results? Are you seeking to benefit the other person? Will it glorify God?

"Before you speak", my father in the ministry Olus Holder would always say, consider: "Is it true? Is it kind? Does it need to be said?" We have all been told since we were little (and my oldest son said it one weekend) if you don't have anything nice to say, don't say anything at all. So you do have the right to remain silent! Anything that you say will be held against you.

God Bless

Promise Keeper

> "The LORD had said to Abram; Go from your country, your people, and your father's household to the land I will show you. I will make you into a great nation, and I will bless you; I will make your name great, and you will be a blessing. I will bless those who bless you, and whoever curses you I will curse; and all peoples on earth will be blessed through you."
> - **Genesis 12:1-3**

It is funny how the world has a view that rules are made to be broken. However, from childhood when you make a promise to someone, to break it is like a sin. Think back to when you were younger and someone promised to get you something or take you somewhere; you placed all of your hope on that promise. My boys ask me sometimes in the morning, "Daddy will you play the Wii with us when you get home?" I can imagine the whole day their minds are locked into the promise that Daddy made until it happens.

Here in the story, God made a promise to Abram, who later became Abraham as a result of the covenant that they made. Abraham was so loyal to God that we benefit today from God's promise to him. God told him that he would be the father of many nations and they would possess the land the Lord had for him forever. It is so awesome to know that our heavenly father is always true to His promise even today.

God promised us that He would be with us always even until the end. He says that He will give us the desires of our heart and that we would reap a harvest if we just don't give up. All of God's promises are attached to a condition and keeping up our end of the deal will only be as hard as we make it. Abraham was able to do it so we surely have the capabilities to do the same thing. I look forward to God coming through on His promises and just like Grandma would do every now and then, He throws a little bit extra in. God made at least seven promises to Abraham in the text above and He kept every one of them. God wants to do the same for you and me. He has so much in store for us as long as we are willing to do our part. Never give up on God because He will come through and never give up on you.

God Bless

The Job Experience

> "But he knows the way that I take; when he has tested me,
> I will come forth as gold. My feet have closely followed
> his steps; I have kept to his way without turning aside."
> **- Job 23:10-11**

For about three weeks earlier this year, I haven't said much about what I've been dealing with to others. I just asked friends and family to pray for me because I discovered that I had a staph infection. Well, I wasn't just dealing a staph infection; I was dealing with MRSA, the worst kind of staph there is. It is flesh eating and often immune to antibiotics. The first antibiotic didn't work so the doctor prescribed a second one that actually did. Without going through all of the details I will tell you that I was in serious pain for at least two weeks. The infected areas were under my left arm and on my right knee.

My first doctor was so passive in her approach with treating me that after visiting the doctor four times in three day, I switched doctors. The new doctor looked at my knee and immediately performed out patient surgery. On top of all this, the doctor told me that I had low enzymes in my liver, insufficient vitamin D (that I have to take pills), very high blood pressure, and elevated cholesterol levels. When it rained, it poured. I have never had that much going on with my health in my life. To make matters worse my leg began to swell; so there was a threat of blood clots in my leg, which is life threatening.

In the midst of all of that I had to make a decision because the enemy was trying to take advantage of this opportunity. Do I continue to trust God and stay the course or do I fall for the enemy's trap and create an environment that would justify what I'm going through? I say it that way because the cards that I had been dealt, wasn't a result of sin. Much like Job, the Lord was using me to silence the enemy. From the outside looking in it appeared that I must really be a sinful man to have so much coming against me.

I lift this up because Job is a great example of holding fast to beliefs in a tough phase. It is not going to be easy because your mind will be filled with questions, starting with why. It is ok to ask God "why", however we have to be willing to trust Him and know that everything that God does is by design for a greater purpose and outcome. The Bible says in Hebrews 10:36 that we have to persevere so that when we have done the will of God we will receive what He has promised. James 1:4 goes on to say that perseverance must finish its work so that we can be mature and complete, not lacking anything.

When you experience trials in your life it is not always linked to how much sin you have in your life. It is a time to reflect and get yourself together as well as focus on the will of God for your life. He is trying to get your attention and get something out of you to make room for what's to come. Job didn't turn his back on God like he was being encouraged to do. He stood on what He believed. Job made it really clear that he was confident that God knew him and his ways and once God delivered him he would be like pure gold.

Purifying gold is a dangerous process that not just anybody can do. The heat in purifying gold can reach temperatures of 2000 degrees Fahrenheit. So we have to go through some heated situations sometimes for the Lord to refine us. Our job is to stay the course and not turn away from God. I am recovering from my surgery and getting my health in order. I know that God is not finished yet, however when this chapter ends I will be stronger. I also trust and believe that the Lord has a major breakthrough on the other side of this purification process.

God Bless

The Heart is Deceitful

> "The heart is deceitful above all things and beyond cure. Who can understand it? "I the LORD search the heart and examine the mind, to reward a man according to his conduct, according to what his deeds deserve."
> **- Jeremiah 17:9-10**

I have often said to others when I was supposed to do something and I didn't do it to charge it to my head not my heart. I have heard it many times and I have used it myself to paint the picture that I really care about what happened, but just forgot. However when I think about it, if my heart was really in it, I would have done whatever it was that I said I forgot to do. Just reading this text and having a flashback of my life has convicted me so much because I never really realized how deceitful the heart could be. I really cared about the situation and wanted to be a part; however, now I realize the heart wasn't fully in it.

The heart and mind really work closely together because God made it clear that he has to protect our hearts and minds in Christ Jesus. If He doesn't, we would completely lose it. His protection is what gives us peace that surpasses all understanding. The majority of what we do is a matter of the heart. The Bible says that out of the heart flows the issues of life and that is displayed by some of the decisions that we make.

According to Jeremiah, our hearts have been inclined to sin since were born. It is easy to fall into a routine of forgetting and forsaking God. Where human nature kicks in and our heart is revealed is the fact that we still have the choice whether to continue in sin. We can fall to a specific temptation or we can ask God to help us resist temptation. The choice is ours to make; it's an issue of the heart.

The awesome part about God is that He knows what is in our hearts and our minds and rewards us according to what we deserve. The only way for us to know is to line up with God and His word so that He can reveal it to us. We have to allow His word to work in us to purify our heart and keep our motives pure. That is why David asked God in Psalms 51:10 to create in him a clean heart and renew a right spirit in him because he knew he needed to correct his sinful nature before it spiraled out of control. Our goal should be to have a pure heart because the Bible says that the pure in heart are blessed and they will see God. So let us stop deceiving others and ourselves and allow God to scan our hearts and cleanse them with His word. That way, when we make decisions, as long as we are true to God, we will be able to consciously be true to ourselves and to others.

God Bless

The Giver

> "And I have been a constant example of how you can help those in need by working hard. You should remember the words of the Lord Jesus: 'It is more blessed to give than to receive.' -**Acts 20:35**

Growing up, we were never well off. As a matter of fact, we were limited to about three or four shirts, matching pants, and a pair of shoes for the whole school year. When it came to Christmas I always dreamed of getting a lot of stuff; however I was content with one big gift and few small ones like socks. All of this happened after my parents divorced, so we found ourselves on the receiving end sometimes. As a result of so many people always willing to give to us, one thing that I never want to fall short on especially around Christmas, is giving.

Since my oldest son was about three, we have been teaching him the principle of giving. My wife and I always have Him pick out toys that are in good working condition to give away to someone who doesn't have much. Next year his little brother will be joining him in this effort. It is funny how his giving spreads throughout the year. If he sees a homeless person asking for money while we are driving, he turns to me and says, "Daddy do you have any money for me to give to him?" Giving is very contagious and something that we should practice doing all of the time, since God already provided the model for us.

Here today the author is saying that he has been an example for the people on helping those who are in need. The desire to help those who are in need has to be in your heart. The Bible says that God loves a cheerful giver. The thought the author left with them was that it is better to give than to receive. To always receive and never give is selfish and reveals that what you want is all that matters to you. A person with this mindset could see someone in need and never even blink or show an ounce of care or concern. In my opinion, there is really nothing Godly about that, considering that God gave His all for us.

Giving makes you feel good inside; it defines purpose in your life and draws you closer to the Father because He desires for us to serve others. He says in His word for us to consider others better than we do ourselves. So my wife and I always find ourselves giving, even out of our lack. Don't let people take advantage of you, though. Don't allow someone taking advantage of your kindness to stop you from desiring to give. It is better to give than receive because you are duplicating what God did for us. He wouldn't say it in His word if hadn't already done it. Be imitators of God and give because it will stir hope in others and inspire them to grow to become givers too.

Who would have thought that those who were such a blessing to me when I was younger would be such an inspiration for me to want to give as well? Once you give once you will never want to stop. During Christmas, we adopt families through a non-profit I am a part of and during the Christmas holidays of 2010 we adopted 23 families with over 85 children. The money we raise and spend is nothing compared to the smile on those faces. We give those families hope to keep pressing on. Be a blessing this year and don't forget it is better to give than to receive.

God Bless

The Choice is Yours

"For the wages of sin is death, but the gift of God is eternal life in Christ Jesus our Lord."- **Romans 6:23**

There are some messages that we get that are hard to receive. Most of the time, the message is hard to receive because there is no beating around the bush or sugar-coating the truth. A number of people tend to want to fantasize sometimes and not deal with reality; however you eventually come face-to-face with it and are left to make a decision.

This is one of those hard messages from the Lord that we all have to deal with, whether we want to or not. Paul puts this word so plainly that a child could get it. Yet we still have some who have either not heard the word or they ignore it. Here he breaks down how before we accepted Jesus Christ as Lord and Savior, we were slaves to sin. The Lord is clear that no matter how you look at it being a slave to sin will eventually lead to death.

Some would say that we all are going to die anyway, so what's the use? The answer is: though life is short and death is certain, how you spend eternity is what you are living for. It is true we are all going to pass away at God's appointed time. However the way we live our lives today determines how we spend eternity. The awesome part about God is that He gives us the freedom to choose: the freedom to choose to live with Him in eternity or spend it being tormented with the enemy. The message is very clear in verses 21-22. Paul asks the question, "What do you benefit being a slave to sin?" His answer: death. On flip side, by being a slave to God in Christ Jesus, we reap holiness. The result is eternal life.

The writing is on the wall and the message is very clear. We have all reached that fork in the road where we have to choose our destination. Quite honestly, I have to say that eternal life is a very appealing offer versus the alternative. To know that we have the power to put ourselves in positions to receive eternal life changes my focus on life. We have to understand that we are at cause for our lives and our actions and no one can *make* us do anything that we don't want to do. We have to be willing to give in before anything happens. In saying that, I believe that when you sin it is because you wanted to, not because someone forced you to do it. God gave the disciples power and authority to drive out demons and cure diseases and he gave us the authority to overcome the power of the enemy, according to Luke 10:19. Saying that the devil made us do it, is nothing but an excuse. He doesn't deserve that much credit.

James 4:17 says," he who knows what he ought to do and doesn't do it, sins." We are accountable for what we know and therefore accountable for the decisions we make.

Choose you this day whom you will serve, but as for my house and me we WILL SERVE THE LORD.

God Bless

The Benediction

"May the grace of the Lord Jesus Christ, and the love of
God, and the fellowship of the Holy Spirit be with you all."
- **2 Corinthians 13:14**

Normally, after your worship service is over you will hear the preacher say something like," To him who is able to keep you from falling and to present you faultless and with great joy to the only God our Savior be glory, majesty, power, and authority, through Jesus Christ our Lord, before all ages, now and forevermore! Amen." Some will even sing "World without end Amen, Amen."

That of course is your benediction. It is a short prayer for divine help, blessing, and guidance as you go your separate ways. Most people really don't know what it means though, they just think it is a part of the service and that is the way it is suppose to end every week.

You are all in agreement with this prayer to the Lord to seal within you, what has been shared with you that day by way of the message and the entire worship experience. You are also joining in together to say to the Lord please continue to impart you blessings upon us and to cover everyone not knowing if it is the last time you will see one another.

In Paul's benediction, he is proving the existence of the Holy Trinity in recognizing God the Father, the Son, and the Holy Spirit. He spells out how we need God's grace through Jesus Christ; whom we would never have in our lives if it wasn't for God's love for us. He wraps it up by recognizing that we need to also have ongoing fellowship or communication with the Holy Spirit who gives us guidance, direction, and comfort.

What better prayer to pray than this one covering all, even those who are strangers to one another and asking the Lord's blessings on everyone. It also asks that all of the Heavenly influences guide us all on the same path of righteousness to our eternal destination.

In other words, this is the Pastor's way of speaking life into us and blessings upon our lives as we leave from our public worship. That is why you may hear some of your pastor's saying not to leave before the benediction. So the next time you are in the service and you really want to beat the traffic out of there so that you can race home and start dinner or watch the game just remember the Pastor is trying to pray peace and blessings over you and your family to make it through the week.

God Bless

The Answer Is

"But in your hearts set apart Christ as Lord. Always be prepared to give an answer to everyone who asks you to give the reason for the hope that you have. But do this with gentleness and respect,"- **1 Peter 3:15**

In 1997 I started a marketing company named "Jacobs Ladder Communications" and it was under the umbrella of a marketing company known as "Tag Team Marketing." My mentor was a multimillionaire and he trained me personally, so of course I had a passion to succeed. I learned so much that there was not suppose to be anyway that I would fail. We were always trained to look for the opportunity to promote and we should always promote the next event.

So, when someone would ask me what I did, my response would always be "I'm glad that you asked." I would create an environment that would cause people to ask what I did just so that I could tell them. We were taught that if you don't have confidence in your product or service, who is really going to believe you. So it was in our best interest to try the services for ourselves. In training we learned that when we first started our businesses, was the best time to promote and be successful because we were the most excited then. The other part was, as more people become a part of your team, then you all could grow your business together.

"I really wish I could preach this thing."

Needless to say I went all over the country promoting my business, doing seminars, and training others on how to start their own business. The Lord allowed me to create a huge following and I was always willing to tell whoever about what I was doing in hopes that they would want to try the services or be a part of the business.

I said all of that to say, that if any of us can do this for our businesses or employer, then why not for the Lord. First, recognizing that God is in control of our lives, He has done everything for us. Just what God has done for you in the last month ought to be enough for you to want to tell everybody about the hope you have Him. We were all called to make disciples, according to the Gospel of Matthew. Just as I described above, if you believe in what you are talking about then you will speak with passion and there will be this fire burning inside of you. Feeling excited like that, who wouldn't want to experience that same hope that you have.

A lot of times when people first start their walk with the Lord, they shy away from talking to others about Him because they fear that they won't know enough. In actuality, that is the best time because you are excited about your new journey.

That is when you are in church consistently, you are reading your word, and you are praying like nobody's business.

We are called to be Ambassadors for Christ, let us go out and not be ashamed to promote Jesus better than we do anything else.

God Bless

Thank you Lord

"When I said, "My foot is slipping," your love, O LORD, supported me. When anxiety was great within me, your consolation brought joy to my soul."- **Psalm 94:18-19**

As a child of God, it is very important that we recognize where we are in our relationship with Him. One way that we measure the strength of our relationship with God is when we see someone going through a tough time, our ability to be able to minster to him or her shows us where we stand. In that opportunity, we do our best to let the Lord use us to either bring that person into an intimate relationship with the Lord or help them realize that He never left their side. The interesting part is, we tend to really feel strong and confident in the Lord in those times and when the person we minister to come through their situation, we tend to have our own praise party.

What about you, though? What about when you are going through a tough time, maybe the toughest situation that you have ever been through? Sometimes, whatever we are dealing with can really get the best of us and we find ourselves falling fast. When I was diagnosed with narcolepsy, soon after, the bottom started falling out. In that same season, my roommate moved out and we have 6 months left on the lease. I lost my job, eviction notice was on the door, the doctor labeled me totally disabled, my car was reposed, and my electricity was cut off, I mean it was bad. I didn't know the Lord then, like I know Him now. I didn't want to go on; anxiety had kicked in so bad, I told the Lord to take me out. The relationship I did have with Him strengthened me to make it through. I found my self-saying to the Lord, that I was falling fast down a slippery slope, but because of His love for me, I would fight through it. God was true to His word and He did support me, console me, and in the midst of my storm I found joy and peace. As a result of the Jesus in me that just wouldn't let me quit, by the grace of God, I overcame my situation. At first I didn't want to fight; because I felt like what's the use, life wasn't going to get better. It seems as if the pressure just wouldn't let up. I felt that someone had their foot on my back and wouldn't let me up. I was still evicted, with nowhere to go; but I had peace. I had no source of income, but the Lord provided so that allowed me to be able to get my car back. The first place I went to was the church. I found that the reason we develop such a strong relationship with the Lord, is so that we can truly have a source of strength when we are going through. We can also be a source of strength when someone else is going through.

I don't know what you are dealing with today, however we are all dealing with something. Trust in the Lord with all your heart and lean not to your own understanding because your own understanding will have you hopeless and ready to quit. The Lord has already walked the path for you, so He knows just what you need to make it through what you are dealing with. He has an endless supply of it for you. Let us not forget who is in control and the fact that He willingly chose to make the sacrifice to be our very present help in our time of trouble. Whatever you are dealing with today, just be real with yourself and God and let Him handle it. This is why the battle is not yours, but His because you can't handle it. He wants us to cast all of our cares on Him. He wants to prove Himself worthy of all of the glory and honor and the praise.

Recognize where you are and know that God loves you more than you could ever love yourself. He wants you to have joy and peace. The only way to receive it is to let Him know and let your issues go. I have tried Him for myself and I know He will come through. Will you try Him today? Don't treat Him like a stranger. Don't insult the Lord acting as if He is incapable of handling your issue. If you can't find peace in the middle of your storm and you know the Lord, it is because you chose not to open your hands and let your issues go.

He's Able!
God Bless

Teach me to do your will

"Teach me to do your will, for you are my God; may your good Spirit lead me on level ground."- **Psalm 143:10**

Here is a prayer of someone who is in deep need of the Lord's touch and presence. If you read the entire Psalm, you can tell that they are on their last leg. It is like they have been broken to the point of wanting to let go. Yet, there is enough Jesus in him to cry out to the Lord. That mustard seed of faith, that moves mountains, have stirred up the gift in him giving him a glimmer of hope. It is amazing how when you are down, you really find the right words to say to the Lord. I believe that it is because you aren't trying so hard to say the right thing anymore; it becomes a real conversation between you and God. We even find ourselves during that time of prayer, getting stronger and feeling better before we end our prayer, like God has breath more life into us.

The Psalmist recognizes that in his deep despair, he can't do this alone. He really needs the Lord's help. He says that his spirit is getting faint, his heart is dismayed, and his soul thirsts for the Lord like a parched land. I really love when he says to the Lord, answer me quickly Father because my spirit fails. Rescue me from my enemy so that I can hide in you.

We all have rough days sometimes, rough weeks or months. We have to realize as children of God our power is in prayer. Lord, I love the way you love me, unconditionally. Wholeheartedly, emphatically, you gave your only son to prove to me, you do. Today Lord, I need you; we need you more than we know. We live in a world where sometimes every step we take feels like quicksand and we need your helping hand to pull us out. The world is sinking fast, only the strong will survive but how will we last, without you. True leadership is few and far in between, so we have no choice but to trust our Risen King. So please don't take your love away. We are not perfect as you can see. Thank God, tomorrow doesn't depend on me because sometimes I'm such a mess, blinded by the lies of the world I can hardly see the road. Thank you Father, for your beacon light, reading and applying your word allows my light to shine so bright. Maybe it will burn on and on, long enough for someone else to catch on fire. After all, it only takes your one touch to lift us out of our distress and you will because you love us so much. Lead us all along the guided path and if we stray leave your footprints, it will bring us back, to you. Never take you Spirit away, for it guides us and gives us hope to make it from day to day. We know that the Bible is not fictional we will be delivered to. Continue to bring us out of trouble, silence our enemies because we will never stop believing in you. Your will is our will, so please teach us your ways. May your good Spirit lead us on level ground, just as the psalmist say. There is one reality that always proves to be true, no matter what our situation; we will overcome as long as our hope in you. Thank you God, we now believe that you will make a way. Though we struggle and strain. We push and we fight. We have been delivered before, so we just have to continue to believe with all our might.

Open you heart and mind, and allow the Lord to move.

God Bless

Take one for the Team

> "But he was pierced for our transgressions, he was crushed for our iniquities; the punishment that brought us peace was upon him, and by his wounds we are healed. We all, like sheep, have gone astray, each of us has turned to his own way; and the LORD has laid on him the iniquity of us all."
> **- Isaiah 53:5-6**

In Football, we would always say," Leave it on the field." What is meant by this; is when you play, you play hard. Once the game is over and you know you have given everything in you, and then you left it on the field.

When playing baseball we would often say, "Take one for the team." I have done this several times my self without trying. Here these words mean; to sacrifice you for the teams benefit. For example, if you are up to bat and there is a wild pitcher, when they throw the ball and it is coming for you, instead of getting out of the way allow the ball to hit you, so that you can advance to first base. This puts the team in a position for a better chance at scoring, because now there is a man on base who got there because of his sacrifice. Taking one for the team never felt good but the results were gratifying, because I knew by doing it my team has a better chance at winning.

A master at taking one for the team is Jesus Christ, no one knows how to do that better than He. The results for Him were gratifying as well and it is a guaranteed victory for all on His team. Jesus' goal was to win and He was willing to make the ultimate sacrifice in order to make it happen.

In Baseball the coach would always say cheer on your teammate so that they know that they have your support, especially when they are up to bat. The team cheering would always encourage the batter to stay focused, so that they could get on base and score.

In Life, God is our coach and He tells us in His word, to encourage the Lord by how we live. He tells us this because Jesus went to bat for us and He took one for the team and we are already victorious. You would think that being on a winning team would cause one to stick their chest out and walk; talk, and act like a winner daily, knowing that your team is the best. When I played baseball and we had a major victory, I couldn't stop talking about it, because it felt so good. I wanted everybody to know. I wouldn't spare any details.

Now I have a chance to do the same thing for the best team that I have ever been a member of, and I am not ashamed to tell anybody.

Aren't you on the same team? Can anybody tell how victorious you are? Read the text above and think about how Jesus took that for you. Think about what it would have been like if you had to take that yourself, instead.

Let's get in the word of God and get geared up, so that we can run and tell everybody about how victorious we are. I can't tell everybody by myself but because of Jesus' sacrifice, I am willing to try if I have to.

Now are you ready?

God Bless

Take me as I am

"For the Son of Man came to seek and to save what was lost."- **Luke 19:10**

Here is an awesome story, of how God is willing to take our shame as His own, hoping that we understand and repent, allowing His love to change us. This is a case for why reading the whole story benefits us more than just this one verse.

Here we have the tax collector Zacchaeus, in the city of Jericho. He is viewed by the people, as a sinner, because the tax collector was known to be a crook, a person who took from others to pad their own pockets and become wealthy. One would think that a sinner doesn't know who Jesus is and if they did they would be trying to stay as far away from Him as possible, but not Zacchaeus. When he heard that Jesus was passing through, he wanted to see Him, in the Greek "wanted" means," to devote serious effort to realize one's desire." So he was on a mission, realizing his desires, after all his name means "righteous one". Since the tax collector was short and couldn't see over the crowd, he ran ahead and climbed a sycamore-fig tree. These trees are known to grow about forty feet high, with branches spreading far and wide. This further emphasizes Zacchaeus' desire to see Jesus and possibly be seen by Him as well. Jesus passes by and calls out Zacchaeus' name and invites Himself to stay at Zacchaeus' house for dinner. Jesus was passing through and He had not planned to stop, but for Zacchaeus He did.

Recognizing Jesus' love for him, Zacchaeus was moved to repent and promised half of his wealth to the poor and he said that if he cheated anybody he would pay them four times what he took from them. The wealth obviously meant nothing compared to not bringing shame to his guest, Jesus Christ. It was kind of like doing whatever you have to do not to bring shame to your family especially your parents. Guilty or not, Zacchaeus wanted to take advantage of the opportunity to at least see Jesus and the fact that he had Jesus to his house for dinner made his efforts well worth it.

There are times in our lives, when we think or know that we have done wrong and brought so much shame to ourselves and others that we tend to want to hide. This feeling sometimes causes you to move away from God and people, so that you won't be exposed. Here, this story helps all of us realize that Jesus will take the shame away, because we too desire to be the righteous one. We allow what others think of us to stop us and put us in a box, but Jesus came so that we can be free, even from the guilt and the shame. We have all sinned and fallen short of the glory of God, so everybody has a past and something that they are ashamed about. We have to have the same desire that Zacchaeus had, to see Jesus and at least put yourself in position to be forgiven and to clear your name. It took for Zacchaeus to move to action and for Jesus to be his guest for him to repent. How many of you know that since the Holy Spirit dwells within us, that God is our guest daily, so we should repent daily? We don't have to wait for Him to come to get right because He is already with us. It doesn't matter if the world doesn't see who we really are because we still mean the world to Jesus and He will take us as we are. You don't have to clean yourself up, because Jesus will change you from the inside out. You just have to be like Zacchaeus and put yourself in position to be made whole again. If you are willing, He will take you as you are.

God Bless

Subject to Authority

"Let everyone be subject to the governing authorities, for there is no authority except that which God has established. The authorities that exist have been established by God."
- **Romans 13:1**

I found this interpretation on the Internet, quoted by Barclay, "Let everyone render due obedience to those who occupy positions of outstanding authority, for there is no authority which is not allotted its place by God." Let every person place themselves habitually in subjection to the persons placed in control is the central theme here and the bottom line is leadership.

When looking at this text, parenting comes to mind, marriages, and even roles in the workplace. Children are to submit to their parent's authority, mostly because the Bible says so. They may not always like it, but at the end of the day the parents have the responsibility to lead their children. However, they train them up will be the foundation on which they stand when they grow older. Will parents always be right? In their eyes most of the time yes, however that is not always true but the children still have to submit regardless.

In marriages, the men are called to lead. It doesn't mean that the wife don't have a say because she does; marriage is a team effort. Women are called to follow their husband's lead, because God placed the responsibility on the man. So for those women, who have husbands that are leading God's way to the best of their ability, trust their leadership. If a man makes a decision that is not favorable for your family, he gets the heavy on that in God's eyes. In other words he was called to lead and he will have to take the heat for it.

I had a situation at work last week where I was 10 minutes late and my new manager walked in and said, "The work day starts at 6:30 around here, is there a reason that you can't make it on time?" I have to be honest, the God in me kept me from making matters worse. I did ask him why is it that no one has anything to say about all of the overtime I give and time on the weekends when I should be with my family. There is often a double standard in the work place, because so many people where I work abuse their time like lunch for example. This same guy who asked me about being on time was late to work and a meeting, called by upper management the next day and no one said a word. I realized that it is not my place to find weakness in the authority over me to justify my position. My job, even though I think it is not right, is to do my best to abide by the rule of those who have been placed in authority over me. If I do my part and we still have some problems, then the responsibility goes to the person in charge. We have to submit because God says so and we want to please Him. Once it is all said and done, the bottom line is pleasing God and doing everything we can to accomplish that goal. We are called to submit to the authority in place and if they don't do their part, you still have to do your part because God established this order.

If you are in leadership, make it a point to lead with integrity and with excellence. Most importantly, our goal hopefully is to be a servant leader, one who works hard to not be self serving, but to think harder on how to respect, value and motivate those you lead. In Jesus Name.

God Bless

Stop Taking Jesus for Granted

"He was despised and rejected by men, a man of sorrows, and familiar with suffering. Like one from whom men hide their faces he was despised, and we esteemed him not. Surely he took up our infirmities and carried our sorrows, yet we considered him stricken by God, smitten by him, and afflicted."- **Isaiah 53:3-4**

We know the story of Jesus or at least we have been exposed to some aspects of the story. Many didn't favor Jesus, which is why the scripture says that he was despised and rejected by men. I believe that Jesus had sadness or sorrow, because His life had purpose and it was to live for us and to die to save us, yet so many people were against him. It is just like when I use to teach high school math, I was there to help pave the way for a brighter future for my students, yet there were some who were so unappreciative. They knew why I was there and that I was genuine, yet at the time some of them still only saw things the way they wanted to see them no matter what I said or did. Once I was ostracized from the school, by no fault of mine, then the message was clear on why I was there and many told me that I was truly missed. Ultimately, they wanted me out of the school because I was for the students and would fight for them and that was favored.

It was the same way with Jesus. He was their teacher, instructing them on living a life with the Lord yet so many just didn't care. It is amazing how He had to die for some of them to finally get the big picture. What is even more amazing is how many people today know the whole story and still live their lives any kind of way, as if Jesus never did anything for them.

He took our weaknesses as His own and His death was meant for us, yet He died. So many today, treat Jesus as if, He was cursed by God. When you read the verses following verse four, it makes it clearer. Despite being treated unfairly, being misunderstood, considered guilty for something that He didn't do, being beaten, tortured, spit on, and talked about and the list goes on; Jesus still took on the sins of the WORLD. He didn't just do it for a certain area but He took on everybody's sin, even those of us who hadn't been born yet. He knew that we would get caught up in sin too, so He took our sins as well. Jesus has even taking on the sins of our children's children, because He loves us and the Bible says that through it all He never said a word.

We have to get to the point of recognizing that Jesus came because of us and He laid the path for us to follow. As a result of the coming of Jesus Christ, our steps have been ordered and if we think that we are missing a step, His word is a lamp unto out feet and a light unto our pathway. I was looking at books the other day and I saw one written by Craig Groeschel called," the Christian atheist." What he is saying, is simply this, there are Christians who believe in God but are living as if He doesn't exist. Christians have to stop despising Jesus and taking His suffering for granted. I have said it before and I will say it again, using a common colloquialism; we need to stop pimping grace. Let us not forget what Jesus so unselfishly did for us, by honoring Him with the way we live our lives. We should think like Paul in **Philippians 3:10**

"I want to know Christ and the power of his resurrection and the fellowship of sharing in his sufferings, becoming like him in his death"

God Bless

We all Fall short

"For all have sinned and fall short of the glory of God."
- **Romans 3:23**

There is a saying by Alexander Pope: "To err is human, to forgive is divine." We all make mistakes at some point in our lives and here Alexander Pope is saying that it is in our human nature. However, to forgive is one choice that has to be made; it is wanted, accepted, and necessary.

The word today is clear in explaining that no one is perfect. "All" have sinned really refers to everyone starting with Adam. To sin is to miss the mark or to get off the path of the will of God, to act in a way that is contrary to what God expects. We all have skeletons in our closets and the one thing that we must acknowledge is that we all have a past and a not-so-perfect track record, if we are honest about it. We all fall short, fail at something, or just have difficulty reaching some of our goals. However, God is so awesome that He has already allowed room for that to happen and He understands, because he made us. To do the same thing over and over again consistently becomes a different thing all together.

God doesn't expect us to be perfect; He does, however, expect us to strive for perfection everyday. With man sometimes this is different. We tend to give each other a really hard time when things don't go the way that we think that they should go. We persecute others and hold their shortcomings over their heads (sometimes forever) as if we have never fallen short ourselves. If God has already made room to forgive us for straying off the path that He has laid out for us, let us think about this and understand that no one is perfect. We have to do our best to understand that and to make every effort to help other people by building them up and encouraging them to get better.

Let us make sure that we are not so hard on others because if the shoe were on the other foot, we would want someone to understanding our circumstances and help us to redeem ourselves.

God Bless

Stay the Course

"Therefore he is able to save completely those who come to God through him, because he always lives to intercede for them."- **Hebrews 7:25**

There are several times in our lives that we have choices to make and depending on what we decide, dictate the direction of our lives. The interesting part is just like when we are in a car driving, after we have made a decision to go one way, we can always change our minds and turn around. It may take a little longer to get to our destination because of the wrong turn; however we still have a chance to get on the right track, if we make the decision to turn around. It is interesting how sometimes; not turning around fast enough discourages some people from turning around period. They just decide to keep going just to see where the road is going to lead them.

Of course, this is similar to us when we are traveling on the road of life. We always have to make a decision and one wrong turn can get us off course. The determination of our lives and where our paths end is all determined by the decisions that we make daily. Choosing to follow God is the only way the He can completely save you and just like it is written above, He lives to look out for us and to take care of us. We are left with the decision to either, follow Him or not and we have to decide that daily.

Following God's path is similar to Dorothy in the "Wizard of Oz", except there is no one playing God at the end. There was a set course for her to follow and it was the yellow brick road. Here instructions were to never stray away from the path and she will find her way home. Now, traveling on the path wasn't always easy and she found herself getting off course a time or two. We travel the set path that God has for us but we sometimes deviate from the course and like Dorothy in the movie, we start scrambling trying to get back on track because it is the only way to make it to our destination. The interesting part is that, Dorothy picked up some folks along the way kind, of like a disciple. She tells them her mission and invites them to travel with her, so that they can get their hearts desire. They choose to travel the course with her and no matter how challenging it was along the way, nothing stopped them from following the yellow brick road. They stay the course because they had faith that what they were seeking, they would find. They all did. Even though the wizard was a fake and they went through a lot of hardship, seemingly for nothing, it turned out that the more determined they were to finish the course, the stronger they became and as a result they all got what they were looking for. Their mistake was following man at first, and then they begin to follow their heart.

We can all find what we are looking for if we choose to be saved by grace through faith in Jesus Christ. We have to be willing to pick some people up along the way, to take this journey with us as well. Everyone deserves to fulfill they're hurts desire. They too have to grow in their faith by going through some challenges along life's journey, but if they endure to the end no one will be disappointed. It is all in choosing to go to God through Jesus. Dorothy was determined to get home and quite honestly I am too. My destination is Heaven and any one who wants to come along for the journey, choose today to stay the course. It won't be easy but what in life is easy? Let's follow the path the Jesus laid out for us. He made it so easy that He left light to guide us through the path. Allow Jesus to intercede on your behalf daily and no matter how big the challenge is, chose to stay the course and disciple some people along the way. I'm headed home, who's coming with me?

God Bless

Stay in God's Grace

"Be glad, O people of Zion, rejoice in the LORD your God, for he has given you the autumn rains in righteousness. He sends you abundant showers, both autumn and spring rains, as before."- **Joel 2:23**

This is an awesome text this morning and you get a better understanding of its meaning if you go back to Hosea 11 and read up to the text today. Israel is clearly God's chosen people; however they have upset the Lord in a bad way. Look at the following text.

But the people of Israel have bitterly provoked the Lord, so their Lord will now sentence them to death in payment for their sins. Hosea 12:14

"I have been the Lord your God ever since I brought you out of Egypt. You must acknowledge no God but me, for there is no other savior. I took care of you in the wilderness, in that dry and thirsty land. But when you had eaten and were satisfied, you became proud and forgot me. So now I will attack you like a lion, like a leopard that lurks along the road. Like a bear whose cubs have been taken away, I will tear out your heart. I will devour you like a hungry lioness and mangle you like a wild animal. "You are about to be destroyed, O Israel—yes, by me, your only helper. Now where is your king? Let him save you!" Hosea 13: 4-10

As a result of Israel's unfaithfulness, the Lord allowed them to feel His wrath. In the beginning of Ch. 2, the Bible describes the locust plague that hit the land, taking everything from the people. The interesting part is that the Lord really pleaded with them before it happened, but pride was still prevalent among the people. All they had to do was repent, because they already knew God and had been beneficiaries of His favor. Our text today shows the Lord having compassion for the Israelites and restoring everything that had been taken away.

We sometimes find ourselves in situations, where our lives may not exactly resemble God's vision for us. Even as Christians, we may have a moment where we find ourselves back sliding regardless to if it is premeditated or not. Looking at the Israelites and what they went through, we can't afford to take everything that the Lord has done for us for granted. I don't know about you, but I don't ever want to get to the point where I feel like I have done everything myself and have to feel the wrath of God. I think about the people that I love and care about. I can only imagine how I would feel if I consistently put out for them and they turn their back on me and show very little appreciation, if at all. I know for a fact, that if this was to happen I would be furious and would be willing to cut them off all together. If you put yourself in that situation and seeing how it would make you feel, just imagine how much more what we do to God upsets Him. There is a song my parents used to listen to by the Stylistics that said, "We break up to make up, that's all we do. First you love me then you hate me, that's a game for fools." I couldn't have put it better myself. Even though their context was different the message is so on point.

We are in a relationship with the Lord and the truth of the matter is we should do everything we can to serve Him in excellence. Playing this game with the Lord like we do with people, will do nothing but cause us a lot of heartache and who knows what else. Let us do our part to be in a position, to always receive the autumn and the spring rain, as before.

God Bless

Stand for Jesus

> "Then know this, you and all the people of Israel: It is by the name of Jesus Christ of Nazareth, whom you crucified but whom God raised from the dead, that this man stands before you healed. Salvation is found in no one else, for there is no other name under heaven given to men by which we must be saved."- **Acts 4:10, 12**

These are some strong, bold words by Peter and John, and they stood before the Sanhedrin council. I say that because it is so important to this text.

The Sanhedrin was an assembly of judges, who were appointed to judge in every city in Israel. There were 23 men appointed and then there was the great Sanhedrin which had 71 members appointed to it.

This is the same Sanhedrin, where Jesus was on trial, so that tells you where they stand on Jesus Christ or anyone who believes in Him. Peter and John were teaching the gospel of Jesus Christ to the people and the temple guards and the Sadducees because of the content of their message seized them. Really I can stop here, because a few things have happened already that we can learn from.

One is that Peter and John already knew that environment and the potential of what could happen by speaking so boldly for Jesus Christ. Even knowing this, they made a conscious decision to do it anyway and accept the consequences of their actions, whatever it would be. This says that they were totally convinced about Jesus Christ, as Lord and Savior and were sold out on getting His message to the masses.

We, as children of God have several opportunities daily, to lift up the name of Jesus and proclaim the truth, however many people shy away. They do this because they are not sure what people will think of them (shame) or they have a certain level of fear about the consequences. Everything must be done in order, so depending on where you are, you may not want to shout out loud, however there is a proper way to share Christ in any environment. We have to set it in our mind that we are sold out no matter what and will take advantage of every situation. I am a little more radical than others; so just pray for me. However, the Bible does say clearly that we should not be ashamed of the Gospel of Jesus Christ. "But whoever shall deny me before men, I will also deny him before My Father who is in heaven." So Jesus was very clear and Peter and John refuse to be denied, what about you?

The second important thing to learn here is simply this; if we make up our mind to share Jesus with others, then we too can possibly help someone get healed. As you can see in this text that all it took was a word and it changed the cripple man's life forever. This word is so powerful; that even in this text it grew to over 5000 that begin to believe by the time Peter and John went to jail. The word is so powerful that the Sanhedrin realized that they couldn't deny it; all they could do was order Peter and John to stop talking. We live in a country that says we have the freedom to speak and I firmly believe in exercising that right. Take advantage of an opportunity to share Christ everyday, you never know whose life you may save. Actually the life you save could be your own.

God Bless

Take a Stand

"Now, brothers, I want to remind you of the gospel I preached to you, which you received and on which you have taken your stand."- **1 Corinthians 15:1, 3-4**

We all have heard and been told, that if you stand for nothing, you will fall for anything. Often times, it is easy to tell what a person stands for. Most of us are family oriented and no one is going to do anything to our family. So we have strong family values. In the same breath, that also means that you will do everything you can to see your family grow, as well as protect them. There are people who take a strong stand on the fact that we must work hard for what we need and want. Those people are really driven to do their best and refuse to settle for setbacks. I even know some people, who take a strong stand politically. Once they establish their view they are like that tree in the Bible, they shall not be moved.

Well, the Apostle Paul is talking about taking the same kind of stand here, in his conversation with the church of Corinth. Just in case everyone forgot, he starts by reminding them that they received the Gospel message that he preached and they said that they would take their stand on it. What does it mean to take a stand? What is it that Paul is talking about and why is it so important?

To take a stand, is to make it clear that you have strong feelings about something. If someone pushes you on an issue, it is something that you will push back on until they let it go. Taking a stand is something that you believe strongly in and you are so confident, in what you believe that no one can influence you to believe otherwise. So this was important to Paul, because he knew what they said, when he was with them, but now that he is not there it was important for the people in Corinth to take a stand for Christ's sake. More importantly, it is time for us as the children of God, to do the same thing.

Paul made it clear that by the gospel that he preached to them, they are saved, however if they don't stand on it, then they have believed in vain. We all prayerfully have heard that same gospel and received our salvation by accepting Jesus Christ as our Lord and Savior. The days ahead of us are not all going to be easy, just like the Church at Corinth and we have to decide that no matter what, to live is Christ and to die is gain. In other words Christ means everything to me in this life, and when I die, I'll have even more because I believed and took a stand.

Paul is not asking us to do anything that he didn't do and that Christ didn't do for us. He is simply asking them and us, to do something that we ought to do. The word "ought" is used to signify an obligation to. Peter says, "we ought to live holy and Godly lives" and Paul says," So then, men ought to regard us as servants of Christ and as those entrusted with the secret things of God." The message today is simple; stand for Christ because He did it for you. If it were not for God sending Christ to show us how to take a stand, we would not be here. Now is a better time than any to take a stand, push against the enemy, and his demonic schemes. Tye Tribbett says in one of his songs that we need to "stand out." When the enemy comes in like a flood, the Bible says, "that the Spirit of the Lord will raise up a standard against the enemy." We are in a war, who is going to take a stand?

God Bless

Stand and Fight

> "Where, O death, is your victory? Where, O death, is your sting?" The sting of death is sin, and the power of sin is the law. But thanks be to God! He gives us the victory through our Lord Jesus Christ."- **1 Corinthians 15:55-57**

My first karate competition was in Victoria, Texas and it was called "Victoria's Best." My sensei and I set out early that morning to make it on time. Even though I was ready and I felt confident because going to the competition meant that my sensei thought that I was ready too, a little nervousness still rested on me. I had never been in that environment before and to see so many people, who had trained and studied the art just like me, was overwhelming at first. One guy I had to fight knew about me before I knew about him and he decided to come and talk to me to get in my head before the fight. I had been so prepared that it didn't work at all and as a matter of fact, it backfired on him. As a result of our little pre-game warm-up, the Lord graced me with a victory over this guy and I got my first 1st place plaque for Tae Kwon Do. It was an amazing feeling. Even though the fight wasn't fixed, in my mind, I had already won before I started to fight, that is just the way the Bruce trained us. Bruce did such an awesome job at building our minds and bodies to be strong and not to expect defeat. We would always say that, "Winner's never quit and quitters never win. I'm a Soldier for who? Christ. Everybody got it, yes sir." That sticks with me in everything that I do.

Paul was helping the Corinthian's understand the same thing, as well as us today. Sin has no power over you unless you give it power. Even though the enemy comes in like a flood seeking to devour us, if we don't give him power, then he is powerless. Just like when my opponent tried to get in my head, I didn't let him, his plan didn't work. In fact it added more fuel to my fire because he tried to get me and let me know that is what he wanted to do. The difference here though is that just as Paul says, we already have victory in Jesus Christ. In other words, the fight is already fixed and we are victorious before we even start the fight. Our job is to believe and walk in it. When we are in the heat of the battle we have to claim victory and be willing to receive it. We all know how to lose and how to expect the worse to happen, however that is not the way we were designed. We were made to be victorious through Jesus Christ.

When I was diagnosed with Narcolepsy, I expected the worse and guess what? It began to happen. I listened to what the doctor's said about how there is no cure and I will have to take medicine for the rest of my life. I had so many car accidents that the doctor labeled me totally disabled. Till this day the doctor still haven't changed that label and that was 1999. I changed my mind though and stopped acting like a victim and claimed the victory. By the grace of God and the Power of the Holy Spirit, I begin to think, talk, walk, and act like I had already defeated my illness. Before I knew it, I was walking in Victory. Just as the scripture says, we have to stand firm and not be moved, knowing that we have given ourselves fully to the work of the Lord. We have to know that we have not labored in vain and that God will do exactly what He said He would do.

Lift up whatever you are dealing with to God and let Him fight your battle for you. There isn't anything that He can't handle. Trust God because He has already trained us for victory and now it is time to show the world how great our teacher (sensei), Jesus Christ really is. He had the faith in us years ago to be victorious, so now it is time to claim our prize. Fight the good fight of faith and God will work everything out according to His will, on your behalf.

It is time to stand and fight. If you don't fight, how can you claim the victory?

God Bless

Some Plant, Some Water God Will Add the Increase

> "What, after all, is Apollos? And what is Paul? Only servants, through whom, you came to believe—as the Lord has assigned to each his task. I planted the seed, Apollos watered it, but God made it grow. So neither he who plants nor he who waters is anything, but only God, who makes things grow. The man who plants and the man who waters have one purpose, and each will be rewarded according to his own labor. For we are God's fellow workers; you are God's field, God's building." -**1 Corinthians 3:5-9**

Growing up in the country I had the awesome pleasure of seeing the process of planting seeds for all of the different crops in my grandmother's garden. That was probably the most tedious part; because we had to prepare to ground first to make sure it was in the best condition, to allow the growing process to take place. The planting process was the most involved as well, because there were so many steps and if you didn't do something right; then all of your work goes in vain and you have to start over.

The watering process was just about caring for your crop to ensure that it grows. This process requires more of your attention; there is still a little work as well. This process is where consistency takes place because you have to visit your future harvest on a regular basis, providing water and making sure your crop has proper exposure to the sun. As we all know that the sun provides everything that we can't, to complete the process.

Around about midnight, one night I received a phone call from one of my youth. The Lord has used me to plant seeds in his life, for the last four years. The hard part was Lil Wayne was king in his world, so he was a hard shell to crack. He is the oldest of three brothers, so he has a lot of influence over them. Well after planting Godly seeds, fighting against lil Wayne and continuing to water and give him proper exposure to the SON, he called me. Fighting back tears, this young man told me that he just got home from a bible study and he really wanted to apologize to me. Filled with joy, just knowing that he went to bible study on his own, the Lord filled me with peace hearing the rest of his words. He said that he knows that I have been trying to teach him what is right and he has been fighting it. This young man said that he took for granted, that he was too young and he had plenty of time, but now he realizes, that now is the time to get him together. I promise, it felt like I heard the angels in heaven celebrating. I told him that I loved him and his brothers and we will continue this walk together.

There may be someone in your life, who seem like they just don't get it. If you, who are in Christ, continue to work in the garden, caring and nurturing, giving proper exposure to the Son, you too will soon see the fruits of your labor. A mighty harvest is in the works; and when it is all done, how dirty are you? How much work have you put in, to fulfill part of God's will for your life.

Are you planting and watering? There can be no harvest if you don't. God is going to do His part, what about you?

God Bless

Sleep or no sleep

"The sleep of a laborer is sweet, whether he eats little or much, but the abundance of a rich man permits him no sleep." -**Ecclesiastes 5:12**

I was driving listening to the radio and what I heard intrigued me so, that I had to go and find this song. The name of the song is "Billionaire" by Travie Mc Coy featuring Bruno Mars. Listening to this young man's mind and heart through his words was so interesting and it kind of reminded me of myself. The content of this song from such a young person wasn't the typical message that we hear on the radio today. This young man is really talking about being a blessing to others and that is what I try to do daily. He is saying things like:

"And yeah I'll be in a whole new tax bracket
we in recession but let me take a crack at it
I'll probably take whatever's left and just split it up
so everybody that I love can have a couple bucks
and not a single tummy around me would know what hungry was"

Though he has his own special way of communicating his message, you can still see his heart through his words. It reminds me of myself because if I have what a person needs, I don't mind giving it and if I don't have it I will try to find it, so I can give it. If you listen to the song, though, make sure you listen to the edited version, because he really expresses his passion with a few choice words in the lyrics.

Warren Buffet's sister is well known not because her brother is wealthy, but because she is and what she is doing with it. Doris Buffett, founder of *The Sunshine Lady Foundation*, gives away millions to help others get in position to help themselves.

The text today highlights more of a mindset that leads to a better lifestyle. When you have a person who is a laborer, they do sleep well not just because they are tired, but also because they are not consumed with what they have. They serve others and most likely, what they have they are willing to share with others who don't have. As apposed to a typical rich person, who is consumed with keeping and protecting what they have because they feel like they worked hard to get it, it is hard for them to sleep because they are always worried about someone trying to take what they have. The laborer most likely has the peace of God in them allowing them to make it through their days, as they strive to have more, hopefully to give more and His peace allows them to rest at night. I'm not sure what God's will is for your life; however if He blesses you with wealth, keep your laborer's mindset. Know that God is the one who blessed you and where much is given much is required. I don't know if Doris has a relationship with Christ, however what she is doing is pleasing to His sight. As you continue to labor daily, just remember that the abundance of God may come to you in many ways. Though Jesus may not have been wealthy monetarily, He was abundantly blessed and He willingly gave His all to be a blessing to others. Whether you find yourself in a new tax bracket or not, follow Jesus' lead and your sleep will be sweet. The key to it though, is humility and being obedient to God.

God Bless

Send Me

> "Then I heard the voice of the Lord saying, "Whom shall I send? And who will go for us?" And I said, "Here am I. Send me!" -**Isaiah 6:8**

Isaiah opens this text by saying that he has seen the Lord, yet he felt inadequate because he said that he had unclean lips and lived among people with unclean lips. He felt that God couldn't use him because of his past sins and guilt. As a result of what Isaiah expressed, the text says that his lips were touched with coal and he was told that his guilt was taken away and his sins were forgiven. Then he heard the Lord say, "Whom shall I send?" and Isaiah said, "Here I am. Send me."

There are times in our lives when the Lord has called us to do something yet we feel insecure about it because of our pasts. Many times, people look at the things that they have done and allow those things to hang over their heads. So when the call comes they don't feel worthy to deliver the messages that God has laid on their hearts. We don't' realize that God has already forgiven us; we just have to forgive ourselves and turn to God.

You may find yourself feeling that you haven't heard the voice of God calling you to do something and the misconception could be because of your past He hasn't called. Perhaps He is waiting for you to volunteer before He tells you what He wants you to do. The one thing that we didn't read in the text (but has to be true) is that Isaiah was at least willing to be used by God. The minute that he felt confident that his past wasn't hanging over his head, he immediately said that he was ready, without knowing what he was going to do.

Jesus was willing to give His life for us before we were ever born into the world. The point was it didn't matter to Him what our lives would be like because he was serving God. Isaiah didn't know he had such a difficult task in front of him; he just wanted to serve the Lord. We were called to be servants by the example set by Jesus Christ. Part of our job is to carry the torch that Jesus handed to us and complete the race. Everyone has a past; so don't allow that to be a roadblock for your service to the Lord. Just because Jesus was so willing, we to should be willing to serve, even if we don't know what the Lord has in store. That is where trust in the Lord comes in, knowing that He will not harm us but prosper us.

Think back to the last conversation that you had with the Lord; I'm sure that He put something on your heart to do. Have you done it yet? Better yet the Bible says that the work if plentiful but the laborers are few. There is plenty of work to do so maybe it is time to pray about your unknown assignment and answer God by saying "Here I am, send me."

God Bless

Seek Him First

"But seek first his kingdom and his righteousness, and all these things will be given to you as well."- **Matthew 6:33**

We are so bombarded by the media with stuff on a daily basis, be it by television, radio, internet, or print. Some of this stuff is dressed up and presented as an essential for our lives. So what we were once not concerned with all of a sudden becomes a necessity, and we try to figure out how we can best obtain it in the shortest time.

By the end of a television commercial, my son will ask me to buy the advertised product; he is unable to even explain why he wants it when I ask him. Here in the text Jesus was addressing the disciples, as well as the many who had gathered. He was teaching them not to worry about things in life that they felt they needed or wanted, but instead to redirect their focus. This is why He started with the word "but."

To seek means to be in pursuit of or to attempt to learn something by investigation. It first is simply pointing out to make something a priority over everything else. So here Jesus was telling them not to worry about what they would eat or wear, but instead to make kingdom living and being in right standing with God a priority. In other words, the antidote to worrying about these things is God's kingdom and His righteousness. The temptation to concern ourselves with the pleasures of the world is going to be present because the world will keep putting it before us. However, to seek is a heart issue and if we seek fellowship with God, we are provided protection against the bait the world uses in an attempt to get us hooked. Jesus is commanding us, asking us to stop making material gain our focus in life. Our pursuit should be the very presence and person of Jesus Christ.

Receiving from God often is very conditional, meaning that if you do this, He will do that. Here it is no different and the reason is that God wants us to show Him where our hearts and minds really are. Even though He can see what we feel and He knows our thoughts before we think them, we still get a chance to show Him how much we trust Him. Today's text is no different because it is simply saying that if we make pursuing God our priority, He will provide all that we need. Now the text says as well which would suggest that we already have some of the necessities of life so as we continue to live and grow and a need arises then the Lord will provide that as well. We sometimes make what is very simple really hard. Those folk who choose to take what they want because their desire to have it is seemingly so great, fall quickly to the sometimes-deadly circumstances of their decisions. Sometimes desire causes us to make some very irrational and irreversible decisions. By seeking God first, we receive needed peace and regain focus. We avoid temporary desires that have permanent consequences.

We are all creatures of habit and we all have our moments of wanting things. There is nothing wrong with that. When my son is obedient, I find myself as his father wanting to reward him sometimes with things that he wants. The Bible says that God will reward those who diligently seek Him, so let us redirect our focus. It is very simple. When in darkness, we are feverously searching for light so that we can see. So in this dark world, let us focus on running to the light.

God Bless

Pride comes before destruction

"In his pride the wicked does not seek him; in all his thoughts there is no room for God." -**Psalms 10:4**

I was once in a situation where I let my pride get the best of me. My roommate had just bailed out on me and there were six months left on our lease. I was diagnosed with narcolepsy (uncontrollable sleep attacks, it is a sleeping disorder) and suddenly laid off. Things were rough. My roommate took everything when he left, including food; all I was left with was what I brought with me, which wasn't much. As the days passed the electricity was disconnected and the repo man was looking for my car, I didn't have much money for food and to top it all off, I found an eviction notice on the door.

With this entire going on I still didn't want to ask anybody for help because I didn't want to feel that I owed anybody anything. Needless to say I found myself homeless and it wasn't because I didn't have anywhere to go. Now that I look back on this period, I realize how backwards I was thinking to allow this to happen; it could have been avoided. Proverbs 16:18 say that "Pride comes before destruction", and I was in a fast and serious downward spiral. As a result of my ignorance at the age of twenty-four I found myself bankrupt, homeless, disabled, and rejected (the government denied aid). I endured all of this turmoil in secrecy.

I quickly came to my senses and had a close encounter with God, to whom I completely surrendered. I knew God before this situation but I hadn't totally submitted. I was saved, baptized, blood bought, and sealed by the Holy Spirit but I wasn't letting God have control of all of me. Pride causes a person to resist God rather than seek to be like Him. As much as I don't want to admit it, I was resisting God and He showed me. After my confession to the Lord He immediately began to open doors for me. One of my friends had just gotten married and was buying his first house. He called to offer me a rent-free room, refusing to take "no" for an answer. I got involved with ministry for the first time and it completely changed my life. About six months later, I started working again, got my car back, and met my wife. Since then, life as I know it has never been the same; however in that moment I was ready to die because of my pride.

All that life has offered me and God have given me since then could have been forfeited because I let my pride get in the way. I once heard a preacher say that when pride gets in the way, it is really one's ego. To him "ego" meant edging God out. It makes sense. Allowing pride to get in the way can truly lead to destruction. God didn't design us to do life all by ourselves. We have to depend on Him. When it comes to God being in our lives we should have nothing but space and opportunity for Him to do whatever He wants. How can we deny the one who gave us life and the opportunity to be a part of it? How can a person be one with God without seeking Him? Put your pride aside, stop edging God out, open your heart and mind, and surrender all of yourself the Lord. He is more than trustworthy.

God Bless

Persevere Under Trial

> "Blessed is the man who perseveres under trial, because when he has stood the test, he will receive the crown of life that God has promised to those who love him."- **James 1:12**

Being in Christ under trial puts us all in great positions. It is something like a litmus test and God has something in store that will make you a better person when you come out of it. James says here that we are blessed when we persevere under trial. The first question is what kind of trial. In verse 2 he clearly states "many trials", so that whatever the reader is going through can relate to this text.

Why should we be joyful? Why are we considered blessed because we are going through something? Here James refers to testing our faith and that is the key to this verse. When we were in school, we all went day in and day out learning certain methods and procedures from our instructors. Of course they would test us to see if we had grasped the concepts taught. In that testing we were able to identify our strengths and weaknesses. Many times the teacher would give us the opportunity to re-take the test so that we could master that particular part of the lesson. Even though developing study habits were tough and there were more distractions than anyone could deal with, we still saw the value in staying focused and studying hard even, if we didn't do so well. The key to school was always having the confidence that we could do it in order to stay focused to accomplish our goals.

God sent Jesus to be our Teacher (Rabbi) and show us how to live this Christian life. For those who love God presumably have been studying to show themselves approved. So we find ourselves being tried to test our Faith in Christ and our beliefs. We are blessed because we can persevere through our trials. In other words, if we have the lasting consistency, tenacity, steadfastness, and confidence, we will prevail in victory over our trial and become stronger and wiser. We will receive the promises of God and His grace to move to the next level in our faith. We will find ourselves maturing in Christ.

Not having Christ is like going through a class and preparing for a test without a book. Non-believers have nothing to stand on or refer to for guidance or direction. So when they fail, they get discouraged and often times they want to give up because they are hopeless. They feel isolated and lonely because there is no one there to encourage them along the way.

Everybody has a choice to want to grow in his or her faith or not. James is expressing that nothing but good will result from continuing to grow in the Christian faith. As a result of many trials, I am stronger and wiser. I see God at work in my life daily because I chose to be a student of His word. I acknowledge that if I study the word, at some point I will be tested on what I have studied. How else can I claim that all the good that happened in the Bible for others who persevered can happen for me if it is not tested? Being a child of God and being blessed does not come easily; Jesus was tried, so why wouldn't we be?

God Bless

Paul's Prayer

> "And this is my prayer: that your love may abound more and more in knowledge and depth of insight, so that you may be able to discern what is best and may be pure and blameless until the day of Christ," -**Philippians 1:9-10**

The Apostle Paul was in prison when he wrote this letter to the church in Philippi to encourage them, express his love and gratitude to them, and equip them with Godly wisdom to continue their journey. He talked to them about having no boundaries when it comes to expressing their love to God and one another and making sure that they stay focused on their destination: Heaven.

Paul even covers in this book how they are to be imitators of Christ and how they should pray to have the same mindset and attitude that Jesus Christ had. Basically Paul wanted them to know that if anyone had to stand for Christ and be examples that they were the ones to do it. In his prayer above he is saying that he hopes that their love for one another will be abundant or overflowing as they continue to grow in the knowledge and understand of God's word, His will for their lives and each other. He wants them to understand what really matters in life what is really going to count. If they focus on what really matters then they will be able to live pure and blameless lives in Jesus Christ. He wanted to see them live their lives full of goodness, produced by the power that Jesus Christ gives them to bring glory and honor to God.

My prayer for you is the same. There is a song by Steven Fee that says it best.

"We are the people of God, the sons and daughters of love. Forgiven, restored and redeemed, living our lives to the praise of our King. We are the ones who will shine, His light in the darkness of the night. The hopeless, the broken, the poor, they will be hopeless and broken no more. Because, you are the light, the light of the world, and we shine You, Lord."

We all have to shine like stars in the universe for a risen savior who gave His all for us. I know that it is in you because spiritually we share the same DNA. I want us all to live lives full of God's abundant love, grace, and mercy, so that we can be blessed and be blessings to others as well. We may experience some hardship but, if we stand together in God's love, we can withstand anything. My brothers and sisters let us be willing to shine our light on this dark world and bond in unity for Christ's sake to support one another in our journeys. I pray your strength in the Lord for the assignment ahead of us is great, but because He who is in us is greater than he who is in the world, we are made for this. As we have come out of darkness into the light, decide today to live your lives in such a way that your actions line up with your words. Hopefully as a result, our light will shine on others so they can be hopeless and broken no more.

God Bless

One Shot

> "A few days later, when Jesus again entered Capernaum, the people heard that he had come home. So many gathered that there was no room left, not even outside the door, and he preached the word to them. Some men came, bringing to him a paralytic, carried by four of them. Since they could not get him to Jesus because of the crowd, they made an opening in the roof above Jesus and, after digging through it, lowered the mat the paralyzed man was lying on. When Jesus saw their faith, he said to the paralytic, "Son, your sins are forgiven." -**Mark 2: 1-5**

Jesus went back to Capernaum and the word got out that He was coming.

Because this was an once-in-a-lifetime opportunity, everybody wanted to see Him. The Bible never mentioned these men's names. There were four men carrying a friend on a stretcher who really needed to see Jesus badly.

They recognized that the crowd was too big and that if they got in line, they would be waiting forever. So instead of waiting for the opportunity they decided to create one instead. They went to the top of the house and lowered the man through the roof with Jesus and when He saw this act of faith Jesus said that the man's sins were forgiven. In other words, his past was now erased. So He dealt with the man's Spirit before he dealt with him physically.

The most valuable part of this story is how they took the initiative to make something happen. There were too many people waiting so they had to exert more of an effort to get in. Either way, there was a sense of urgency for them. Now, because they took the initiative to do what no one else did their outcome was favorable. They even recognized that it had to be a team effort in order to accomplish the goal, which at one point seemed impossible.

Eminem, a platinum selling rap artist said:" If you had one shot, or one opportunity to seize everything you ever wanted- one moment. Would you capture it or just let it slip?"

You only get one shot; don't miss your chance. Everyday we get the opportunity to experience life with new challenges. The fact of the matter is we only get one chance each day to get it as right as we possibly can. Whatever your goals are, they should be approached with a sense of urgency. Put your best effort forward.

On another note we should be pressing in to get closer to the Lord just like these men were. They took a united initiative to make it happen. There are too many of us running the same race but, separately. There really is strength in numbers. How hard is it to run a relay by yourself? Let us work on pulling together to press in and get closer to Jesus. If someone falls, there will be someone there to help carry us to the finish line. We have moments when we know for sure that Jesus is present. Take advantage of those moments. We don't know what tomorrow may bring; all we have is right now. The Bible says in **Matthew 6:34** "Therefore do not worry about tomorrow, for tomorrow will worry about itself. Each day has enough trouble of its own." Focus on today, use your time wisely and know that you can get more accomplished if there is a team effort.

God Bless

Make the Most of Every Opportunity

"Be wise in the way you act toward outsiders; make the most of every opportunity." -**Colossians 4:5**

Being a part of an organization or even a big family comes with some conditions. The Bible says that a good name is to be chosen rather than great riches. So in essence there is a lot in whom you are connected with. The big emphasis is that you can no longer think and act as if you are only representing yourself, because you are not. Anything that you do or say, once you are affiliated with a group, affects that entire group. It is no longer all about you. It is called the dynamics of life. It is an unfair assessment and a lot of responsibility but it is also inescapable.

Most people identify us by our families, social organizations, jobsites, and church affiliation. So how we carry ourselves automatically becomes a reflection of whom or what we are associated with. If someone in your circle does something ungodly and people know that you are connected they sometimes might tend to question you as well and the same vice versa. There are some situations where the label goes to the individual only however the whole body is still held accountable for that one person's actions.

Paul, who was in prison when he wrote this letter, is placing major emphasis on being wise in how we act towards non-Christians. Being wise as Christians, is properly applying the knowledge that God revealed to us. We are not just talking about Biblical wisdom here; we are looking at spiritual wisdom as well. We all know right from wrong and those who are really in tune with God know how to present themselves to others genuinely. Every sermon is more about our relationships getting stronger with the Lord so that we can be vessels, used by Him to draw others. So Paul says that we should make the most of every opportunity that we get to represent for the Kingdom of God.

We don't all realize it, but sometimes we are amongst people who have been hurt by the church or just don't go at all. We may be the source of the only scripture they will get exposure to. It is so important for us to be wise in how we treat others and talk to others, because we risk not confirming what they think they already know. It is important not to be ashamed of the gospel of Jesus Christ, especially at work. I am not telling you to get fired for Jesus' sake; however everywhere you go, Christ is there with you and people ought to at least sense it. You don't have to be overbearing towards others, but don't allow anyone or anything to cause you to deny Jesus Christ.

If you were put on trial for being a Christian, would there be enough "evidence" to convict you?

Make the most of every opportunity.

God Bless

Lord, Lord

> "Why do you call me, 'Lord, Lord,' and do not do what I say?" -**Luke 6:46**

From my research I find that most people, when it comes to your faith, want to be challenged. Most of the time they prefer the challenge come from the pulpit and not so much on a one-on-one basis. A challenge is easier to except from the pulpit because no one can really hold you accountable, as opposed to a direct challenge from an individual, which makes you accountable to someone who will be in your face on a regular basis. This thought process refers to the believers and the non-believers alike.

Most people want true leadership, especially when a lot of growth is taking place because it really benefits them. However when they are leaned on some people tend to shy away because it is no longer convenient or wanted. This even happens with most friendships; you expect that the person you consider to be your friend will be true to you, no matter what. The basis that they will be real with you is the foundation that helped you choose to be best friends with them in the first place. However, the minute that people begin to do things out of order, they tend to create distance between themselves and their true friends to start hanging with people who are willing to compromise their lives just to hang out and have fun for the moment.

Foundations are important. When you build a house if the foundation is shaky, the house is guaranteed to fall when the smallest storm comes. However, if you have a solid foundation, you stand a better chance to weather the storm and see another day. The text today is talking about the integrity of your spiritual foundation. Jesus is talking about the wise and the foolish builder, but it is a metaphor compared to how we apply His word in our lives and allow it to be our foundation. He says that if we take His word and apply it in our lives, we are like builders who dig deep to create solid foundations. When the storm comes, it will not shake you because you are well built. The one, who hears God's word and doesn't apply it, is a person who builds a house with no foundation. The first storm that comes will destroy it because it would be too weak to withstand storms.

The relationships that God allows us to create with others are very important because they are like pillars to help hold us up when the storms of life come. If we remove those pillars and replace them with something like plywood, we won't last at all. There is no other relationship more important than the one we create with Jesus Christ. He is the rock of our salvation, the one who empowers us to be steadfast and unmovable. The Bible says unless the Lord builds the house, the builder's labor in vain. Why create an awesome relationship with the Lord and then, when it is convenient you, compromise your foundation for something that won't last?

The relationship with our friends often reflects the relationship we have with the Lord. When we find ourselves out of His will we sometimes tend to shy away from God, stop going to church like we used to, and are easily annoyed by friends who tell us the truth. Back in the day, we called you two-faced and didn't want to be around you. Why do we treat God that way? That is the question that He is asking today. You can't hide from God when you are out of His will. He will create an opportunity for you to get back on track and it is up to you to choose. He does it because He loves you, not because He is obligated to. Your friends know when you are out of line too. Allow the words that come from your mouth to be reflected in your heart and your actions. Don't stray from your solid foundation, because it is what got you to where you are today and it will allow you to withstand many more storms that are sure to come.

God Bless

Live Life on Purpose

"As a prisoner for the Lord, then, I urge you to live a life worthy of the calling you have received." -**Ephesians 4:1**

Considering the tragic event from yesterday I have been inspired by this verse. Yesterday, Mr. Stack flew his plane into an IRS building in Austin, Texas because his passion had become a feud with them and it had him so wrapped up that it drove him to commit suicide. As we pray for his family, let us learn a lesson from this.

I know for a fact that this guy knew the Lord because he was an usher at his church. A friend of mine went to church with him and she told me that when she asked me to pray for his family. At some point the circumstances got so tough that his focus began to shift.

We sometimes find ourselves in the same place and there is a big fork in the road in front of us. We have a choice: live our lives as God has called us to or take measures in our own hands.

I can remember when I was in the 10th grade; I thought I was so in love with this young lady. When I found her at the movies waiting to meet another dude, I was so crushed that I decided I was going to show her. I went home and overdosed on some of my mom's pills on her birthday. By the grace of God, I didn't have to get my stomach pumped and I survived that situation. After the fact, I realized that it wasn't worth my being willing to take my life. I almost cheated myself out of a chance to be great; a chance to be a husband, a father, friend, leader, preacher and the list goes on. The girl didn't even know that I did it and she still doesn't to this day. Some point I'm making.

God has given us the gift of life. Normally, we are so excited to open most gifts. We should be excited about life because there is something new and different every 24 hours and we should not take that for granted. Everyday we get to unwrap the gift and our job is to use that gift wisely and give thanks to God for giving it to us; He will do the rest. I have read that time is a nonrenewable resource and so many people live like they have a thousands years of life. Some try to speed up the process. We should enjoy every waking moment and live life to the fullest.

Once we really learn how to play the hand that we have been dealt, we will find ourselves in a much better position and have a better outlook on life. God called us to live, so that means He has a purpose for us to fulfill. When we choose to live in accordance with God's plan for our lives, we experience His peace and abundance. Many of you know me so you know that I am blessed beyond measure. All that I have been through in my life has shaped me to be the person that I am today and I almost cheated the lives that I have touched and me. I realize that progress without struggle, is no progress at all.

Embrace what you are going through and change perspective about it. Live life to the fullest, it won't let you down. Live life on purpose.

God Bless

Live for Today

"Do not boast about tomorrow, for you do not know what a day may bring forth."- **Proverbs 27:1**

I normally wouldn't deal with this type of text until a funeral but it is still relevant for all of the living. Often I tell people not to take life for granted because we don't know what tomorrow will bring. We all make so many plans to accomplish so much. We all have great hopes for our futures. There are some who hesitate moving on an opportunity because they want to wait until they get themselves in a certain position. Then there are those who just think that they have plenty of time so they just aimlessly cruise through life.

The text tells us not to count so much on tomorrow because it is not promised. I have even heard Thomas Jefferson's quote on the cartoons about "not putting off till tomorrow what you can do today." All life has a beginning and an end but what matters most is that dash in between. There are a lot of people who took their great plans and high hopes with them and never got the chance to live them out. We all have to make the most of our days and live out our dreams because we only get one life to do it. If you have accomplished your biggest dream, it is time to dream more. If you haven't, it's past time to start pressing to make it happen. You can't wait for your dream to come true, because it is waiting for you to come and get it. We have to line our lives up with the Lord and live for Him in order to accomplish our goals because He is the only one who can release it in our lives. That is why it is so important for us to be serious about living Christ-like now and leading others as to do the same. I had the opportunity to watch someone really special to me live out his life's dream yesterday and one of the greatest highlights was the exclamation point at the end. He plays football and once the game was over he waited on the field to kneel and pray with all of the other players from both teams, thanking God for the privilege.

The Bible says that if we delight in the Lord then He will give us the desires of our heart and as you can see, it is conditional. We have to be willing to do our part; we have to totally commit ourselves to Him and have Faith that He will honor His promise. Without faith it is impossible to please God, and quite honestly without Faith it is impossible to fulfill your dreams. The call is today and the time is now to line our lives up with God and press towards causing our dreams to manifest in our lives on earth. Remember, if you don't live today because you are constantly worried about tomorrow, sooner or later you will realize that all you have are a bunch of empty yesterdays. Live life to the fullest today in Jesus name and trust that He will lead you through the path to make your dreams become real. If you believe just enough and trust God enough, tomorrow could be the day your dreams come true.

God Bless

Let the Word save you

"Therefore, get rid of all moral filth and the evil that is so prevalent and humbly accept the word planted in you, which can save you."- **James 1:21**

In verse 20 James is talking about accomplishing the righteousness of God, which is equivalent to either receiving salvation or growing in your state of being set aside for a holy purpose (Sanctification). Anything that is not of God can create a screen that blinds you from seeing what God's plan for you. In achieving the righteousness of God, we can't afford to get side tracked because it lessens our quality of life.

Picture this; if you are in a race, as long as you have the finish line in view, you will stay focused until the end. However, if while you are running you happen to focus on the sideline you now create an opportunity to stop before the end of the race. To get rid of "moral filth" is to put it away all things immoral, which could become a hindrance. Well, while you are running it is difficult to act like the sideline doesn't exist, however if you allow your desire to finish supersede what is on the sideline, then you can stay focus and stay the course. Understanding that anything on the sideline is a distraction to slow you down or eventually cause you to stop. Distractions take the form of anger, people, materialism, selfish desires, and the list goes on. The only way to stay focused is to walk closely with the Lord because He will give you strength to avoid the traps of the enemy.

God's word is designed to regenerate us. However, it requires the right response, which is a test of our faith. Receiving the word however and allowing it to work in our lives to move us towards spiritual maturity are two different things. We must first be willing and eager to hear the word and then process it without having any premature reactions to it. This means that we must be open enough not to angrily reject the Lord's revelations. This is why we stated earlier that in order for God's word to move in our lives we have to remove all that hinders its operation.

If we humbly accept the word of God and allow it to purge us, it can save us even from ourselves. Accomplishing the righteousness of God will become more attainable because we will have the Word of God as the light unto our feet. According to the word, our steps have already been ordered. We just have to remove those things that are in our way so that God can better use us. So we have to heed the words that James shared in this text. If we learn to be quick to listen, slow to speak, and slow to become angry, it won't be hard for us separate ourselves from the evil that hinders us from accepting God's word.

If you listen when you talk, you will learn more when you listen. Are you making it easier or harder to allow the word of God that is already in you to save you?

God Bless

Keep the Light on

> Your word is a lamp to my feet and a light for my path."
> **- Psalm 119:105**

When planning a long road trip most of us always make sure that we have our maps. Even if we go on Map Quest to get directions, we tend to make sure that we get reliable directions so that we won't get lost. We all know that feeling of getting lost. It only took one time and I knew that I didn't want to get lost ever again. Honestly, you drive with more confidence and assurance when you know where you are going. Here, this text is telling us that the Bible, the word of God, is our road map to life. If we just follow the **B**asic **I**nstructions **B**efore **L**eaving **E**arth it will guarantee our arriving safely to our desired destination.

In this, we also have to trust God and know that he won't lead us down the wrong path. We hear about God being light and how we are to be light. Ironically, some take that lightly. Think about it. If you were traveling in darkness what would be the first thing that you would do? When you walk into you house at night what is the first thing that you do? If you find yourself in the middle of nowhere without any power, what is it that you wish you had to find your way? Of course the answer for all preceding questions is light. God says that His word will be a lamp for our feet and a light for our paths. With Him there is no way that we can get lost because HE is the source of light. All we have to do is connect with Him to be plugged in with unlimited power. LaQuinta Inn had these commercials that would always end with their saying, "We'll keep the light on for you" emphasizing that they would take care of those who find their way to their locations. Not only is God saying that He will keep the light on for us, He is saying that we can be a source of light for others.

Our life's mission is to be a reflection of Him. When you look in the mirror, what do you see? When others look at you who do they see, you or a reflection of the SON? We should be working harder to do everything to keep the light on. Get in the word and hide it in your heart so that the Holy Spirit has something to work with. Be light in a world full of darkness.

God Bless

I Love Myself

> "So God created mankind in his own image, in the image of God he created them; male and female he created them. God saw all that he had made, and it was very good. And there was evening, and there was morning—the sixth day."
> **Genesis 1:27, 31**

I can remember as a child playing with Play-Doh creating and shaping and molding. The most common thing to make was my own little people when I got tired of putting it in the applicator, almost like a cookie cutter, that came with it where you had to squeeze the play-do through a shape and get a long star or some other odd shape. I can even remember mixing the colors only to find out that afterwards I wasn't able to separate them completely.

Either way I had the freedom to create what I wanted or in my eyes what I created was perfect so it didn't matter if someone else didn't like it because I did. In our text today God says that the same concept applies. On day six God created man and woman and this was an all day event. Once God spent the entire day shaping and molding man and woman He said it is very good. In other words he had created a masterpiece and was well pleased with His work. God had put so much into shaping man and woman that the seventh day He considered a Holy day and took a rest. We can almost consider that God saved the best for last knowing that once he finished His greatest work he would need a rest.

For some reason there are many people who are not comfortable in their skin. As a matter of fact, some are so uncomfortable that they consciously augment their features or body to try to make God's completed masterpiece better in their eyes. Please understand that when God made us in His eyes we were so perfect that He broke the mold after us. So there won't be another "you" made. When you think about it, even identical twins are different: so we are truly all fearfully and wonderfully made.

Our student ministry had tough questions for the leadership and one of the gray areas of the Bible for them was whether wearing tattoos is a sin. If we go with Leviticus 19:28, the answer is "yes", but if you go deeper and understand the context of the scripture, reading the four or five verses before it the answer is "no." Making augmentations to our bodies is not forbidden in the Bible, however 1 Corinthians 10:23 says that everything is permissible but not everything is beneficial. Standing in line at the grocery store, I observed the cover of one of the tabloids and the headlines dealt with plastic surgery gone badly. Some of those pictures were so horrible. The people who underwent plastic surgery never imagined that long-term consequences would cause problems.

It is up to you to risk getting wings tattooed on your body that, ten years later, may look like two moons. The point here is that God already considers you perfect. If we can accept His approval and love ourselves, we can be free to live the life that He has called us to live. No one should allow himself to fall victim to society's standard of perfection. God loves you just the way you are. So, now you have to love yourself just the same. I have gained a few pounds, so I have to work out to get back to God's original vision. However, I love myself. We are made in God's image. If we truly love God, how could we not love ourselves?

God Bless

I am Not Ashamed

> "I am not ashamed of the gospel, because it is the power of God for the salvation of everyone who believes: first for the Jew, then for the Gentile." -**Romans 1:16**

The Apostle Paul was serious about his commitment to the Lord; he was sold out for Christ. He was unashamed of the Gospel, even though it created many scandals for him. Paul had been imprisoned in Philippi, chased out of Thessalonica, smuggled out of Berea, mocked at in Athens, regarded as a fool in Corinth, and stoned in Galatia, but he remained eager to preach the gospel, even in Rome, (which is the seat of contemporary political power and pagan religion). Neither ridicule, nor criticism, or physical persecution could shake his boldness to present the Gospel to the world. When people dealt with Paul, it was very clear where he stood and he would not try to adapt to anyone else to fit in, no matter where he was.

So that leaves a question of how serious we are about the Gospel of Jesus Christ. How far are we willing to go to stand for the gospel? How far should we go? Being serious about the gospel doesn't mean that we have to be overbearing with people to share the gospel; however we have to be willing to assist those who are lost. Often when we have the opportunity to speak for Christ, we don't. Many think that they have to create the opportunity, when in fact Jesus Christ will do that for us. Many people don't want to offend those who are unsaved or anybody, for that matter, so they shy away from those opportunities. It is said that if you draw white chalk around a goose on the floor it won't venture outside of that circle because of fear of crossing the white mark. Many Christians don't want to deal with the ridicule, criticism, and rejection, so they rather stay secure in their Christian fellowship instead of not ministering to the unsaved.

In the workplace there are people who are in Christ, however they shy away from communicating what they believe. In my opinion it has to be difficult to turn your faith on and off for the sake of not offending someone. Should there be a time and place that you are to share the gospel or just pray for somebody and a time not to? If so, who really has the power or position to say so, considering that the Bible says to go and make disciples.

Paul made a declaration that he stands firm in his decision. It was a continual attitude that he wasn't planning on changing. He didn't fear humiliation; neither did he lack courage to stand up for the gospel. Rightfully so, there shouldn't be any fear standing up for the gospel since it is the power that we need to receive and expose others to eternal life. We have to make a conscious decision to not allow fear to paralyze us in situations where opportunity is created to stand firm on beliefs. Based on your faith and trust in God, you have to decide are you going to stand by any means or if there is a point where you back down. The gospel is what gives you the power to push through your opposition and overcome; it equips you to fight in this daily spiritual warfare. Look at how God's people act. Yet He has never disowned us. How could we be ashamed to stand for someone who gave so much to us? Jesus says that if we are ashamed to stand for Him before the world, He will be ashamed of you before my Father. Jesus Christ is the last person whose support you'd want to live without. In all you do, stand for truth. Don't be ashamed of the gospel. It is the power of God for the salvation of everyone who believes.

God Bless

Help Everyone Prepare

"We proclaim him, admonishing and teaching everyone with all wisdom, so that we may present everyone perfect in Christ."- **Colossians 1:28**

There is a saying that I have heard a few times; each one teaches one. Formally working in the educational system and now being an educator on life, I strongly believe in this statement. Often we teach unknowingly, unaware of whom is watching us. However, intentionally teach certain people specific things. Whatever your reason is the purpose for taking the time out to share with them is because you care about their well being and don't' want them to fail. That is an awesome attitude to have and we would hope that it is contagious with those that you share with.

I am reminded of a movie "Pay it Forward" in which a little boy cared so much for others that he did kind deeds yet asked them to pay it forward to three other people instead of repaying him. In other words, he would ask a person to be a blessing to someone else without expecting anything in return. Our text today covers the same concept, making sure that we who are in Christ do our parts to be blessings to others.

Paul says first of all, "We proclaim", so those of us who are in Christ must make a public declaration about the crucified Christ. We must know Him and not just memorize 100 passages of scripture or participate regularly in Bible study. Our walk is not about religion, but our relationships with our Lord and risen Savior. Much like the character in the movie, we should care enough to expose everyone we meet to the truth. We should warn them and teach them about Christ so that they may be equipped to make conscious decisions of faith. We have all been called to make disciples, however many people pick and choose whom they tell about the gospel and when they want to talk to them about it. Here is a question for you. Would you warn others to prepare for unavoidable danger? Well, here we have the same situation. Jesus Christ is coming back and no one knows when, however we have a mission to warn and teach as many willing listeners as possible to be ready when He returns. We are all God's creation but we are not all God's children. Only those who receive His son are a part of the family so we have a lot of work to do. J.B. Phillips summarized this text this way: "So, naturally, we proclaim Christ! We warn everyone we meet, and we teach everyone we can, all that we know about him, so that, if possible, we may bring every man up to his full maturity in Christ."

I had the pleasure to counsel and baptize my grandmother on my wife's side of the family a few weeks ago. Even though she didn't say much, I knew that she understood and acknowledged that Jesus Christ is her Lord and Savior with a head nod as she lay in her hospital bed. By the grace of God she is still with us. However, we don't have to worry about her eternal security because she is a part of the family of God. Do your part to help present everyone you encounter perfect in Christ.

God Bless

He will keep you

"The LORD will keep you from all harm— he will watch over your life; the LORD will watch over your coming and going both now and forevermore."- **Psalm 121:7-8**

There are so many people who are unsure of God's love for and commitment to us. It is our duty to introduce Christ to them and equip them with the necessary tools to build a strong relationship with the Lord. Once it is all said and done, we all want assurance that God is true to His word and that we will overcome our struggles.

Here we are once again reminded that it is inevitable that God will keep us, and not just from some harm; also, He will watch over our lives. Many times we experience hardship and trials and some question where God is. I thought He was protecting me? If He is, why am I going through this? God has a funny way of strengthening us and building our character. He allows us to struggle so that when we come out of it we will know for sure that it was only Him who could deliver us.

I made some new friends this weekend, who are family like now. One person in particular has endured a lot. Drive had a rough life as a child, but his mom told him to never quit. So he never stopped believing in his dream and trusting God. Even when they found themselves sleeping in a U-haul, he never threw in the towel. Many people would blame God and turn their backs on Him; however we must keep in mind the He knows what's best. Drive is now very well known and very successful at speaking and playing football. He knows that scripture is true because he never doubted the Lord. He always knew that God was watching over him because his situation could have worsened. When you are going through something, if you hold on a little while longer your blessings might be literally seconds away. Drive is doing great things in his community and in the world all because he never doubted God.

Just know that in everything you do God "got you", even when it doesn't seem that way. When you are going through and it seems that you have reached your breaking point, God is standing by, waiting for the right moment to rescue you. We have to endure hardships as good soldiers for the Lord Jesus Christ, which are designed to develop character and unrelenting will and desire. God wants you to be relentless when it comes to your faith. Never forget that God is watching you, keeping you both in your comings and goings from now and forevermore.

God Bless

Have Faith

> "Have faith in God," Jesus answered. "Truly I tell you, if anyone says to this mountain, 'Go, throw yourself into the sea,' and does not doubt in their heart but believes that what they say will happen, it will be done for them. Therefore I tell you, whatever you ask for in prayer, believe that you have received it, and it will be yours." -**Mark 11:22-24**

The Bible says, "Faith is the substance of things hoped for and the evidence of things not seen." When you break the word substance down to define it, it is reality or the actual matter of a thing. The word reality is simply something that appears to be real. So faith is having great expectations in something that appears to be or is real and the manifestation or the sign of things not seen. So faith is an understanding that what you have great expectation for, can become real for you.

Based off of this definition, we all experience faith everyday. We have hoped to wake up in the morning, have safe travel to and from our set destination, and to be able to provide for our families. There are many people with their back up against the wall and they have hope that the bills will be paid even though they don't know where the money is coming from. Faith is something that we exercise daily even though we really don't pay much attention to it. However, when it comes to having faith in God all of a sudden that becomes something so hard for many people to imagine.

The key to faith believes in something that has a real possibility to happen in your life. I'm not saying that you can't become a millionaire tomorrow however; the reality that you will have more money than Donald Trump, is not something that is likely to happen over night. It can happen over time and if you believe and work hard at executing your plan, then overtime it can happen. We have to get away from thinking that things are just supposed to happen and that is a way of life.

Most of the time, we will something into our lives. Your will is your mental ability to carefully choose your next course of action. That again, requires that you believe that it can happen and God is saying for us to believe in Him to manifest the things that we pray for in our lives. We don't think so hard about waking up in the morning; we claim it for our lives and expect it to happen and to date by the grace of God, it manifests itself daily. So let us get in the habit of letting go and letting God. Let's believe more in the power of faith, the power that God will manifest what we believe in our lives. Let us stop over thinking this thing and start exercising our Faith in God.

God Bless

Half cleaned house is still dirty

"Do you not know that your body is a temple of the Holy Spirit, who is in you, whom you have received from God? You are not your own; you were bought at a price. Therefore honor God with your body." -**1 Corinthians 6:19-20**

I am sure that when you have company over for a visit or have dinner, your normal plan of action is to clean you house. No one wants to have company with a dirty house, am I right? It's not about impressing them, but it is a reflection of who you are and how well you keep your house together. Some people go as far as to just hide stuff under the bed or in the closet until their company leaves. There may even be a designated room that holds everything in until you open the door. Either way, your house only has the appearance of being clean at that point. The truth of the matter is if you are not in a habit of regularly cleaning your house, then it is really always only half clean. Just for the record, a half clean house is still dirty.

Well, your body is like your home and the Holy Spirit dwells within you. The question is: Did you clean up before the Holy Spirit arrived? For most of us, probably all of us, the answer is no, so the Holy Spirit became our motivation to get it clean. We could have been at our lowest point when we received Jesus Christ in our lives and being blessed with the presence and power of the Holy Spirit. So now that the Holy Spirit dwells within you, how well are you keeping your house now? The Holy Spirit is a guest that you have invited in and the truth is the Holy Spirit deserves to dwell in a clean environment. So the question is: Are you just doing spring-cleaning? Has your temple become something that you do your best to keep clean daily? We have all kept some anger, frustration, possibly jealousy, and envy in our house and it made it dirty.

We can all get in the habit of doing a daily cleaning no matter how tired we get some times. No houseguest wants to stay in a home that is dirty or unclean. I guarantee, if you just make the effort to clean up daily your holy guest will be more than willing to help.

We can't afford to keep pushing all of the jealousy, hate, and all of the other things that keep us dirty, under the bed or in the closet. The Holy Spirit will expose it and you will have a decision to make. Many of us don't like to do anything half way because we don't like for people to halfway do anything for us. No matter how we look at it, a half clean house will always still be dirty. Let us get into a habit of really cleaning our Spiritual house up on a daily basis.

God Bless

God's Protection

> "Even when I walk through the darkest valley, I will not be afraid, for you are close beside me.
> Your rod and your staff protect and comfort me. You prepare a feast for me in the presence of my enemies. You honor me by anointing my head with oil. My cup overflows with blessings." **-Psalm 23:4-5**

One of our greatest concerns is protection from the dangers of the world. As the media perpetuate an image of the rise in crime, unemployment and homelessness, many of our concerns grow daily. People find themselves in the midst of hardships wondering when it will end. Even as Christians some of us may have experienced some anxiety about this. I am more than sure that there are some non-believers and believers alike, who question where is God in the midst of all of this? How can He allow such hurt and devastation to take place?

Young David gives us some great insight to God's protection in this passage that will give many of us that peace that surpasses all understanding. David uses a metaphor comparing God to a shepherd in verse one. David knows the relationship between a shepherd and his sheep. Psalm 100:3 uses a metaphor comparing us to sheep when it states, "Acknowledge that the Lord is God! He made us, and we are his. We are his people, the sheep of his pasture." Sheep depend solely on their shepherd for everything. He supplies their needs and protection. Sheep have no defense mechanism; so the shepherd walks the land before they go to graze to look for holes. In my study, vipers live in holes and they stick their heads up to bite the sheep on their nose, which kills them. What the shepherd does is pour olive oil in the entrance of the holes and he anoints the sheep's head with oil. This causes the snake's body to be slippery so they can't get out of the hole to attack the sheep. Here is a perfect picture of how God prepares a feast for us in the presence of our enemy.

God loves us so much that He provides this same protection for us. He anoints our heads with oil; He uses His rod to protect us from the enemy, and His staff to comfort us. In the same way the shepherd walks the land, the Lord walked our lives out before us. This is why according to the scripture, our steps are ordered. We just have to walk the path that He has already laid out for us, by stepping in His footprints. David was confident just like the sheep were because he knew that God was right beside him all the way. He says even when he walks through the valley, which would suggest that we won't always be in a valley but regardless to if we are or not God is still always with us. We don't have to fear our valley situation; we too can walk through it with the assurance that we have God's protection.

In the NIV version of the Bible, this text says that we walk through the valley of the shadow of death. A shadow is defined as an imperfect imitation, so it is a fake. So that thing that stands in front of us as a potential threat to our lives, are really an imperfect imitation, it appears to be real but it is a fake. Does your shadow give a true representation of who you are? Of course not so why should we fear the enemies shadow? The best way to set us up with protection is to put ourselves in the right position with God. Clearly stated in Psalm 91:1, "Those who live in the shelter of the Most High, will find rest in the shadow of the Almighty." There has to be a light source in order for a shadow to be casted. Our source of light physically comes from the sun, but our source of light spiritually comes from the SON. If we submit to the Lord's authority, we can live in His protection. There we will find rest in His shadow. There is nothing imperfect about God, so that is the shadow that we all want to find rest in.

Fear God, not your situation because He is in control of it. The Lord has already provided what you need to make it through your situation. Remember, without faith it is impossible to please God and our faith is like a rubber band. It is stretched as far as it can go creating a lot of tension, but once it is released it expands a little more. Our faith expands like that allowing us to be stronger and able to handle more than we thought we could deal with. Trust God because He is all the protection we need, He is our shepherd.

God Bless

Godly Attributes

"Therefore, as God's chosen people, holy and dearly loved, clothe yourselves with compassion, kindness, humility, gentleness and patience."- **Colossians 3:12**

All of the text in chapter 3 prior to this text gives instructions on what life should be for the people in Colossae now that they are in Christ. It tells them to set their minds on things above and not on earthly things and to put certain things to death in order to make room for their new selves.

In order for the people of Colossae to be more like Christ, they really need to focus on putting these things to death: anger, rage, malice, slander, and filthy language. The same applies to us. When others see us, it will be hard for them to see Christ in us if we are covered with all of these life-threatening ways.

The text encourages them because it starts off with "therefore", which means that as a result of putting those things to death they should now be clothed with Christ-like characteristics. First, this suggests that they can do it if they put their minds to it because God has already equipped them. Second, God has obviously given them victory because the text states that they are already God's chosen, holy and dearly loved.

All of this applies to us as well. We are God's chosen people and He has great expectations for our lives. In order for us to operate in the fullness of God we have to let some things go. There are some things that we should be shedding daily to rid ourselves of all of the dead weight that has been holding us back from living Godly lives. We have to see ourselves being more like Christ in order for it to happen. The text gives us the formula to do it; we have to clothe ourselves with compassion, kindness, humility, gentleness, and patience.

These are all characteristics of Christ. We have to embrace these attributes and make them a part of our being and show these things to others. Christ was the perfect model because if it weren't for His compassion towards us and His desire to alleviate our suffering, where would we be? His humility is a road map on how we should be and it allows us to see how kind and gentle Christ is. We all know that dealing with ourselves, a person has to have patience and God showed us how to do that through Christ's patience with others.

The truth of the matter is this; I want people to be more Christ-like when they are dealing with me. That would put me in a position to stay away from behavior that we should be avoiding like anger, for example. In order for people to handle us like Christ, we ought to exemplify the same characteristics towards them. The Golden Rule is "Do unto others as you would have them do unto you." There is a reason this is so true. If you are patient with others, most likely they will be patient with you. If you are kind, gentle, and compassionate, it would open the door for someone else to reciprocate. We should all walk in humility just because the Bible says that the humble will be exalted. Let us heed the words that the Lord shared with the Church in Colossae. Embrace the new you by being more like Christ daily.

    God Bless

God Will Finish What He Started.

"Being confident of this, that he who began a good work in you will carry it on to completion until the day of Christ Jesus."- **Philippians 1:6**

There are so many people who have come to a place in their lives where they feel like this is it. Nothing is going to change. Everything is just going to be the way it is. They have settled in the position of complacency and decided in their minds that they have reached the peak of their lives; it is all downhill from there, especially in today's economy where it seems as if nothing is going to get better. Circumstances have people bowing out as if it is not possible for things to improve.

Just to know that in the word of God that He is not finished with us yet is truly exciting. To know that we are really a building under construction until the day of Christ means that I have so much more to look forward to and so do you. Don't fool yourself into thinking that "this is it" because God says that He has begun a good work in you and the blueprints show signs of more construction. So clean up the site and prepare it for a mighty work by God.

One thing that we know for sure and that is our God is not one who will quit. Everything that He starts, He finishes. The Israelites were in captivity and through God they were released. He promised that they would get to the Promised Land, even though it didn't look promising for them. It took so long, but a few of them still made it. Those who didn't make it were blocked because of their own disobedience. We have a role to play in God's work being complete. The text starts by saying, "being confident" and that is our part. Those Israelites who didn't make it to the land flowing with milk and honey failed due to their lack of confidence in God's promises. It is possible to talk or think your way out of being blessed. The more we try God and trust Him at His word, the more we will believe that he is able and will do what He said that He would do. So don't grow impatient with God because He is constantly at work. Instead, stand firm on His promises and know that he will finish what He started.

God Bless

God will Exalt You

"But, Let him who boasts boast in the Lord." For it is not the one who commends himself who is approved, but the one whom the Lord commends."- **2 Corinthians 10:17-18**

There are many of us who don't get caught up in self-promotion. However, there are many who subscribe to the same mindset that Martin Lawrence had in the movie "Welcome Home Roscoe Jenkins" the power of me. Here Paul says that it is not wise to compare yourself to yourself. More important, the Bible says that the humble will be exalted.

It is true, especially in the working world, where so many are focused on doing their best to get ahead. Well, so many get caught up in doing whatever it takes to put himself or herself ahead of everyone else. They are willing to step on whomever, praise themselves, and throw others under the bus just for position, status, money and supposed power. The sad part about this is that there are many Christians who are right in the middle of this rat race. They all feel that they have to stand out in order to be considered and they are right. But it is how you go about doing it that matters especially to God.

This text is a reminder that we ought to humble ourselves. It really doesn't matter what we think of ourselves or what others think of us; it is really about what God thinks. We should be living our lives to honor and please God. If we focus and concentrate on blowing God's mind, everything else will fall into place. Any promotion or elevation that takes place in your life is going to be because God is at work and allowed it. There is a practical side to this, of course. We have to work hard in order to maintain; that should be standard. There will be moments when you will be given the opportunity to stand up and stand out, however you don't take that time to promote the power of you. People see your hard work and what your worth is by how you carry yourself. Most importantly, God sees it and just like the Bible says "the king's heart is in the hand of the Lord; He directs it like a watercourse wherever He pleases." We don't have to try so hard to outshine others if we just focus on pleasing God. God is in charge of whoever is in charge of you. Our path is already predestined; we just have to follow God's plan.

Remember, God is not a magician we have to put in work and do our part in order to enjoy the fruits of our labor. We don't have to be big promoters of self to the point that we appear conceited. Don't forget the Bible says that pride comes before destruction. It means a lot more and has a stronger foundation when someone else praises you because you humble yourself and work hard. It is far greater when God promotes you because that is a promotion that no one can change. Stop beating yourself up, trying to figure out how to get ahead and make yourself look better than everyone else. God has already laid a plan out for you and all you have to do is get on course with His plan. He will commend and exalt you.

God Bless

God moves on our behalf

This is what Cyrus king of Persia says: "The LORD, the God of heaven, has given me all the kingdoms of the earth and he has appointed me to build a temple for him at Jerusalem in Judah. Any of his people among you may go up to Jerusalem in Judah and build the temple of the LORD, the God of Israel, the God who is in Jerusalem, and may their God be with them. And in any locality where survivors may now be living, the people are to provide them with silver and gold, with goods and livestock, and with freewill offerings for the temple of God in Jerusalem." -**Ezra 1: 2-4**

The Book of Ezra has a unique history behind it. It is considered a book of the Hebrew Bible and was originally combined with the book of Nehemiah in a single book: Ezra-Nehemiah. The two became separated in the early Christians years. The first chapter is about God's people returning to Zion after the Babylonian captivity. If you read through 2 Chronicles you will see that the leadership changed hands several times and many of them did evil in God's eyes. In the last chapter the people of God had still rejected Him and God did not spare many of them at all, from young men to young women.

However, by the end of the last chapter God moved on the heart of Cyrus, King of Persia, to start the movement of rebuilding the temple in Jerusalem. All of God's people who remained received the promise of God spoken to them through Jeremiah to be free after seventy years. God showed them favor by providing them with silver, gold, livestock, and free will offerings as the Bible says, for the temple. So here, even though God's people turned their backs on God, He still fulfilled His promise to those who remained by allowing them to go back home and rebuild the temple. Though the Jewish people had the free will to choose to go back, many of them did not.

Scripture is shown to be true here in this text because the King's heart is in the hand of the Master. God moved on his heart to show favor to His chosen people. We too are God's chosen people and God is always making moves on our behalf, despite how we treat him. Many Christians act like God's people acted in this text and reject Him on a regular basis and yet He still shows you love. A lot of our heartache could be avoided if we just stop rejecting God and start accepting His will for our lives. God has made provisions for us to rebuild our lives and to get a fresh start. It is up to each of us individually to decide to accept or reject His offer. We have all been bound under the power and penalty of sin and it is Jesus Christ who offered Himself so that we can be free. Whosoever will, by repentance and faith, return to God, Jesus Christ has opened the way for him, and will raise him out of the slavery of sin into the liberty promised for the children of God.

God has made the offer for you and me to rebuild. What are you going to do? As for me and my house, we will serve the Lord.

God Bless

God Has Remembered

> "The LORD will be king over the whole earth. On that day there will be one LORD, and his name the only name."
> - **Zechariah 14:9**

I can't do this text any justice without sharing the background about what caused Zechariah to make this statement.

In the Book of Jeremiah, Nebuchadnezzar captured the people living in Jerusalem and they were exiled from their land and forced to live in Babylon. The prophet Jeremiah told the survivors of the exile, in chapter 29, to make the best of their situation. He prophesied to them to live their lives as normal as possible and after 70 years the Lord would return them to Jerusalem and rebuild the Temple that was destroyed. During the exile, there were many false prophets leading God's people astray. So prior to this text Cyrus the great overtook Babylon and those who were exiled were allowed to return to Jerusalem. When Zechariah prophesied, Darius the Great took over office and his mission was to rebuild the Temple in hopes that it would strengthen the authorities and the Jews saw this as a blessing from God.

Zechariah means "God has remembered" and of course the name alone should have given the captives hope. He painted the picture for them that God didn't forget about them and at that point He was proving that He is true to His word.

We all experience some rough times during which we just have to make the best of it. We have all heard the phrase "when you get lemons, make lemonade" and that still holds true today. Our current economy is the backdrop that allows many of us to feel what the captives felt in this text. We find ourselves having to submit to the authorities over us; the job market is tight, so the thought of moving around is out of the question. There are many living from paycheck to paycheck but find themselves content because they are still working. Times right now look really rough and some are wondering where is God. I just found out yesterday that the first five hours of overtime that I work must be given to the company. So in order to see any fruit from my extra labor, I have to work more than five hours.

God gives us hope today just in our knowing that He has remembered us. Just like those in captivity the Lord will restore us if we just hold on. It is important for us not to fall victim to false prophets, but instead to continue to find our hope and faith in the Lord. The Bible is clear when it says that without Faith it is impossible to please God. He promised us in Jeremiah as well that He has plans for our lives and it is for hope and a future, plans to prosper us and not harm us. I went home last night and found out that our gas was off for a $43.75

bill that was due four days ago. It won't be turned back on until sometime today. Though we had the money to pay the bill, the reality that these folks didn't care about our situation is disheartening and frustrating. The fact still remains that this is a sign of the times and we need to have Jesus Christ as Lord and Savior if we are going to make. Galatians 6:9 says, "Let us not become weary in doing good, for at the proper time we will reap a harvest if we do not give up."

The Lord remembers you and He will restore you. Our job is to line up with His will and stay the course by any means necessary. Let me encourage you, while I encourage me.

God Bless

God Alone

> "Again, the devil took him to a very high mountain and showed him all the kingdoms of the world and their splendor." "All this I will give you," he said, "if you will bow down and worship me." "Jesus said to him, "Away from me, Satan! For it is written: 'Worship the Lord your God, and serve him only.'" Then the devil left him, and angels came and attended him." -**Matthew 4:8-11**

Yesterday we visited First Metropolitan Church, with family, where the Pastor is John Ogletree. His message was titled "God Alone" and he focused on worship. As I sat and listened, it made me think about how we all are bombarded by stuff and the value that we place on it versus giving God our total focus. First, worship is derived from an Old English word, "worthscipe," which means worthiness. It is simply to give worth to something and from the Christian perspective to give total reverence to God. Either way the Pastor was right when he said that worship is both an act and an attitude. The act many people have down pat because so many Christians are programmed to raise their hands or to shout. There are some you can count on to shout out or take off running every Sunday after the Pastor says something like "Ain't He, Ain't He, Ain't He" and they knock everything over in their way, including people.

There are many people who worship the wrong things like their cars, homes, jobs, and education. The preacher put it perfectly yesterday when he said, "those folks are worshipping mortgages and car notes, something that can't save them or answer their prayers." This is far too common in our society and we have to become conscious enough to recognize if we are falling into that same trap.

The text starts off by saying; "again, the devil took Him to a very high mountain." This is the story of the enemy trying to tempt Jesus to separate Him from His relationship with God. This one statement simply points out that the devil made multiple attempts to get Jesus to fall, so what would make you and I think that he wouldn't put in that same effort with us? We are not as solid as Jesus so we have to be really careful and prayerful about our decisions. If the enemy had the audacity to offer Jesus something that His Father already owned, who's to say that he won't do the same to us? As a matter of fact, he does. The enemy wants us to bow down and worship him by worshipping the material possessions that he offers us.

We have to continue to study to show ourselves approved unto God, rightly dividing the word of truth. The more we get in the word and the word get in us and we apply it in our lives daily, we will be able to build the resistance to stand and say to the enemy, "Leave me alone satan. I worship God and God alone."

When I truly get into the worship experience, nothing else matters. I get so lost in the Lord that I forget about all of my issues, hurts, bills, or whatever and I am at a place of peace that is so hard to put into words. When I am there, in that moment, I never want to leave because I really feel the joy of the Lord flowing through me and I am spiritually stronger than ever. If we can get ourselves to that place of worshipping God alone we will be strong enough to tell the enemy to flee. Just as the text states, he will leave. The warning here is that he will be back, so we have to continue to focus our worship on God. He is the only one who can strengthen us to stand against the enemy. In other words, we have to develop an attitude that God is the only one truly worthy to be worshipped. If we strive to serve God with all that is within us, we will find ourselves in a position to blow His mind. Thus, He will meet our needs according to His Glorious riches in Christ Jesus. True Worship is to God and God Alone.

God Bless

Give Thanks

"Give thanks in all circumstances; for this is God's will for you in Christ Jesus." -**1 Thessalonians 5:18**

A few years ago I had the awesome opportunity to assist in teaching in children's church. We had a very creative approach to ministry and getting the children to learn scripture. We would always try our best to get them to sing the scriptures because we learned that they would have a better chance at learning them. This particular text the children were so successful at learning, not because it was short, but because of the way they learned it with handclaps and singing. I can still see their happy faces singing loudly and proudly, because they knew the scripture and they knew how to apply it in their lives.

The Apostle Paul introduced this text to us to paint a very clear picture. First, Paul shared with us in Philippians 4:11 that he was content in all circumstances. He was saying that he was satisfied with where he was in life and what he had. You may have heard people say that if God never blesses them with anything else they will be satisfied and this is what Paul was saying. So when we get to today's text it makes sense for Paul, who is content in everything, to give thanks in all circumstances.

Simply stated, no matter where we are in life or what we have or want, we should be thankful that we are here. If you stop and take a look at your life you will find that there is always going to be something that you still want to accomplish or something that you want either for yourself or your family. You may find that you are not where you want to be in your career or in life in general or you may even be at the lowest point of your life ever. Either way, the truth is that God wants us all to be thankful for the little things.

Our lives could be so different right now, no matter where we are. There are people who are in far worse situations than we could ever imagine, yet are thankful just for having life. I haven't accomplished all that I want to however I am so thankful that I am still able to provide for my family. I am thankful that even though my wife may not have everything that I want her to have, everything that we do have, including our children, we have together. I am so thankful that we have family and friends who care so much for us and pray for us consistently. I am so thankful that we serve a risen savior who sacrificed everything so that we could live abundantly by His grace and mercy.

I recently left the hospital visiting with a mother of an amazing high school junior. She has been in and out of the hospital at least the last three years and now they have figured out what is going on. She shared with me heartbreak and disappointment that they are dealing with right now and how there is nothing that she can do it about it because she is sick. Not once did she complain. Neither is her son complaining about their circumstances. They are so thankful just to have life and each other that their circumstances have to take a number to get recognized. As I prayed with her I could feel that she was so grateful that she had God in her life, she still had her family, and that I was there to visit her. Your current circumstances are only a comma in your life, not meant to be the end. God has the final say in everything, so we just have to operate in His will and He will place the period in our lives as He see fit.

Be grateful for where you are and what you have and give thanks no matter what; your situation could be worse. If nothing else, be thankful that you have the one and only true God in your life. I can't imagine life without Him.

God Bless

Gift vs. Talent

> "God has given each of you a gift from his great variety of spiritual gifts. Use them well to serve one another."
> - **1 Peter 4:10**

There are many talented people in the world who use their talents in different ways. We mostly know people to use their talent in good ways to get ahead in life and make something of themselves. Talents are basically abilities we were born with that we later discover and develop over time. There are people who have great ability in athletics, music, acting, speaking, writing, cooking and the list goes on.

When a person discovers his talents he has the right to use them however he chooses. Many people us them for good while some use talents for selfish or evil reasons. Those people waste their talents.

When you accept Jesus Christ as Lord and Savior He begins to bless you with spiritual abilities that are called gifts. Christ allows His love to flow through us so that it can be shared with others through our spiritual gifts. As stated in the text above, God gave us these special gifts so that we can serve one another.

There is a difference between a spiritual gift and a talent. The Holy Spirit empowers us to use our special abilities to bring God glory and to help the Body of Christ function and stay in line with the Will of God. However, again a talent is something that you were born with that can be used as a form of expression however you choose to use it. A talent can become a means by which you choose to express a spiritual gift. For example, I have a friend who is an awesome singer. He is extremely talented in that area and he chooses to use it to glorify God. The Holy Spirit empowers him to lead all into worship and open their eyes and hearts to the Love of Jesus Christ. I have another friend who is an awesome comedian and we all know how comedy can be. However, every time he does a show it is clean and God-filled, leading others towards God. He uses his gift to show the world that we can have a good time in Christ and we don't have to place ourselves in a box.

Do an assessment of the things that you have a special ability to do. Then, make note of it and ask yourself if this is a talent or a gift? Since you are in Christ ask yourself how can you take your talent and express the Love of God towards others and pray that God allow you to grow in that area. There are other gifts that God releases to us such as the gift of discernment, knowledge, teaching, preaching, and shepherding etc. To help you discover those gifts you need to take a spiritual assessment and pray for God to reveal your special abilities He has released to you by the Power of the Holy Spirit. The Bible is very clear when it says that your gift will make room for you and bring you before great men, so choose today how you will use your special abilities to glorify God.

God Bless

Get on the Right Path

"The path of the righteous is like the first gleam of dawn, shining ever brighter till the full light of day." -**Proverbs 4:18**

When you line your life up with the Lord you place your feet on the path of righteousness. The awesome part is that the word of God says that the Lord orders our steps and His word is a light unto our feet and a lamp unto our pathway. So in essence, God has already made provisions for us to be successful with staying the course. He has already established every step for us. Our job is to stay focused and in His presence so that we can stay on the path.

Part of staying the course that the Lord has already laid for us is helping others find their way. Not only is it pleasing to God and part of what we have been charged to do, it also opens the door for someone to take this journey with us creating accountability partners. This past week was an awesome week for my family and me. We had the opportunity to assist with a close encounter with the Lord for a little over a hundred high school boys and girls. As we went through the week and strategically broke down barriers that these children had, so much truth was revealed. Between the young men and young ladies there were issues of teen pregnancy, miscarriages, molestation by family members and rape. It is no wonder that our world is so corrupt and many have no hope in the future generation. Look at what those responsible have allowed to happen to these babies. Through praise and worship, awesome guest speakers, life skills sessions, powerful small group sessions, and one-on-one sessions, many chose on their own to give their issues and lives to the Lord. Now they are well on their way. By the power of the Holy Spirit we were able to help these young folks see that a brighter day will come if they just stay on the path.

Our job is not done because the children that we spent time with this week are not even scratching the surface. So many others out there need hope. There are many adults in the same position and as children of God we have a great task ahead. I challenge you to take the time to consider others better than you do yourself and pour into someone's life hope and take the journey with them. At day break, when get that first sight of light we know that as the day goes it will get brighter. Our lives are the same way. All we need is a little beacon of light that will lead us on our paths and allow us to have great expectations as we travel.

We have been called to be the light of the world so we have to be willing to go out and be contagious turning on the light for others. Not only should we turn on the light, sometimes we have to take their hands and lead them until they can stand on their own. Before we left the camp, we had 7 boys and 3 girls to give their lives to the Lord. We also had one of the young men to call a meeting amongst the other campers and there were about 30 young men having a testimony session where they committed to hold each other accountable. Are you up for the challenge? If we put in the work the results will come.

    Let Him use you.
    God Bless

Friends Can be Trusted

> "Wounds from a friend can be trusted, but an enemy multiplies kisses." -**Proverbs 27:6**

There are so many people who really don't know what qualities they want in a friend. It is amazing how people can have a friend for years as long as they aren't challenging or truthful. However the minute they cross that line, they are viewed as an enemy or foe because they have said something that you didn't like. The other amazing thing is how people can become so close to fake people who most likely are around because you have something that they want or need.

We have to do a better job at picking and choosing our friends. To have someone in your life who is just going with the flow and being like a "yes man" will do you no good at all. I have seen people who surround themselves with people who feel inferior to them and will go along with the program. They, as a result, have found themselves in turmoil. Let's really look at it. Do you really want people around who won't come through in the end when you really need them?

The text talks about true friendship today and the characteristic of friendship that most people don't want to deal with. It says that wounds from a friend can be trusted. This means that true friends may have to cut you sometimes as long as they season their words with grace and give you the truth in love. Once they've been honest, it is going to hurt and you will probably be wounded. But wounds heal, provided they are taken care of the right way. A true friend will not just cut you then leave you to bleed to death, yet an enemy won't care.

An enemy will speak kind words to your face and tell lies behind your back. Just like the O'Jays said, "They smile in your face, all the time they want to take your place Backstabbers." We have to be careful whom we allow in our inner circle. Understand this too. Sometimes your friends want to tell you information you may not be ready to hear. That doesn't make them bad friends; they know that the information will crush you, so timing is important. If I fall off or do something that is totally out of my character, I expect my friends to say something and not let me continue to look like a fool.

Take a look at your circle of friends and determine whom you can really count on. Make sure that you have accountability and are open to constructive criticism. Noah had three sons and while two of them covered his nakedness when he got drunk, one of then was accused of exposing his nakedness and he was cursed. Your true friends will cover and protect you while exposing you to the truth. If your friends won't tell you the truth (even about you), you have to question the sincerity of their friendship.

Remember wounds heal and when they do you have something to remind you to never go down that road again. So in essence, you become a stronger person who can help someone else to avoid undergoing the same painful experience.

God Bless

Free Indeed

"So if the Son sets you free, you will be free indeed."
- **John 8:36**

Feeling enslaved or in bondage is not a good feeling for anyone. However there are so many people who want to be free but won't allow themselves the privilege. There are so many people (who are in emotional, spiritual, and mental enslavement) looking for a way out and refuse to accept the terms of the only one who can really loose them. I wrote a poem entitled "Life with no Parole" and it talks specifically to mental enslavement and how we tend to sentence ourselves, being locked down for life because we don't want to be free if we don't like the Lord's terms.

The son here is of course the Son of God who is the heir of all things. He is the one who is forever with God and therefore has unlimited power to liberate anyone from bondage. Those who find themselves trapped have a way out; it is just a matter of making a decision. Jesus is the only one who can deliver you from bondage of sin. The word says you will be free indeed, which would suggest that if you are seeking freedom, Jesus Christ is the way. Freedom is guaranteed if you want it.

Jesus is willing to adopt you into the family and give you all the rights and privileges that come with it. All we have to do is accept His terms to be family forever. No matter where we are in life, there are some rules that we have to abide by. The difference is that there is no guarantee (with your willingness to follow the guidelines) like there is with God. The text is talking about being a slave to sin and it says that a slave has no permanent place in a family. But if the Lord considers you a son, you are family for good.

People who have been released from jail are not really free because they are constantly being watched. Most times, they have to check in with their parole officers to update their status and progress but they have a criminal record that will never be erased, following them for the rest of their lives and making it difficult to get ahead. With Jesus, that is not the case. When he sets you free, your past is erased and you have a fresh start. Whatever you have done can be used to help you grow and empower others as well, so your negative has the potential to become a positive. If you have to depend on your friends to bail you out when you are in trouble, you will most likely have to pay them back. Jesus says that He has paid the price and you are debt free. When I was a slave to sin I went to the Lord and Jesus bailed me out and life has never been the same. I am a living testimony that whoever the Son sets free is truly free indeed. If you or someone you know is locked up in sin, I have Jesus' contact information; just call Him you will be glad you did.

God Bless

Fork in the Road

> "Enter through the narrow gate. For wide is the gate and broad is the road that leads to destruction, and many enter through it. But small is the gate and narrow the road that leads to life and only a few find it."- **Matthew 7:13-14**

Famous poet Robert Frost wrote the poem "The Road Not Taken". In this poem you find a traveler who runs into this fork in the road. He stops and stares for a while, trying to decide which road to take. At one point the poet claims that the two roads were the same and then he comes back and says that one looks less traveled by. He makes a decision on which road he will travel but he wonders about the other road, even making the comment that he may come back and try it one day knowing that life happens so that may not happen. At the end of the poem he says that he is telling his story with a sigh because he took the road less traveled by and it has made all of the difference.

Interpretation of poetry is on the reader and being a poet makes it so awesome. How you read our work dictates your perception of what we mean. Well, regardless of all of the different perceptions about Robert Frost's poem, he brings up a great thought. We have all had a fork in the road at one time or another and our outcome depended solely on the decision that we made up front.

There are many people who don't like being alone and instead of standing out in a crowd they would rather find a way to hide in the midst of everyone else. Those people would much rather travel the road that has more ware because many have gone that way before. However, there are trailblazers who would rather create a standard than be a part of one already created. Either road has its ups and its downs. Depending on your perception of the situation, either road could be a good choice.

When we look at it from a biblical perspective things change a bit when it comes to making decisions. The Bible tells us for every temptation there is always a way of escape. What is implied here is a contrast between good and evil or sin and holiness. The wide gate would be representative of the phrase that everybody is doing it and so should you. The narrow gate would represent one who makes the conscious decision to go against the grain and be different, not desiring to be like everyone else. To stand out and be different, especially in a society where most sin is expected and accepted is a hard decision for some. Many people find it easier to just go with the flow for the sake of fitting in. I realize that the path less traveled is not popular because everyone is not doing it. People follow people if they share the same views, passions, and desires and honestly there aren't enough people willing to take the narrow road. There are so many people scared of the responsibility that comes with making that decision. Here the text has made it clear for us that the decision could cost us our lives.

I am a rebel, meaning that I am going to make a conscious effort to stand for Christ no matter what, in a world where many are still nailing Him to the cross daily. It may not be easy, but anything worth having is worth fighting for and eternity with God is worth it. Is there anybody coming with me?

God Bless

Forgive Because He forgives

"Be kind and compassionate to one another, forgiving each other, just as in Christ God forgave you."- **Ephesians 4:32**

When a person has been hurt or crossed by someone, for some reason, it seems so hard to forgive. There are a lot of people who feel that forgiveness is an emotion, when in fact it is a choice. One has to choose to forgive first and foremost before anything can happen. The main thing you are always up against, though, is that desire for the other person to feel what you felt and for some they never really know when to stop.

It is really clear that when you get hurt your thought may be that you are a really good person so you question why anybody would mistreat you. Being hurt is an unavoidable part of life. For many of us it is like an alarm that goes off helping us to see a truth and turning the light on to avoid going through what you went through. It is a natural part of life that helps us to grow and to become stronger. The way we handle pain determines whether we grow.

Many times we focus on who hurt us versus how to handle it and get past it. I have been hurt by many people and can truly say that choosing to forgive was the hardest thing in many of those situations. The only way that I was able to find the strength to forgive was through Jesus Christ. I always think about what I have done to hurt the Lord and how no matter what, He still forgives me. The scripture today says that we should be loving and sympathetic towards others. The Lord wants us to be sensitive to others' emotions and in all situations; He wants us to forgive like Christ forgives us.

Jesus is the perfect example of how to forgive even if you can't forget. There are so many people who hurt Christ so much. It is almost like putting Him back on the cross and yet He still is open to forgive in love. Sit down and recount your life and think about all the times the Lord showed you grace. Think about all of the things that should have happened to you because of what you did but were blocked by God. If you take the time to really look at those situations for what they are worth, you will get a true picture of kindness and compassion. You will clearly understand, at that point, how to forgive like Christ forgave. Just think, if you don't let it go, you are really holding a grudge, even though Paul reminds us that there is no condemnation in Jesus Christ. I even understand you do not want to take a chance at getting hurt again. However, we have to follow the example of Christ and trust that He has everything under control.

God didn't have to forgive us and truthfully even if we do something today to hurt Him, He will still forgive us. If you look outside your window right now, you will see the sun's reflection off of all of the vehicles or windows. When others see us we ought to be a reflection of the SON as well. Let us be more willing to choose to forgive, not just because God expects us to, but also because He has done it for you.

God Bless

Fixed Fight

"But thanks be to God! He gives us the victory through our Lord Jesus Christ." -**1 Corinthians 15:57**

Everyday that you awake and leave your house there is a fight. There's a fight to get what you need to provide for your household, a fight to get ahead, a fight just to survive. For some reason it seems as if you get no peace of mind until you get back to your house. Sometimes that fight continues at home, but your home should be your safe haven.

Whenever you know that you have to fight, there are a few things that have to take place. I know that as a student of martial arts I have to do some intense training (both mental and physical) just to get prepared. My sensei would always have us go through one of our training routines in front of everyone to get into the mindset of our opponent. It works every time.

When we look at this, though, from a spiritual aspect we still have to train for the fight. However, God has already proclaimed you as a winner before the fight ever start. Our training consists of being consistent in reading and applying the word of God to our lives and sharing it with others. Having a lot of the word in us will allow us to have that much more fight when we are backed into a corner. God is saying here that the fights that we face daily are fixed; All we have to do is follow the instructions given in training.

God reveals for us the enemy's game plan in our training, so there isn't a move that the enemy can make that we haven't already been exposed to. The awesome part is our opponent already knows that he doesn't have a chance to beat us with God on our side. The problem is that we don't always know it. Normally it isn't until we have gone through some cataclysmic situation that we believe that God has our backs. Here, God is telling us before we go through anything that we have it in the bag. We just have to believe and walk it out in our faith. There is so much that we can accomplish if we just believe. Look at the woman with the issue of blood. It took here twelve years to be healed but it only took a mustard seed of faith for her situation to change.

Before you leave your house every morning, it is good to spar with your trainer and get some of this word in you so that once you walk out of your door, you are ready. The Bible says that if you don't do what is right, sin is crouching at your door because it desires to have you. For some reason when we don't get geared up before we leave the house, many people get tripped up by sin and fall every time. Just know that you can trust God at His word and if He said you are victorious, it is true. It is up to us to do our parts to claim the victory.

I am working on being one of the heavyweight champions of the world. How about you?

God Bless

Firecracker or Firefighter

> "A man who burns with anger stirs up fights. But a person who is patient calms things down." -**Proverbs 15:18**

Many times when we find ourselves angry about something we often times don't take the time out to think. So many people are impulsive and before they know it they have found themselves in the middle of a situation that they never wanted to be in. Look at this story that was reported in a special on violence by James Tillman.

"**Derrion Albert was a 16-year-old high-school student who unknowingly found himself in the middle of a school fight that involved over a 100 students. He was struck in the head twice with a stick and suffered head trauma as result of the melee. As you can imagine, his family is having a very difficult time dealing with the fact that Derrion is no longer with them and why his life came to such a violent end. According to family members, he was an honor-roll student, wasn't involved in any gangs, and that he was a person who never even raised his voice to anyone. Derrion's grandfather, who has raised him since he was an infant, describes him as quiet person and that he spent most evenings either doing school work or on his computer**" (Tillman, 2009)

Here, an innocent person passing through became victim to someone else's anger. Somebody in that crowd burned with anger for whatever reason, but there was a person there to put the fire out. The text today in plain words is asking whether you are a firecracker or a firefighter? You know once you light the fuse of a firecracker it is difficult to stop it if you don't move quickly. More often than not, the firecracker will not stop itself because it was designed to create an intense environment before exploding. I can only imagine what really happened in this situation before Derrion even arrived on the scene and I would imagine that the young men were so angry that when they saw him, they just went after him.

Anger causes us to be very irrational and there is often no positive energy flowing at the time. Normally our actions, when we are angry, are the catalyst to our regret once we come to our senses. When we allow our anger to get the best of us. Everything that we have been holding in all comes out at that moment and whatever or whoever becomes the target of our release. That is why many professionals say to those who have children: Never discipline them when you are angry. It's true because you don't know how far you will really go.

God has equipped you with the power to deal with your anger in the proper manner. He shares it with us in the book of James when he said to be quick to listen, slow to speak, and slow to become angry. This text causes you to listen and think first before you react. It is an awesome recipe for creating firefighters.

Firefighters approach fires with no fear and with the intent to put it out. They are also very equipped to handle the job; no matter how big it is, even if they have to call for back up. They normally know how to find the core of the fire to extinguish it and part of their mission is to control the fire in order to save lives. Imagine how much happier the ending would have been, had there been a firefighter around before Derrion even arrived on the scene.

When people start gossiping, complaining, arguing, or fighting with anyone, are you a spark to that firecracker or a firefighter? God wants more firefighters and today He is making an appeal to you. Become a firefighter today. You never know; the life you save could be your own.

God Bless

Feet like Deer

"The Sovereign LORD is my strength; he makes my feet like the feet of a deer, he enables me to go on the heights. On my stringed instruments."- **Habakkuk 3:19**

Have you ever been in a situation where you sensed danger or hardship and questioned the Lord? You found yourself wondering why God would allow this to happen and what you should do. How did knowing what would possibly happen affect your faith? Were you angry with God? For example, it amazes me that we work hard everyday to make ends meet and then some, yet there are some folks doing half of what we are doing and have no threat of foreclosure, overdraft fees, repossession, and so on. In my carnal way of thinking I ask, "Why am I doing this if I can just do what they do and supposedly live better? Maybe that is how I escape what I see coming my way?"

Habakkuk saw disaster-approaching Judah and questioned the Lord about it in Chapters one through two and found himself praying and praising in chapter three. Habakkuk shows us that his faith was being tested; yet he wasn't moved by it. We have all heard that Faith is the substance of things hoped for and the evidence of things not seen. Simply put, Faith is your ability to trust God and have comfort in Him when everything in your world seems to crumble around you. The bible makes it clear in chapter 2:4 that we should still trust in God's sovereignty, regardless of the circumstances.

Habakkuk is an awesome example of how we should stand in the face of an oncoming threat. He declared that even if the Lord sends suffering and losses, that He would still trust in the Lord and praise his way through it. Instead of breaking down and surrendering, he will stand firm and believe. He is so descriptive here in his metaphor where he says that the Lord makes his feet like deer and enables him to go on the heights. He is basically saying that when danger approaches the Lord will allow him to be as swift as a deer and elude the danger. The gazelle, for example, is surefooted and swift so that it readily escapes its pursuers and Habakkuk is saying that the Lord has prepared him to be the same way. If the truth were told, this stands true for us as well.

God wants to use difficult times to strengthen our faith. So even when we are facing something as major as sickness, foreclosure, unemployment, or overdraft fees, God still has a plan. When you are in your darkest hours, don't doubt what the Lord told you in the light. Remember, the just shall live by faith. Don't step down and do what everyone else is doing to get ahead, do what the Lord planned for you to do and while you are waiting for your change, never stop doubting that God has greater plans in store. Your valley situation will only last for a little while before your change comes; you just have to hold on in order to reap a harvest. Allow the joy of the Lord to be your strength and stand firm on the promises of God.

God Bless

Fear the Lord

"The fear of the LORD is the beginning of knowledge, but fools despise wisdom and discipline." -**Proverbs 1:7**

I have often heard the phrase "It's not what you know but who you know" and "Who you know will get you in and what you know will keep you there." Both phrases have some truth, especially in the business world. Depending on whom you know a door can open wide for you without much effort on your part. I was able to get back into engineering from teaching high school math because of my connection. This goes to show that relationship really is very important, not so much because you can benefit from it, but you will never know when you will genuinely need somebody in your corner.

Depending on the foundation of your relationship and the strength of it almost anything can happen and you and that person will still support one another and build each other up. Some people create relationships solely to benefit themselves and in most cases they aren't successful. Someone ends up getting hurt. Either way, the time and energy you invest building a relationship with someone should reflect the kind of relationship you have with the Lord.

Here the text is saying to us that a right relationship with God opens to door to knowledge beyond our years. In any relationship, especially in one with God, we have to humble ourselves and be willing to learn His ways. No one knows better than God so it would be very foolish for us not to heed His wisdom and directions. We should not seek to develop a relationship with the Lord just because we heard it could get us to Heaven. That foundation would not be solid and at some point the bottom would fall out. Our goal is Heaven; however we should really want to know the Father and want Him to really know us. Having a genuine relationship with Him empowers us to endure the hard times and stay focused in the good times because He is right there with us. Just like most of us, God doesn't like fake people; it doesn't stop Him from loving them though. In this relationship, whom you know will get you lined up and what you know will empower you to stay the course with Heaven as your final destination.

Value your relationships with others the same way because you don't know everything. The people who are great friends can impart some wisdom on you that can help you in so many ways, but if you don't have a great relationship with them you would not be exposed to that wisdom. People really don't care what you know until they know that you care. At that point they are open to share life with you on any level. So we don't have to be fearful of people to get to know them. However, we do have to humble ourselves and be open-minded in getting to know them. Handle your relationships as if they were fragile. You don't want to break them. Really good relationships are valuable, so be fearful not to cause any damage to them.

God Bless

Favor Happens

> "During the time Mordecai was sitting at the king's gate, Bigthana and Teresh, two of the king's officers who guarded the doorway, became angry and conspired to assassinate King Xerxes. But Mordecai found out about the plot and told Queen Esther, who in turn reported it to the king, giving credit to Mordecai." -**Esther 2:21-22**

Mordecai, who resided in Susa, the metropolis of Persia, which is now Iran, adopted his orphan cousin Esther and raised her as his own daughter. He was a part of the Tribe of Benjamin. Mordecai was a part of the Jewish people who were held captive and after 70 years were freed and allowed to go home. Mordecai and many others chose to stay in Persia. While God was never mentioned in the book of Esther by reading the story you know that He was present.

Mordecai, in this particular text, helps us to see how when you are in the will of God, favor happens. Since Mordecai was Esther's cousin and adopted father, when he heard of the King's plan to find a new queen, he gave wise counsel to Esther and that helped her become the Queen of Persia. Remember they were enslaved prior to this. Mordecai was promoted to the position of royal court advisor after deliberately trying to gain the favor of the king. His position was referred to as one of those who sat at the King's gate which indicated his position of closeness to the king. While holding this position, Mordecai overheard two of the king's eunuchs plotting to kill the king. As a result of Mordecai's faithfulness to the king, the plan was foiled and Mordecai's service was recorded in the royal chronicles.

This is kind of deep because the story is so rich with information, however I will get to the point that I want to make with this part of the story. The text starts out with "in those days while Mordecai sat within the king's gate". Now this indicates two things for me.

Mordecai was in a position that we all find ourselves in sometimes; trapped feeling like there is no escape. First, in those days, the word "sat" meant that Mordecai didn't stay in that position forever. Surrendering to God will put you in line for an automatic promotion. With God you can't do anything but excel, be delivered; be set aside for His glory. We just have to be willing to surrender to God.

Not only that, it also indicates that Mordecai, a former prisoner, had to have a position of importance if he was trusted to watch the king's gate. We are all important to God and we are right where He can use us most. All of us are keepers of the gate and don't even realize it. We have the favor of the king and deny ourselves the right to enjoy it. God trusts us all to be good stewards, managers of everything He has given us and it is our job to honor Him.

What if Mordecai was out of position? He wouldn't have heard their plan and would not have been able to be used by God? How many times has God caught you out of position but spared you anyway? Stop taking God for granted and don't move until God gives the green light. Even though Mordecai didn't have a high-ranking position with the king, he was still grateful until his change. The promise here is that his change is coming but he is not trying to rush it. By the end of the story he was exalted by God. Many of us are not in a high position in our jobs or wherever, but that doesn't mean that God can't use us. When God places you somewhere, even if there is some discomfort, we have to learn to be still because God is up to something. I'm sure sitting at the gate wasn't comfortable but Mordecai was pleased to do it and the Lord showed him favor as a result. So, my brothers and sisters, be joyful in your current positions. God is trying to make you complete, so that you won't lack anything.

God Bless

Father's Compassion

"As a father has compassion on his children, so the LORD has compassion on those who fear him."- **Psalm 103:13**

My boys always want to know that I care. If I am just sitting watching television they will come in and sit with me or climb all over me. Sometimes when I may be really busy they will come and start some kind of conversation, including our then one-year-old with his limited vocabulary. When they fall and hurt themselves or get in trouble, they want to come and hang all over me and be hugged even if they get in trouble with me. It never fails that if they get in trouble with me they will go to my wife first, wait a little while, and finally come to me so that I can embrace them and reassure them that daddy still cares.

What children don't want to know if their fathers really care for them, especially if they are hurt or down for any reason? I believe that this is mostly because most men don't always show a lot of emotion. So just as your wife or girlfriend wants to be sure that you love her, your children will do the same thing.

Webster says that compassion is "consciousness of others' distress together with a desire to alleviate it." If my children are going through anything I want to take the stress from them and put it on me so that they don't have to deal with it. My oldest has to use a C-Pap machine at night and it drives me crazy to see him have to deal with that night after night. I would just rather switch breathing patterns with him. I would use the machine every night, however I can't do that.

Either way that is compassion and the truth is just as we hope our earthly father has that for us, we can be sure that our Heavenly one does. That perfect picture that you have in your head of a father's love for his child is real with God and then some. We can't measure the love and compassion that God has for us who are His children. Can you imagine how difficult it is for the Lord to sit back and allow us to go through some of the things we have to go through knowing that He can fix it? However He knows that if He fix everything then we will never really learn or grow in the Lord. So instead He allows us to go through until we reach our limit then He steps in saves and embraces us. Through His embrace we are encouraged to keep on pressing because each time we are convinced that He must really love us. The Bible says that nothing can separate us from the Love of God and that He will be with us until the end. If you didn't know before now you can be sure that your Heavenly Father has so much compassion and love for you that He sent Jesus Christ to take for us what should have been for us just to prove it.

Show the same compassion and love towards your children as best you can and they will always honor you and be by your side.

God Bless

Exposed

"What you have said in the dark will be heard in the daylight, and what you have whispered in the ear in the inner rooms will be proclaimed from the roofs." -**Luke 12:3**

There is a very thin line between gossip and the truth. Gossip is idle talk or rumor, especially about the personal or private affairs of others. It is a form of sharing unproven facts and views about others, which leaves room for error and is often done with an ulterior motive.

The truth, however, is just that, the truth. It is fact, something that you can prove and repeat in front of the person about whom you have spoken.

Many of us have been involved in rumors before, regardless of whether we just listened and shook our heads, carried misinformation to others, or were the victims of misinformation being spread. Either way, we have all been connected to gossip at some point and time. I'm not talking about the latest celebrity gossip; I'm talking about common folk like you and me.

We have to be careful how we handle information because if it gets to the wrong person, what we thought was innocent conversation can end up turning someone's life around in a bad way. What the scripture is sharing with us this morning is that anything that happens in the dark will come to the light. So anything that you do will eventually be exposed, especially if you are in Christ. How can you have a relationship with Christ and be the light of the world and not get exposed? It is not possible. What is possible is that it doesn't have to be everybody's business.

I have been heard saying that "truth crushed to the ground will soon rise" so we should all be more accountable by what we say and do. Anything that you discuss with someone in confidence should be with someone that you trust to take the information and pray for the individual. Everyone is not always prepared to handle the delicate information that is being shared. Normally, when that untrustworthy person gets the information, before too long everybody knows it.

Information disseminated to the wrong people in the wrong way usually leaves someone hurt and embarrassed, sometimes triggering even worse consequences or emotions. The best way to handle these situations is to approach that person to discuss the matter. Let him know what the word on the street is to prepare him to handle it. However, make sure that you don't stir up anger. If you don't have a great relationship with the person being discussed, you should stay out of it. You can have a conversation with the person without divulging the source, because most time, the original source is not who told you the information.

Either way, always consider how you would feel if it were you being discussed. How would you want the information to come to you? Would you appreciate someone close to you telling you the truth in love? Would you want people who are not directly affected by the situation to know what is going on? If someone is directly affected by whatever is happening, should he know and who should be the one to share the information? If you don't share the information, does someone else have the right to do it for you? There is a lot to consider when talking to people about what is going on with you or with someone else.

The truth of the matter is what is done in the dark will come to the light. Your exposure could just be with the individuals directly involved or to more people than you expected. The objective here is to stop operating in darkness. Then, you won't have to worry about being exposed.

God Bless

Expectations

> "In the sixth month of Elizabeth's pregnancy, God sent the angel Gabriel to Nazareth, a town in Galilee, to a virgin pledged to be married to a man named Joseph, a descendant of David. The virgin's name was Mary. The angel went to her and said, "Greetings, you who are highly favored! The Lord is with you." -**Luke 1:26-38**

Mary was greatly troubled by his words and wondered what kind of greeting this might have been. But the angel said to her, "Do not be afraid, Mary; you have found favor with God. You will conceive and give birth to a son, and you are to call him Jesus. He will be great and will be called the Son of the Most High. The Lord God will give him the throne of his father David, and he will reign over Jacob's descendants forever; his kingdom will never end."

"How will this be," Mary asked the angel, "since I am a virgin?"

The angel answered, "The Holy Spirit will come on you, and the power of the Most High will overshadow you. So the holy one to be born will be called the Son of God. Even Elizabeth your relative is going to have a child in her old age, and she who was said to be unable to conceive is in her sixth month. For no word from God will ever fail."

"I am the Lord's servant," Mary answered. "May your word to me be fulfilled." Then the angel left her. Luke 1:26-38

When we think about how awesome and powerful God is, sometimes it is hard to take it all in. When you read a story like the text above a clear picture is painted and we are able to gain some understanding of just how great God really is. We have Elizabeth, Mary's sister, who is pregnant and this is significant because of her age. She was well past the age of conceiving and her husband was elderly so Elizabeth gave up hope of having a child. At the same time her sister Mary, who was engaged to Joseph, was a virgin and as the story is told, conceived a child as well but by the power of the Holy Spirit.

Elizabeth's child was John the Baptist and of course Mary gave Birth to Jesus Christ. Both Jesus and John played very important roles in our being who we are more specifically Jesus Christ. If you pay attention to the story Mary questioned the angel Gabriel, however she never rejected what he told her. Instead of her having a "seeing is believing" attitude, she leaned on faith. Mary's thought was, "Use me Lord, for your will." We all know that His will was done.

Though this story is about the birth of Jesus Christ it is also evidence of the favor and power of God. There is nothing that God can't do and here what seemed impossible was possible with God. You may not be in a position to expect a child, however we should all be in a position where we are expecting. We should allow our hearts and minds to be so free that we are expecting God to birth a miracle. As the story illustrates, He is very capable of doing just that. Just like Mary and Elizabeth, don't put God in a box. Instead expect the unexpected and believe in the impossible with God. Wherever you are in your life, just know that God can and will give birth to a blessing that you may not have room enough to receive. If He said that He would do it just believe Him at His word. If He did it for them, He will do it for you.

God Bless

Entering His Presence

"Enter his gates with thanksgiving and his courts with praise; give thanks to him and praise his name. For the LORD is good and his love endures forever; his faithfulness continues through all generations."- **Psalm 100:4-5**

Growing up I learned quickly how to approach people and as I got older and starting doing marketing, I learned that people have so many personality traits. How you handle people determines if they will be open to listen to you and what you say will determine if they buy in. The point here is that we have to be careful how we handle people.

We are currently teaching our boys to be respectful and speak to everyone when they enter a room, mostly because that is what we were taught. Even if we didn't know everyone, we were taught to look at people in their eyes, smile, and speak. If nothing else, it could brighten up their day and show them respect. In business, when you enter a room, use the same approach, but greet people with a firm handshake, as you look them in their eyes. Try to remember their name as a sign of respect.

We were taught these things and much more because a first impression is a lasting one. We were to show respect and honor to those whose presence you were in. These are all learned behaviors that over time become second nature. Every now and then, I find myself having to remind a young person (when I see them for the first time) that they didn't wake up with me, so they better speak.

I don't know if you have ever paid attention to it but how you enter plays a major role in how people receive and perceive you. It is so interesting that most people are so well-versed with coming into others presences, but make it such a difficult task to enter the presence of God. Being in church and being behind the scenes, you get a totally different view of how people come into His presence. I have seen people come in dressed like they just left the club, and those who sport tailor-made suits, yet when we go to work we follow the dress code to the letter. The Bible doesn't say, "Come as you are" literally. However, God did say to dress in modest apparel and that was specifically referring to women.

God is really looking at our hearts when we enter His presence, not our clothes. If He can get to our hearts, everything else will change anyway. He tells us here to enter into His presence with thanksgiving in our hearts and praise flowing out of our mouths. When I enter into true praise and worship, I really don't want to leave because there I am so free. Galatians 1:10 says that we should not seek to please man but God and if our goal is to please man, we should not consider ourselves servants of Christ.

Let us spend more time focusing on how we enter God's presence and how to seek His approval just because He is God. When we show this kind of respect for people some of the time, it is because we want something from them be it a raise, a connection to somebody, or reassurance. I'm not suggesting that there aren't genuinely nice people. It is just not seen most of the time since those who step on others to get ahead seemingly outnumber sincere people. The only one truly worthy of our praise, honor, respect, humility, and appreciation is God. We are His people. So just like when you go to a family reunion or your grandparent's house you should always be excited to be in the presence of God. He is the only one who is truly faithful to us and will love us unconditionally. Sometimes we are so concerned about making an impression on people. Instead focus all of that energy on pleasing God, the one who will be faithful to you and many generations down the line.

God Bless

Don't Worry, Be Happy

"Who of you by worrying can add a single hour to your life?"
- **Luke 12:25**

The more things change the more things stay the same. At work I have been doing my best to be sociable and have limited, but open, communication with my co-workers. They have, of course, shared more than I have and I can look at it two ways. They have done this in an effort to get me to talk more and share more about what I am thinking or they just freely open themselves up to anybody they feel comfortable with. Either way, the more you know about a person, the more you feel that there is some type of trusting relationship being developed. What I have found is for some people, when it comes to work and covering themselves, they will throw you under the bus and keep rolling like nothing happened. So here I am left with the question: Do I still try to be open with them or do I just "do me" and interact only when I have to? What I have learned is that I can't worry about it. If I continue to keep an open line of communication, I may open the door to win them to Christ and that is far more important than trying to be their best friend.

Here, Jesus is talking to His disciples, encouraging and preparing them for the assignment that He has for them. He told them not to worry about what they will wear or eat because that is small stuff. He wants them to focus more on Him and why He called them. The more time they spend on the things and people of the world, the more it pulls their focus off of His will for their lives.

We are all guilty of concerning ourselves with things that should not be a concern; it is almost a force of habit. Here Jesus poses a question for us, though, by asking what can we add to our lives by worrying. The truth is the only thing that we add is more stress, which is a recipe for disaster. Instead, if we really cast all of our cares on God, it will free us up to serve Him like we should. I believe that the main culprit to this worry that we sometimes face is trying to be in control of everything in our lives. I believe that we think if we are in control we can dictate what happens in any area of our lives and the truth is that we can't. Just like with my co-workers, I have realized that if I allow God to handle it, He will.

Though it is sometimes difficult to resist taking control of challenging situations, if you just allow God to handle them, I guarantee the outcome will be much better. Most of the time that situation involves someone else. So what if you mess up by taking control. You take a chance of never bringing them to a close relationship with Christ.

I watched this movie with my sons called "Shark Tales" and in the movie Will Smith plays a character who is concerned about how the rest of his fish friends see him. So he creates this big story about being a shark killer and everybody believes it, just to learn that it was conjured up in the end. The irony is that Will's character was loved when he was just being himself. So, he prolonged his accomplishments by embellishing his identity. Well, one of the songs in the movie has a line in it from an old Bob Marley song that goes, "Don't worry about a thing, because every little thing, is going to be alright." Bobby McFerrin even made a song that is called, "Don't Worry, Be Happy." Take these words into consideration and allow God to handle your situation. Let go and let God and stop wasting your time worrying.

God Bless

Don't Touch Him

"Do not touch my anointed ones; do my prophets no harm."
- **Psalm 105:15**

In this particular text the Psalmist is making us aware of the covenant the Lord made with Abraham, Isaac, and Jacob. He said that He would give them the land of Canaan. Even though they had gone through a few generations the Lord was still true to His word. The text goes on to say that even though they wandered from nation to nation and kingdom to kingdom, the Lord still wouldn't let anyone oppress them or cause them any hardship. To show His faithfulness and loyalty to them (the text even says that) He rebuked kings for their sake. In other words, He sternly disapproved of (or reprimanded) them if they came against His chosen people.

Even though we are not always this faithful and loyal to God He still stands by His word. Just like the text says in Psalm 100:3: we are "His people, the sheep of His pasture." That means that we belong to the Lord. For those of us who have children this text is saying what you have probably told someone else concerning your child, "If they act up, you don't touch them only I can do that." We tend to get really protective of our children, especially in today's society because it is getting harder to trust anybody else with your child. We even get offended if a person talks about them; we are ready to tear somebody a new one.

Well, God is the same way, especially if you are in covenant with Him. He is very protective of His children and doesn't even want anyone to even think about talking about you, in other words. When he says anointed ones here in the text He is referring to His chosen people and for us, that is all who are in Christ. As a part of the Lord's covering or protection He anoints our heads with oil, giving us a fresh anointing daily. When the text speaks of His prophets it is referring to those who have been called out as leaders, like our preachers. They have been gifted to deliver the word of God to His people.

We have a well-known pastor in the news with some serious allegations against him. This situation, if handled the wrong way, has the potential to shake up the church (as we know it) across the nation. Trust and believe that the media are going to do their jobs at distorting the truth, as they want you to perceive it. Our job as children of God is not to join the bandwagon, but instead to come together as the church and pray. Knowing the truth is important. However it is not as important as coming together as a unified body to defend our faith. The world will paint the picture as if this man is being attacked, but underneath what we believe is really being attacked and it is time that we stop playing a role in our own demise.

If we want to talk about something, let's discuss how a thirteen-year-old won $50K in the National Texting Championship for being the world's fastest text messenger. The crazy part is all she had to text was "**Old McDonald had a farm, EI-EI-O! And on this farm he had a champ. With a text here, and BFF there. Here a text, there a text, everywhere a text-text!**" and she did it in under sixty seconds. What is the world coming to? We pick and choose what we prioritize. Just know that integrity and the solid foundation of what we believe are being attacked daily and God is not pleased. Let us do better by not touching God's anointed ones or doing His prophets any harm. We should do an even better job at not putting ourselves in a position to be a target for an attack. God has provided protection for us. All we have to do is stay under His covering.

God Bless

Don't Move

"Be still, and know that I am God; I will be exalted among the nations, I will be exalted in the earth."- **Psalm 46:10**

Watching my boys throughout the day is one of the greatest things to do. Seeing a couple of little me's running around shows me how amazing God is. They are so full of nonstop energy. Don't let them take a nap. That is like plugging them up so that they can re-energize. I find myself saying to them over and over again to sit down and be still; because the more they go they eventually hurt themselves. They sometimes jump and bounce around so much that they don't pay attention to what they are doing and something almost always happens. So I have been working on being able to tell them one time to be still to protect them from themselves as well as any immediate opportunity for them to get hurt by something or someone.

What I have come to realize is that now that I am grown, I move around just as much as they do. My wife has told me over and over again that I need to slow down or just be still and sit down somewhere and rest. It is almost like saying that a bad habit is hard to break. The truth is that we should all get into that habit because when God says be still it won't be hard for us to do that. God tells us to be still for the same reason that I tell my boys to be still: to protect us. God is always there to help, providing security and peace.

In this Psalm it is believed that Jerusalem was invaded and surrounded by the Assyrian Army. However as we get to chapter 48 they are celebrating victory from their foe. What allowed them to be able to do that?

Learning how to be still and exalt God. Instead of trying to do God's work for Him they just stopped because God said, "Be still and KNOW that I am GOD." We have to trust God and know that He is our protection from any kind of danger. So we have to get into the habit of slowing down and reverently honoring His power and His majesty. I believe that when we are in danger of something threatening us God says "Be Still." For instance, what would be the first thing someone would say to you if they witnessed your encountering a venomous snake? Be still. A way to get into a habit of hearing God when He says, "be still" is to just do it. We should have several moments in our day where we just stop and honor God. This will allow us to draw closer to Him and to tune in to hear Him better when He speaks to us. If we take time daily to be still and exalt God, I believe that we will be better able to hear from God at anytime.

God Bless

Do the Right Thing

"But Zacchaeus stood up and said to the Lord, "Look, Lord! Here and now I give half of my possessions to the poor, and if I have cheated anybody out of anything, I will pay back four times the amount." -**Luke 19:8**

Jesus answered, "If you want to be perfect, go, sell your possessions and give to the poor, and you will have treasure in heaven. Then come, follow me. When the young man heard this, he went away sad, because he had great wealth."
Matthew 19:21-22
Read all of Luke 19:1-10 and Matthew 19:16-30

We have all been charged with doing what is right. Growing up, everyone is taught on some level what is right and wrong and is held accountable at that point for what we know. When you would do right there was often times some kind of celebration to encourage you to continue to do right. That celebration sometimes resulted in you being rewarded however the main idea was to encourage you to have a mindset that doing right would always be the thing to do.

On the other hand when you would do wrong you knew that there were consequences that you had to face. It didn't matter how long you prolonged facing those consequences you still had to deal with them and if you waited too long it just got worse. I wasn't a really bad child however I do recall getting in trouble for calling myself running away from home at about 9 p.m. one night because I was tired of having to always wash the dishes. I know crazy right! I stayed out as long as I could but considering the fact that I was in middle school there wasn't too many places for me to go. So I finally gave up and went back home and to my surprise my father was there waiting for me and the rest went exactly how you picture it in your mind.

Here in the text we have two stories one of the Rich Young Ruler and the other about Zacchaeus. They both had an encounter with the Lord, seeking the same thing however there were two different outcomes. The rich young ruler wanted eternal life but he wasn't willing to give up his possessions to get it. He had no conviction in his heart and mind so it caused him to be said thinking about what he had to give up. The very thing that had him bound he considered it as a tool to be free. His sense of guilt wasn't strong enough for Him to give up ownership of everything and trust God to allow him to use it for His will.

Zaachaeus was a tax collector, so everyone in the town wasn't too fond of him. When Jesus came on the scene Zacchaeus immediately submitted to Him and wanted to know Him better. His guilt was so strong without the Lord saying anything he freely repented and showed that he would give up whatever he had to in order to do the right thing. God honored his heart and mind and set him free that day of all sins.

When we are out of order and we know it, why prolong or contemplate doing what is right like I did when I ran away? I knew that it was wrong and I convinced myself that there was some way around the punishment. Instead we should be like Zacchaeus and immediately recognize the Lord as the only one who can save us and repent quickly relying on the Lord, not man, to set us free from our sin.

What Jessica Tata did was an accident that could have been avoided had she done the right thing. Her running away is a cowardice act and horrible judgment because it appears that she fears man's judgment more than God's. I don't know if she knows the Lord in the pardon of her sins, however if she does, I pray that she has enough conviction in her heart to do the right thing. The longer she runs, the worse it is going to get and the thing that she fears most, man's judgment, will be the very thing that she has to face.

Let this be motivation for you to have a spirit like Zacchaeus and allow it to push you to do the right thing. Before he met Jesus he didn't know Him; you do. After meeting Him his life wasn't the same. How has life been for you? Do the right thing; keeping God's commands is what counts.

God Bless

Confess and be Cleansed

> "If we confess our sins, he is faithful and just and will
> forgive us our sins and purify us from all unrighteousness."
> **- 1 John 1:9**

My oldest son hates getting in trouble. However, because he is young, sometimes he can't avoid it. If he doesn't have much to occupy his time he gets bored quickly and at that point something is bound to happen. I believe that part of his biggest fear is Daddy finding out because he knows that I will deal with it. I still love my son and he knows it; however he knows that if he does something wrong we don't overlook it. To his surprise a lot of time (especially lately) the extent of the situation being dealt with was just the two of us talking. I do my best to mix it up as much as possible so that he won't want to come to me later for anything and so that he knows that he can talk to me about anything. Of course he is young so some things must be learned over time.

The main point though is that he would rather I not know because he doesn't want to face me when he gets in trouble. Either way, I am consistent in helping him to learn the lesson from his actions and to build himself back up once it is all over. My wife still thinks I'm a little hard on him but it will pay off down the road.

Here the text starts of with a condition or a conditional statement; if we confess, He will forgive and purify. The idea is if you take one step, God will do the rest. In order to receive the promise of God stated here we have to be willing to open up and confess our sin. The problem is most of us are operating like my oldest son we don't want anyone to know. A lot times it is because of the consequences we will face; and then there is also the concern of people's opinions and perceptions of us. Most times we don't want people to view us negatively so we try to hide the truth.

The truth is that none of that matters to God. We sometimes get so caught up with what other people think that we forget that God is in control and He is the only one who really matters. People will hear the truth and still have the freedom to decide if they want to forgive you. God says that if you just come to Daddy and tell Him what is happening, no matter how bad it is, as long as you are truly sincere and have a repentant heart, He will be fair and forgive you. Moreover, He will cleanse you from everything and put you back in right standing with Him. The Bible says that keeping God's command is what counts so we have to be obedient to the word. Additionally, Paul says that we are not here to please man but God so we don't have to fight to win the approval of man. No man or woman has a heaven or a hell to put you in so they don't get the final word. God does. He will have the final word, regardless of whether we confess to Him or not.

We don't want to completely disregard the people we may hurt or offend because of our sin so we have to be careful to rebuild those relationships. Sometimes they will forgive and at other times we make it difficult for them to forgive. However, you better believe that they will never forget. So even though they don't have the final say don't totally disregard other's feelings.

Once it is all said and done there is nothing that we can hide from God so it would be in our best interest to go quickly to God and confess so that He can forgive us and cleanse us from all unrighteousness. The bible says in Hebrews 4:13 "Nothing in all creation is hidden from God's sight. Everything is uncovered and laid bare before the eyes of him to whom we must give account." He already knows so just confess and be cleansed.

God Bless

Come Into Light

> "Everyone who does evil hates the light, and will not come into the light for fear that his deeds will be exposed. But whoever lives by the truth comes into the light, so that it may be seen plainly that what he has done has been done through God."- **John 3:20-21**

Here Jesus is talking to Nicodemus and He is teaching him about New Birth, or being born again. Once Nicodemus began to ask questions Jesus started to break it down for him. This leads up to one of the most well-known scriptures across the world and that is John 3:16. I have even seen this scripture displayed at football games. Jesus explained to Nicodemus that He wasn't sent to condemn the world, but to save it. Jesus goes on to say that light has come into the world but men run from it because of their love to do evil deeds. They don't go into the light because they don't want to be exposed. However, those who live by the truth go into the light and everyone sees that they are living for God.

The thought that everyone has skeletons in their closets is a fact because everyone has a past and nothing can be done to change it. What amazes me is how some people feel that they can keep their sinful ways from being exposed. Granted, some of the things that people do go to the grave with them and those that they didn't want the truth exposed to will never know or when they find out it will be too late. The interesting fact here is that for most of the folks who are not in Christ don't care about being exposed. When on the other hand most who are in Christ are the ones with the deepest, darkest secrets and they are doing everything in their power to conceal them.

How is it possible to say that you walk in light and think that there is not even a hint of light on whatever sinful act being hidden? I am a firm believer that truth crushed to the ground will soon raise. So to me it is in the best interest of the believers to do his or her best to clean up their acts. Most of the things that we get caught up in, if handled the right way, can really deliver someone else. We get so caught up in caring about how others will view us, when the one who counts is not even considered at all. The fact of the matter is this: when your porch gets dirty and someone comes stomping around for some answers, once the dust settles, only truth will remain. We know as Christians the best way to handle our indiscretions is to repent. The Bible even says in James 5:16 "Therefore confess your sins to each other and pray for each other so that you may be healed. The prayer of a righteous man is powerful and effective." There is nothing wrong with finding someone whom you trust to express your struggle so that you can be delivered from it.

The main reason many Christians don't want to be exposed is fear of being crucified by others. The sad part is most of those who do the crucifying are believers. Understand that no one is perfect and whatever you may have struggled with in your past could be what someone needs to hear and be delivered from. Being willing to be transparent, can possibly save many. Pray about your past, let it go, and be set you free! Then you may be able to use your story to help someone else. The scripture above says that whoever lives by the truth comes into the light. Where do you think they are coming from?

God Bless

Choose Wisely

"He who walks with the wise grows wise, but a companion of fools suffers harm."- **Proverbs 13:20**

We live in a society today where it benefits you to have someone reliable from whom you gain knowledge and wisdom. It is very wise for anyone who wants to succeed at something to find someone who is successful at that same thing. Ask if that person would be willing to be your mentor and show you the way. Most people prayerfully will be willing to open their hearts and minds and share their experiences with you so that you will avoid some of the pitfalls that they have been through. It is sad to say, on the other hand, that there are a few who are so insecure that they refuse to share anything, mostly because of fear.

This insight that you seek doesn't always have to be related to work or business; it can also be about life. Life deals us all a hand at times that we find hard to play. Having the right individual to help you through can sustain you until a better hand is dealt. There are few people in my life whom I trust to give me guidance and wisdom. These same people will challenge me as well, letting me know when I am wrong and needing to get it together. This is all a recipe for success as long as we put ourselves in the right position.

In the same breath ignorance gives birth to the same thing. If you know that a person is successful but has a bad track record, you don't sacrifice yourself just so that you can try to learn from them. The probability that you will have problems is very high. The Bible says that bad company corrupts good character so we have to be careful of the company that we keep. Everyone is not meant to lead and there are some who know this and some who just ignore it. If you are going to gain wisdom from someone, be willing to do your homework and if that person is really hard on you it may be for your own good.

Be wise in choosing whom you walk with and make sure that you are going in the same direction. Choosing good friends also falls under this scripture as well. Your destiny depends on the company that you keep. Everybody is not always for you so you have to be careful at choosing good friends. Knowing when to let go is difficult, yet necessary for growth. Scripture says that, "You were running a good race. Who cut in on you and kept you from obeying the truth?" **Galatians 5:7.** You don't want to allow someone to get you off the course of what God has called you to do. We should all be focused on running to the finish line and not the sidelines. In keeping with this theme of track, when you have a good friend, he is willing to run a leg for you in this relay because he wants you all to win. That same friend running a leg for you could be encouraging you and pushing you to keep going. Lets be careful who we have running this race with us; choose your friends and mentors wisely.

God Bless

Choose the Way of Truth

"I have chosen the way of truth; I have set my heart on your laws."- **Psalm 119:30**

The Hebrews knew the Book of Psalms as the Hallel, the Book of Praises. God describes praise, an expression of shared joy and exalting the Lord and His works. Hallel emphasizes joy as we exalt God together. The Psalms are like a guide to prayer that presents examples of the intimacy we ought to have in our relationship with God. Psalms helps us recognize that our focus is not on human experience, but on God.

Here the psalmist says that he has chosen the way of truth, which implies that there is a way that is full of lies. He also exclaims that he has set his heart on the laws of God, which indicates that there was an option and he has decided to follow the Lord.

From verses 25 through 32, the psalmist prayed to God because life had become too overwhelming. He had weariness and disappointment and he needed strengthening, understanding, and protection. So in his praying and giving of himself, God gave him understanding and he chose to comply with and trust in the Lord because he treasured His law. We learn here that the times of trouble become the times of prayer. We should fully invest ourselves in prayer at all times. However, when we are down that is the time we need God the most.

The key here for us today is that we do have the freedom to choose the way of truth and in that choice we have to give a lot of ourselves if we truly believe in the path we chose. As we give more and more of ourselves value is now attached to that decision because our belief becomes stronger. It is just like if you own a business. If someone else made the investment for you for a lot of people there really wouldn't be any value created because as an owner you didn't have to do anything to attain the business. Sure you would go through the motions because you see there is an opportunity for you to capitalize on. However because there is no value when you don't get the return you expect when you expect you; it is then easy to give up on it and become an advocate on why it didn't work. The truth is it didn't work because you really didn't invest anything into it.

On the flip side if you make the full investment to get that business started then your perspective changes. There is now created value because you freely gave of yourself, which says that you really believe in what you are doing. No one can cloud your vision because your focus is different. Even when you don't get the return you desire you don't quit because you now understand that it is a process and the more you give of yourself in the end the more you will gain. It becomes more difficult to quit and you really develop the attitude that you will succeed or you will die trying because you gave up so much. As a result of you sacrificing you may lose some money but its ok and you may even lose some friends along the way because they don't believe and think that you are crazy but that is ok to. Your desire to succeed becomes stronger because of the value created in your small investment.

Making that decision to follow Christ is the same way. For most, Jesus Christ paying the ultimate price isn't enough. So many people go through the motions of saying that they are a believer but there is no value created because they haven't truly given themselves to Him. So when going through the motions don't yield the results that they heard it should then they become hypocrites and strongly voice their disbelief in God.

Oh but when you give yourself fully to the Lord, when you chose the way of truth there is more value because not only has the way been paid, you have also made a major deposit. When we choose to follow the Lord, He gives us understanding that it is a process. He promises us that it won't be easy but if we just don't stop believing then in the end we will reap a mighty harvest. Not only does the Lord give His rules to follow, He walks along side of us to encourage us along the way. He sees the potential in us. His promises help us to continue to pray until something happens. Giving of our whole heart allows us to have a relationship with Him that no one can put a wedge in between because the bond is so tight. Just like in the business scenario we lose friends along the way because our commitment becomes stronger and we lose more and more of the wickedness inside of us because we put on more of His Glory. We have great expectations and find ourselves in a position where failure ultimately propels us to success. When we chose to follow the Lord we are fully vested meaning that from day one we have full rights and privileges to all of the benefits of a believer. There is no one who can take those benefits from. The thought of being fully vested is centered on building a strong retirement plan. There is no plan stronger than eternity with the Lord.

My goal is Heaven all the way. I am fully vested because I chose to fully invest myself in the Lord.

Do you have your retirement plan in place? Chose the way of truth and have your heart set on His laws.

God Bless

Brotherly Love

"Be devoted to one another in brotherly love. Honor one another above yourselves."- **Romans 12:10**

I often watch my boys play together to observe how they treat one another. They are brothers, so of course they have their moments; however they really love each other. As the oldest wakes up in the morning he asks if he can awake his little brother. And if the youngest wakes first, he doesn't ask, he just does it. They are always looking for each other, feeding off of each other's energy. The oldest is getting used to following our youngest up and down the stairs to make sure that he doesn't fall. I mean they are really getting this brother thing down, there is still a little ways to go but they are getting it.

They are loyal to each other and will not let anything happen to the other. When they are apart they are excited to meet up again; it is a beautiful thing. One day I took my oldest son to a baseball game while our youngest stayed at home. Well, he had some cotton candy all to himself; yet instead he only took a few bites and decided that he was going to save the rest for his little brother. He never took another bite of it. He cared and thought that much of his little brother without my having to push him to do it, selfless at 5. He wanted his little brother to be able to share some of his baseball experience. As a matter of fact one of my brothers took care of the baseball experience for many of us and our sons on yesterday.

We have to be loyal to one another as well. Loyalty to one another most often times gives us that push to keep going knowing that we have someone in our corner. We want someone who is going to celebrate with us our successes and encourage us through our trials. It is that someone who is willing to consider you better than they consider themselves. We have all experienced this before because Christ did it for us, He was the perfect example. I am not saying that we have to die for someone however sometimes we have to be willing to make sacrifices for others so that they can see Christ. Some of you still question what is brotherly love? And here is the best way to share it with you.

WHAT IS BROTHERLY LOVE?

It's SILENCE when your words would hurt,
It's PATIENCE when you brother is curt,
It's DEAFNESS when some gossip flows,
It's COMPASSION for a brother's woes,
It's COURAGE when misfortune falls,
It's FIRMNESS when one's duty calls,

It's WILLINGNESS to help another,
It's TRUSTING and especially a brother,
It's RESTITUTION made when due,
It's FORGIVING when asked of you.
Author Unknown
God Bless

Bow Down Humbly

> "Therefore God exalted him to the highest place and gave him the name that is above every name, that at the name of Jesus every knee should bow, in heaven and on earth and under the earth, and every tongue confess that Jesus Christ is Lord, to the glory of God the Father."- **Philippians 2:9-11**

Here we find the Apostle Paul speaking with the church at Philippi, challenging them to be imitators of Christ. He opens this text by asking them if they really feel good about uniting with Christ and telling them that they should do more to be like Him. He says for them not to be selfish by only thinking of themselves but instead consider others better than they do themselves. Paul then goes on to say that they should have the same attitude as Christ. He didn't come to *be* served even though He could have, but instead He came to serve.

Even though Jesus Christ is King of Kings and Lord of Lords, He didn't consider Himself equal to God. Instead, He humbled himself and submitted to God's will. He became an example for us and He was obedient to God's word until His death. Jesus' birthright gave Him power and authority yet He never abused it. My oldest son has the youngest by four years so because he is older and understands that he can order his brother around with no resistance and the baby will most likely do it. Instead we have been teaching him to look out for his little brother. So for example, yesterday I fixed him something to eat and his first statement was, "Is my little brother getting ready to eat too?" Another example is my walking in the house from work. He will be quick to tell me to be quiet because his little brother was sleeping or to turn the television down so that we won't wake him up. Jesus Christ is looking out for us and He has always considered us better than He considers Himself. So we too should avoid our own selfish desires even if we feel that we have a right to be and humble ourselves for the sake of others. My son could not care whether his brother eats or sleeps; however at a young age he humbles himself willingly.

As a result God exalted Jesus Christ above all because of His humbleness. Paul was letting the Philippians know that they have a choice and it should be to be more like Christ and we have that same choice. The hard truth though is this we can willingly humble ourselves and submit to God's will or we can be put in situations where we will have to humble ourselves. The word here is plain, it says that every knee should bow and every tongue must confess that Jesus Christ is Lord. Simply put, you can both humble yourself and submit by choice or by force; however there's not a question of whether you will do it.

If a then five-year-old, who really doesn't have a clear understanding so he could do whatever he wants, chooses to humble himself, those of us who are older and wiser should have a much clearer understanding of what God requires of us. The Bible says whoever humbles himself like a child is the greatest in the Kingdom of Heaven. It also says that unless we change and become like little children we will never enter the Kingdom of Heaven, which means we have to have a child-like faith. We can tell children anything and they will believe it and follow with no questions.

Sometimes our children model for us what we should be modeling for them. God Bless

Bear with each other

> "Bear with each other and forgive whatever grievances you may have against one another. Forgive as the Lord forgave you."- **Colossians 3:13**

It is often a difficult task to please people all the time. However it is so easy to get them so upset that they don't want to forgive you. There are some things that people do that are so inhumane it would make you say, "Why should I forgive this person?" Have you ever taken the time, though, to consider if God can forgive, why don't you?

Since God is the maker and creator of all and no one is greater than He, why is it so hard to follow His example? I believe that it's partly because people feel that forgiveness requires forgetting and letting people off the hook as if they are blameless. Our minds sometimes can't wrap themselves around letting people get away with wronging us. Some things would be more difficult to let go than others, however the more you hold on to that memory, the more upset you will become and the longer you'll trap yourself in that frame of mind. I have seen someone so angry that the mention of the offender's name causes a relapse of rage. Remember that forgiveness is a choice, not an emotion. You have to want to do it.

Here the word is instructing us to be patient and tolerant of folks and forgive them no matter what they have done. God is saying to let it go. We have to remember that we don't have the final word; God does and we can't worry about if they seek to change. There is nothing that we can do or say to people to cause them to do something against their will. Forgiving them doesn't mean that everything goes back to normal; you just don't have anger and hate in your heart towards them anymore.

I can think of several people whom I could be still angry with, however the Jesus in me won't let me do it. My father had me angry to the point that I refused to forgive him. I saw him desert us when I was five and live his life like nothing was wrong. I helplessly watched him date other women, marry several times, and treat the children of one of his girlfriends better than me, his flesh and blood. He never came to a baseball game and the only time he showed that he was really proud of me was when I graduated from high school and college and married. He never told me that he loved me from what I can remember; yet I hear him tell my boys that now so freely. God had a conversation with me one day and I choose to forgive him and move in with him to force myself to have a relationship with him. Today you can't tell that we had such a rocky past and though sometimes those old thoughts come up and that old feeling tries to stir up in me, God has equipped me with what I need to quickly put that fire out.

I know what the Lord has forgiven me for so, who am I not to forgive someone else? I am not perfect; none of us is, however I have tried the Lord and applied His word in my life and I can truly say that it works. My circumstance is different from many others because I was able to forgive and still desire to have my father close because he showed that is where he wanted to be. So in my situation I didn't have to force him. The Lord compelled him to get himself together. We never talked about all that happened because I didn't want to and he still hasn't said that he loves me. However, I can tell that he does when I look at the situation through God's eyes.

Work on forgiveness and let everything that God forgave you for be the backdrop that you focus on.

God Bless

Be Strong and Courageous (A.S.A.P. A.S.A.P.)

> "Have I not commanded you? Be strong and courageous. Do not be terrified; do not be discouraged, for the LORD your God will be with you wherever you go."- **Joshua 1:9**

Whenever I find myself going through a tough situation, my wife or some of my close loved ones always reassured me that it is going to be alright. Truthfully at that point I am encouraged and I believe that it will...until something else happens. Then I may find myself asking them if they are sure that everything will be okay? Many times after they encourage me I find that I have to encourage myself as well.

However there is nothing like hearing the Lord say not to worry about it; I got it. When the Lord says, "Don't be scared and no matter where you are I will be there too so you are good," there is more than just comfort, there is assurance and confidence. It's similar to the protection of older siblings against bullies. When your older sibling was there you were more confident that everything was good just because of their presence. God is the same way except He is with you everywhere that you go.

Here in the text Joshua had a reason to fear because the Lord handed him a major responsibility. Moses was dead and he had to lead God's people into the land that had been promised to them by God, the Land Flowing with Milk and Honey. God told Joshua twice to be strong and courageous and when we pick up our text He is basically saying, "by the way, did you hear me say that you need to be strong and courageous? Well I meant that."

Why? He answered before the question was asked and He said that He would be there. God encouraged Joshua that he had everything that he needed to triumph and that no one would be able to come up against him. God's simple request was not to forget about the World. He told him to think on it day and night, apply it in his life, and be careful to be obedient to the word and as a result Joshua would be prosperous and successful in everything that he did.

I want you to know that what God meant for Joshua He also meant for all of us as well. Why would God do all of this for Joshua, tell us about it, and not do it for us? That would be like God was teasing us and we know He won't do that. We have to stop reading stories in the Bible thinking, "I wish that could happen for me," and start embracing that God wants to do the same thing in our lives.

We can't go into a state of panic when we are faced with a challenge because God is always right there to help us in our time of need. Our problem is that we don't communicate with Him like we should. So that disconnection leaves room for doubt so we don't always move immediately when the Lord tells us to. My friend shared this with me yesterday and I will share it with you. We are always asked or pressured to do stuff A.S.A.P. We know that to be "as soon as possible," which means to do something with a sense of urgency.

Well my twist on it with my friend's help is when we are faced with a challenge in our lives and it appears to be more than we can handle, we need to A.S.A.P. A.S.A.P.

<u>Always Say A Prayer As Soon As Possible.</u>

Make that a priority in your life everyday and you will find that you will be able to move immediately to action just like Joshua did without questions because of your confidence in the Lord. Don't be terrified. Be strong and courageous.

God Bless

Attitude Adjustment

"Your attitude should be the same as that of Christ Jesus: Who, being in very nature God, did not consider equality with God something to be grasped, but made himself nothing, taking the very nature of a servant, being made in human likeness. And being found in appearance as a man, he humbled himself and became obedient to death— even death on a cross!"- **Philippians 2:5-8**

I can still remember when I was a high school student and our school was visited by the Dream Team. The Dream Team comprised Montel Williams and one of his partners from the military, who came to the school as motivational speakers. The theme of their message was basically *if you can dream it you could achieve it.* Just because of their energy and *powerful* message, we had hope for a brighter future. One thing they would say over and over again is that your *Attitude determined your Altitude.* They were basically saying that if your attitude was horrible, you wouldn't get far in life or it would be a real struggle. On the other hand, if you humbled yourself and had a positive attitude, the sky was the limit. The message went over well since the other speaker was a fighter pilot. He wore his blue uniform with all of his badges of honor stitched to his suit, a yellow bandanna around his neck, and silver tinted glasses. He was so cool. I never would have imagined that a ninety-minute rap session and motivational speech would be a life-changing event; I decided to carry myself differently and to adjust my attitude.

It is amazing that someone else's accomplishments can inspire you to want to do better and possibly be like them. In fact, that was Jesus' purpose. He came to inspire, be the example, and make the ultimate sacrifice for us with hopes that we would want to be more like Him. One of the things that stand out most about Christ is His attitude and His approach. Many outcomes would have been drastically different had we been confronted with all that He faced. For example, the ambush at the Garden of Gethsemane would have been so different if it were I instead of Jesus. Peter wouldn't have had a chance to cut anybody because there would have been a beat down on site, delivered by me to everyone of them I could have put my hands on. If that were the case, though, prophecy would not have been fulfilled and none of us would have been saved because of my actions. God is so awesome. So we have to trust that He knows what He is doing.

Instead Jesus showed us how we should approach life and all of its challenges and successes. Even though he had the power to do whatever He wanted He didn't even consider Himself equal to God. But He knew that He was less than. He could have had everybody serve Him yet He chose to serve instead. He showed us how to humble ourselves and still accomplish our goals, and how our attitudes can dictate the outcome of any situation. Just consider if Jesus would have been cocky and rude to the soldiers and the entire group of priests who came to get Him in the garden. He wouldn't have made it out of there alive. His reason for being there in the first place was to pray and prepare for what was coming. Jesus showed us so much, in just that story alone that will forever be more inspiring than the 90 minutes I spent with the Dream Team in high school. The more I read the word the more I am inspired to be more like Christ. He is so cool and the way that He handled opposition was so amazing. His mindset alone on starting something and choosing to finish it (even knowing the consequences) moved me to believe that if I just adjusted my attitude, I could do anything. Jesus' attitude did determine His altitude and there is no one higher than He. So my goal is to become more like Jesus Christ daily. What about you? Has He done anything to inspire you to be more like Him?

God Bless

A Virtuous Woman

> "A wife of noble character who can find? She is worth far more than rubies. She watches over the affairs of her household and does not eat the bread of idleness. Her children arise and call her blessed; her husband also, and he praises her:"- **Proverbs 31:10, 27-28**

The Proverb of the virtuous woman is a well-known scripture. I have heard many men say that *they want* one and many women say that they want *to be* one. Here the text gives a brief description of the characteristics of the Proverbs 31 woman.

First we begin with "a wife of noble character who can find." When we look at the words, *noble* is defined as possessing outstanding qualities, illustrious. Character truly defines who you are so the text is starting off by asking who can find a wife who possesses outstanding qualities. I am sure that if I was standing in a room full of men, somebody would say *amen*. The truth of the matter is that as men we can bring out the best and the worst in women; it works the same vice versa. Men, we have to be careful to use wisdom when finding a wife. This woman with outstanding qualities exists; it is all in the way that we treat women. All women want to give and receive love. As men we have to prove ourselves worthy (by God's standard) of receiving it by the way we carry ourselves and how we treat women. I had a few relationships prior to my marriage. As I sit back and reflect on them, I admit that I brought out good and bad in those few women. It was all a result of how I treated them.

God told Adam that it wasn't good for him to be alone so He would make him a suitable helper. That proves that there is someone for everyone. God has laid out the framework for us to unite as one. From a man's perspective, we have to find the value in the woman we choose and make sure that she realizes that we know her true worth. It has to be genuine, though and the way to discover a woman's true value is to love her, spend time with her and nurture that relationship. When a woman feels truly loved she'll be a supportive companion for life who highly respects her mate. At that point she will be more than willing to handle the affairs of the household. She won't get caught up in mess and gossip because she won't have time for it. She will find herself more interested in being diligent, wise, caring, and devoted to her husband and her family.

The key in this verse that is often overlooked is the man's role in helping his wife to be virtuous. My wife does an awesome job handling the affairs of our household. Our children hold her in high regard because they don't see Daddy disrespecting her. She has her days just like everyone else does but that doesn't change who she is and who she has become. I still have room for improvement;

however, we are working together to be better. As a result of how I treat my wife, I recognize this noble character to which the Bible refers.

Women, you are virtuous and your worth is far more valuable than the most precious stones. The question is: do you really believe that and are you willing to show your true value to the man in your life by requiring him to prove himself worthy by God's standards?

God Bless

A Spiritual Movement (Rom 15:5-6)

> "May the God who gives endurance and encouragement give you a spirit of unity among yourselves as you follow Christ Jesus, so that with one heart and mouth you may glorify the God and Father of our Lord Jesus Christ."- **Romans 15:5-6**

The civil rights movement was a fight for equality that occurred between 1950-1980. Specifically, the "Southern Freedom Movement" was about far more than just civil rights under law; it was also about fundamental issues of freedom, respect, dignity, and economic and social equality as stated in Wikipedia. This movement was a fight of endurance and unity; it showed the world that only the strong survive. Though the motivation was mostly politically driven, all involved were on the same mission. Their life represented what was in their hearts and they knew that the only way to make a true stand was to do it together. There really is strength in numbers. The battle became tougher as each day came, however they leaned on their leadership, each other, and most importantly, Christ to encourage them to continue the fight.

When I was in college, there were nineteen students who wanted to do an absentee vote in the city of Prairie View, Texas. "Since we are all living here why not have voices?" The city refused to allow it to happen so the student body came together with the same mission and one voice to fight. It's ironic that I wasn't even interested in voting at the time because I was so radical and militant-minded. However I still marched with them. We marched to city hall in a protest. As a result of our pulling together, the "P.V. 19" was able to vote.

Things that matter to us most always seem to supersede any and everything else going on in our lives. When we choose to take a stand, it is the strength of God, on which we rely to encourage ourselves to push until change comes. People of all nationalities and religious backgrounds have stood together to fight for what was strongly pressing on their hearts. Yet we all have a hard time coming together to fight for the lives of the lost.

Just like in everything, God gives us the endurance and the encouragement to unite and take a stand for our causes. So why not do it for Him? As believers, we all say that we are daily striving to be more Christlike, so let us do so(in the same spirit of unity as those in the civil rights movement) and pull together with one voice and one heart. Let us take a stand to glorify God in all we do until we win. The mouth is important because with it we confess. The heart is the source of life issues. Let us heed the words of Paul and have hope in the word of God that we can rebel together for *Christ sake*, knowing that we can look to the hills from which cometh our help.

Let us stand together to encourage the lost to come to know Christ today. There is a spiritual war raging but we are already victorious. All we have to do now is believe that we are victorious, stand, fight the good fight of faith.

God Bless

A Privilege to Suffer

> "For it has been granted to you on behalf of Christ
> not only to believe on him, but also to suffer for him,"
> **- Philippians 1:29**

Paul's epistles are full of passion and conviction. When you read the words that the Lord gave him you can almost feel what he is feeling. We can all attribute that to experience.

In business, I was told that in order to be a great leader, one has to be willing to fail and to push through the opposition. I find myself telling people that, "Progress without struggle is really no progress at all." So no matter how it is worded, the truth is, "in order for you to be a stronger person, leader, parent, business owner, or you name it, you must endure some hardship." When you undergo hardship it is your passion and desire to succeed that drive you to it. Once you survive the storm, peace means so much more because you can look back and marvel at how you made it through. At the same time, you can rejoice because through the struggle you discovered that you were much stronger than you realized.

It seems like backwards thinking, but many people want to earn their stripes, per se, to prove that they are qualified to fulfill the job at hand. Think about it. When you talk with someone about trouble with your marriage, do you consult someone who has never been married? No! You confide in someone who is married, thus credible enough to advise you. Experience matters whether we seek solutions to issues with parenting, employment, relationships, and friendships.

Here Paul says that it *has been granted to us on behalf of Christ,* meaning that we have been permitted the right, privilege, or favor to not only believe in Christ, but to suffer for Him as well. So it is a privilege to "go through" for Christ because it makes our conviction stronger and we can speak with passion after suffering a trial and coming out victorious. Most of Paul's letters were written while he was imprisoned, suffering for Christ. Think about how many lives have been saved because of his struggle. Consider how your lives have been saved or changed by reading Paul's words.

The next time you are going through a hardship after you ask GOD why it has to be you and when it is going to end, thank God for allowing you to go through it and ask him to reveal what are you supposed to learn from it. Therefore you and others may grow. We suffer to be strengthened and developed. Consequently, others do the same. So I consider it a privilege to suffer for Christ. Not only did He do it for me, He is the only one who can and will bring me out of it for His namesake.

God Bless

A Father's Joy

"The father of a righteous man has great joy; he who has a wise son delights in him."- **Proverbs 23:24**

Every *father* wants to have great joy in his children and especially in a son. To know that you groomed your son to be a great man of character and integrity is an awesome reward to any man because it shows that he did something right in raising his son. Also, having a son to grow into a great man means that he actually listened to what you said and applied it in his life. The Bible says that children are a reward from the Lord and a son is a heritage from Him. In other words, a son is an inheritance from the Lord, so one should handle him with care and train him up in the way that he should go.

The reason a father of a righteous man has great joy is that the Bible has countless verses about righteousness like:

The LORD has rewarded me according to my righteousness, according to my cleanness in his sight. 2 Samuel 22:25
Psalm 37:29
the righteous will inherit the land and dwell in it forever.

A father should have great delight in a wise son if he has taken the time to teach his child the word of God and how to submit to the Lord's will. The Bible says, "A wise son heeds his father's instruction; if you are wise, your wisdom will reward you; Wisdom makes one wise man more powerful than ten rulers in a city; the fear of the LORD is the beginning of knowledge, but fools despise wisdom and discipline."

There is nothing like bearing good fruit and as a parent, which should always be your aim. Whatever you have to endure to train your child up, just know that it is your responsibility to do so. God trusted you enough to allow you to participate in bringing a life into this world. That means that He has full confidence in you and has equipped you with everything that you need to train your child to fear the Lord and to grow in wisdom. Your child will learn to live a righteous life by watching you; our actions are like tutorials for our children. Here, the text is saying that it is possible for us all to have joy and delight in the way that we raise our children.

Solomon gave specific instructions to his sons to watch their walks and in their doing so would bring him great joy and delight so their mother would rejoice. We should do the same to ours as well. One of my great desires is to be an awesome example for my boys so that when they are on their own they will bring joy and delight, not only to me and my wife, but also to the Lord. I pray that they live their lives in such a way that it absolutely pleases God and are a blessing to those around them; I pray the same for you.

Are you living your life in such a way that shows your child (or any child) to be righteous and to fear the Lord?

God Bless

Will Your Name Be There

> "The Lord is not slow in keeping his promise, as some understand slowness. Instead he is patient with you, not wanting anyone to perish, but everyone to come to repentance." -**2 Peter 3:9**

On last Sunday I was blessed with the opportunity to teach a lesson to the youth based on questions they posed. My challenge was, "Why does God send good people to hell?" Immediately I received the revelation that they understood that some good people may find themselves in hell. One of the first things the Lord gave me to share with them is that "good" is not enough for God. Good is defined on a worldly level as morally excellent or satisfactory in quality. So good is really just average. When I say that good is not enough, I am not speaking of works; I'm talking about lifestyle. When we look at Matthew 25:31-46 Jesus is sharing a parable about believers and non-believers, comparing them to sheep and goat.

We know that though sheep sometimes stray, they are very loyal to their shepherd, whom they completely trust with their lives and depend on for protection, food, shelter, and guidance. The goat, on the other hand, is very stubborn. They have minds of their own and are only about self. It is difficult to get them to follow because they love to lead or be independent. God placed them on either side and then gave them judgment. While neither of them questioned their position, they did question His judgment and it was based on how they treated Christ. In Matthew25: 41, it states that God basically prepared hell for the devil and the fallen angles. Those who chose to reject God's offering of forgiveness are destined for the same place. It is true that we have all sinned and fallen short of the glory of God, so we all deserve to go to hell. However God sent Jesus Christ to be the standard and there is no one else who can measure up to Him. God gave us the way to secure our place with Him in eternity and it is through Jesus Christ, according to John 14:6. Jesus is the way, the truth, and the life and all we have to do is accept Him as our Lord and Savior and trust Him like the sheep do. We have to be willing to get in the passenger seat and just ride instead of being back seat drivers.

According to Romans 1:18-20, there are no excuses for not knowing about God and the way to eternal life, because God's eternal power and divine nature have been clearly seen by all. Since He has revealed himself what is important is how we respond. God bases His judgment off of the truth that we have heard and what we do with that truth. So why does God send good people to hell? They are just good, average, and still overwhelmed with a goat mentality.

The text today says that God is not slow but instead he is patient. He can very well come and snatch us all up today without warning and if you haven't gotten your life together and lined up it, will be too late. Don't turn a blind eye to God. Instead, surrender to His love, His will, and His way. Stop going against the grain thinking that you have time because the truth is we don't know when He is coming back. Choose you this day whom you will serve. As for my house and me we will serve the Lord.

Why should God settle for good when he sent Jesus Christ to be the standard for all? We make power moves to secure a position to further our careers and to earn the salaries we want to make. Accepting Jesus Christ as Lord and Savior and being committed to following Him wholeheartedly will set you up for a future that is beyond compare to any. The choice is yours and your destiny is truly in your hands. The Bible says in Revelation 20:15 "And if anyone's name was not found written in the book of life, he was thrown into the lake of fire." This is that place prepared for the devil and the fallen angels. You don't get in the book by your works, but by your faith.

When God turns the pages of the Book of Life, will your name be there? God Bless

To Seek and Save

"For the Son of Man came to seek and to save the lost."
- **Luke 19:10**

Have you ever been in a situation where you lost your keys? No matter how many times you would back track, those keys never showed up. The thing about it was without the keys you couldn't go anywhere; your plans for the day just changed until you discovered where you left them. Your keys symbolized the importance of moving forward, the power to get on track to accomplish your goals. When you seek you are trying to locate or discover something and it is something that you do with a great passion.

How about driving and all of a sudden you are lost? You are unable to find your way and there appears to be no help in sight. If you could just find your road map, just maybe you could find your way if you know how to read and understand the directions it gives you. At that moment, if you have been there before fear, overtakes you until you see a glimmer of hope and then you finally get that feeling of relief because someone saved you.

In the text Zacchaeus was lost and I believe he knew it. I say that because he heard Jesus was coming and instead of letting Jesus Christ find him, Zacchaeus went looking for Jesus. No matter the obstacle he let nothing get in his way of just trying to see Jesus Christ. As a result of his being willing, Zacchaeus put himself in position to be saved and that is when Jesus Christ proclaimed that He came to seek and save the lost.

There are many people in the world who have gone astray. The have gotten off course or have never been on track and clearly can't find their way. Many of them want to be saved, but instead of being willing like Zacchaeus, they are comfortable or complacent, needing a little push. Jesus Christ came to be that perfect example for all of us and His life was dedicated to seek and save the lost. Jesus Christ is the standard for us and not the exception so we are to model our lives after Christ daily.

Think back to when you were lost and how it felt to be saved. Once you became the salt of the earth and the light of the world, life has never been the same. Now prayerfully you are confident in your salvation; however there are still many who are lost and not looking for a savior. They need one and they just don't know it.

It is our job to search with great passion to find the lost so that we can help get them on track. Just like we would search high and low for our keys, we have to do the same for our brothers and sisters because we hold the key to their futures and they hold the keys to ours. We can't truly complete our journey if we don't follow the example of Christ; that is what we were called to do. We have experienced God's amazing grace and can now proclaim that we once were lost but now we are found. It is time that we share that experience with someone else. Jesus Christ held the key to our future and we were the key to His and He gave us the power to read and understand the road map and we are well on our way. It is past time for us to empower someone else. Turn the light on for somebody today; give them the key to unlock a promising future: eternal life with the Lord. Someone you will encounter is lost in the wilderness and needs a beacon of light to find the way. Are you willing to S.H.I.N.E. today? Make everyday a day that you Serve Him IN Excellence.

God Bless

Spiritual Residue

> "So I find this law at work: Although I want to do good, evil is right there with me. For in my inner being I delight in God's law." -**Romans 7:21**

We are all an ex-something and in many occasions, we think that we have been totally cleansed. But there are signs that show otherwise. Our lives are comparable to when we wash dishes. Many times, we have the water steaming hot and the sink full of suds, we find ourselves wiping away with our towel getting the dishes clean. Then you get to that pot and try to use your towel, and realize that when you finish there is still residue left in the pot. Even after what you consider as a thorough cleaning; there are signs that your pot is still not clean. The reason is not a lack of effort on your part, but the process didn't change. When you are dealing with a different dynamic, your process has to change; otherwise you end up with the same result.

Here, the Apostle Paul is in a position of showing us a human side of himself. He is saved. Yet he recognizes that he is still in the same flesh, prior to salvation. He is sharing with us our two natures, our Godly nature and sinful nature. The point for us is to recognize, even though we are saved by grace through faith, the truth is we still have some *spiritual residue* from our past. At any given moment we can all fall down that slippery slope and become a victim of our sinful nature.

The text says that evil is always present. "Present" in the Greek, is parakeimai, which means: to lie near or to be within reach. So in other words, evil is always ready to turn us from our Godly nature (good) to our sinful nature (evil). We have to be careful of our development and practices as we grow in Christ. Since we do still have some spiritual residue from our past, we have to become conscious of our weaknesses and not allow ourselves to fall to the temptation. Instead, we have to imitate Paul and feel satisfaction on the inside, with God's plan for our lives. We have to find joy in our hearts, to want to be transformed into the image of Christ.

Spiritual residue is not always a bad thing because it can help us stay grounded and never lose sight of how far we have come. If you know anything about cast iron cookware, it is almost a requirement that you don't thoroughly clean them like normal dishes, because the seasoning provides a stick resistant coating to help the cookware last. You will never be able to escape your past and if we put it in the right perspective, our past can be used to thrust us to higher heights in the Lord, if we allow it to and keep it in its proper context. Your past can create a protective barrier in your heart and mind, to keep you from your evil desires. Don't fool yourself into thinking that now that you are in Christ you are invincible, because evil is always right there. We all have some spiritual residue that can take us out if we allow it to.

God Bless

Please act like you Know

> "He is despised and rejected of men; a man of sorrows, and acquainted with grief: and we hid as it were our faces from him; he was despised, and we esteemed him not. Surely he hath borne our griefs, and carried our sorrows: yet we did esteem him stricken, smitten of God, and afflicted."
> **- Isaiah 53:3-4**

When I was younger I was shorter than the average person my age and so that made me a target for bullies. It always amazed me how people would see someone bothering me and would just keep going. As I got older I made a vow to myself that if someone was in danger, (especially if being bothered by someone else) I would do something about it. Now that I am grown with a family, I have to be very cautious about jumping into someone else's domestic dispute. However, that doesn't stop me from intervening. To see someone under attack and do nothing would be very heartless.

When that situation happens to people that we know we tend to respond in a different way. Most of the time, our natural response may be to just jump in and help because we don't want to see them hurt. In other words, there is a certain level of loyalty or allegiance to certain individuals.

Here the text describes what it was like for Jesus Christ. Have you seen the movie 'Passion of the Christ'? If not, you should. Even though the accounts of what happened to Jesus were not all displayed in the scenes, what you witness watching the movie you can't help getting emotional about it, if you really love Him. I took it personally when I saw the torture and brutality that Jesus endured for me. I was so upset that I wanted to jump in the movie screen and fight as many as I could just to get them to leave Jesus alone. That is the kind of relationship I have with the Lord. I recognize daily what he did for us all. The graphic movie scenes, which are engraved in my mind, are a constant reminder that Jesus really gave His all for us. We were in danger, our lives were at stake, and God recognized it. He sent Jesus, who loved us so much that He stepped in and took the blows for us.

Everyday that we breathe and we don't honor God with our lives and everyday that we allow ourselves to do the things that we know wouldn't please the Lord, it is like hiding our faces while Jesus takes the fall for us. We have to make it a priority to honor God with our lives so that we don't get accused of falling out of relationship with Him. The Bible says in Hebrews 6:1-6 that we have to stop operating on a basic level of what we know about Christ and step it up. If we fall it would almost be like crucifying Christ all over again. If your friend is in trouble, you feel obligated to do something about it. Well, Christ died for you and everyday we get the opportunity to do something about it.

Today, how do you respond?

God Bless

Integrity

"May integrity and honesty protect me, for I put my hope in you." -**Psalm 25:21**

The church before has hurt my family and me and I am sure that the church has hurt others as well. When choosing a church home there are many things that we take into consideration, does the pastor teach a solid bible-based word, what ministries do they have, and is there somewhere for our children to be feed the word of God, are just a few. Integrity in the pastor is one of the biggest things that we look for as well. We want to know if he is honest, does he have good character and honor. We want to know is he really trustworthy and does he really have a heart to serve God and His people. The truth is we can't really tell until we trust God enough to sit under that pastor's leadership.

When you have been hurt before it is difficult to fully open up and trust again. Here in this text we find part of a prayer by David. He is proclaiming to God that he knows that He is good and upright and trustworthy. In David's prayer, he asks God not to remember the sins of his youth and his rebellious ways. He acknowledges that he was wrong and now David is humbling himself and telling God that he places all of his hope in God all day long. Hope again is outcomes with great expectations. David is asking God to guard his life and rescue him because he has many enemies. It sounds like David has been hurt before and he is pleading with God to stand firm on His integrity because David is placing all of trust in God. David knows that man sometimes can't be trusted so he is trying to disconnect from that feeling and fully trust God.

We have to have the Spirit of David when it comes to God. When we get hurt by man it is not a reflection of God however many people blame God for it. We can't blame God for something that He gave us fore warning about. In Psalm 146:3 God said, "Do not put your trust in princes, nor the son of man, in whom there is no help." He told us not to put all of our trust in man but in Him because man will let you down. When the church hurt us it was hard to trust man not God because we have a relationship with God. What we had to learn is to trust God in the decision that we made for a church home because we were placing all of our hope in Him not the pastor. We all have to do the same thing. Grow a close relationship with God and learn to trust Him over anybody and anything else and He will guide your steps.

A good example is if you have a really good friend that you absolutely trust and they recommend someone else to do something for you, you trust their word because you know that they have your best interest at heart not the person they recommended. We have to be the same way with God, however the only way to trust God in all things all the time is to try Him for yourself. Don't allow what man has corrupted to stop you from having a trusting and loving relationship with God. The person who may have hurt you is not God, they may be His children but they're not Him. If you have children and you have taught them the righteous way to live and they hurt you do you blame yourself? You shouldn't because they made their own decision to do what they did despite what you taught them. Place all of your hope and trust in God and He will order your steps and your stops.

God Bless

Hide the Word

"I have hidden your word in my heart that I might not sin against you." -**Psalm 119:11**

Most of the things that we deal with in life are a matter of the heart. How we feel has a direct connection to our heart so how we handle life's issues affects our hearts in positive or negative ways. One of the scriptures that supports this thought is Proverbs 4:23. It says to guard your heart, because out of it flow the issues of life. It is so critical for us to create a protective barrier around our heart because it is our lifeline.

Another scripture that comes to mind is in Philippians, which teaches us not to worry about anything, but to pray about everything. It goes on to say that if we stop worrying and start praying, God will give us a peace that surpasses all understanding and He will protect our hearts and our minds in Jesus Christ. So the word is pointing out where the enemy will attack us all and if we don't put ourselves in positions to protect ourselves, we will fall victim to his traps.

So it is very important for us to hide the word of God in our heart because it will help us to stay in line with God's will for our lives. The enemy can't see what you think or how you feel, like God can, so that could be the reason that "hide" is used here in this text. When you have something of value and you want to protect it from thieves, what do you do with it? You hide it in a safe place. You store up your treasures so that they can be safe and at the same time increase in value. We can also look at it from the perspective of farmers because they hide seeds in the ground and over time those seeds produce a great harvest. This is the same with hiding God's word in our hearts; we store up a treasure and the more we put in, the more valuable it becomes and it produces more than we can imagine.

We have to hide God's word in our hearts because it puts us in positions of power when we are up against the enemy. The Word of God keeps us in line with God and His will. You never want to show your opponent your hand, so keep it covered until the opportune time. One of our main goals should be not to offend God and we do that by sinning. The more we learn His word and store it in our hearts, the more we learn and know the mind and will of God. The more we know God, the more empowered we become, because we realize that He dwells within us through His Holy Spirit, which means that we have wonder-working power within us daily.

I discovered something just recently; the human tongue is the strongest muscle in the body. What better than to have the strongest part of you handle the word carefully against the enemy? The Bible says that life and death is in the power of the tongue, so if we don't have ammunition in our hearts, it will be difficult to speak life to our situations or those of others. We have to make it a point to not only read the word, but to also hide it in our hearts so that it can take root and become a part of our being. We should all want to be what some of my friends call me: the "Walking Word."

So be careful how you handle God's word because your life depends on it. God Bless

He Chose You

"…. if my people, who are called by my name…"
- **2 Chronicles 7:14**

There is a common colloquialism used mostly in the streets that refers to people who are single. The common phrase that one might hear is that they are trying "to get chose." To get chose usually is used when single people (mostly women) clean themselves up and dress nicely from head to toe. Nothing is out of place, make up is perfect, and every hair is in line. Their flawless appearance is evidence that they attempt to be recognized, by potential companions. When people really make up their minds that they want to be in relationships, they consistently put their best effort forward with the hopes of catching someone's eye.

The use of "my people" of this verse suggests that God chose the people. God is saying here that everyone that He refers to, as His children are His people. So in essence we are all God's children, having already been chosen. He identifies us by using His name first: God's children. Though we have been called by His name not everyone has answered the call.

See when women are trying to get chosen or men are trying to choose, they normally put their all into it: It is all about making an impression. What I don't understand is how some people will give their all to another person but give God the cold shoulder. With God you don't have to put in work to get chosen because He wants us; we just have to want to be with Him. When you have met the person that you think you really like, you can't wait to talk or be together again. Some people sit by the phone and wait for the call and it barely rings one full time before they answer. However, the savior of the world, who is on speed dial, receives fewer calls than He should; His calls, which He places constantly, often go unanswered.

God deserves our very best, considering what He went through on our behalf. There are too many people saying that God chose them; they didn't choose God. The fact is you want to be chosen by God. You want Him to be the one who desires to be close to you. When you think about it, there should be no other way. When I speak to young women I tell them that they should be so close to God that the man who wants to be with them should have to seek God first to find them. Really, this statement works both ways. I consider it a privilege to be chosen by God and an honor to be called His child.

If you want to look your best for someone, do it for God and everything else will fall in place. Don't gargle with mouthwash and put on your best scents for someone else and then get in God's presence with morning breath. Give God your very best, not someone else's seconds.

God Bless

Follow My Example

"Follow my example, as I follow the example of Christ."
- 1 Corinthians 11

While riding in the truck, I have made the conscious decision to control the music that my boys listen to. Often when I turn on the radio, they both have special requests as if I am their riding DJ. The funny part is that they want to listen to the same artists, yet different songs. Then they go back and forth, about which song will be played until I ask them to hush. Though they listen to several artists in the music world, their favorite is Lecrea. They both like the record on his album entitled "I Just Want to be Like You."

One day while taking my oldest to baseball practice I lowered the volume and asked him, "Whom do you want to be like?" And his response was "nobody." I had mixed emotions because as a father you want to hear "Like you, daddy." However I have been teaching him to just be himself and not try to do what everyone else is doing. Either way, it made me think about how he views me and whether I have done enough to be worthy of his wanting to emulate me.

Here, the Apostle Paul is talking to the Church in Corinth and at the end of chapter 10. He is found saying that we shouldn't do anything to cause others to stumble. He is taking on the responsibility to look out for the good of others so they can be saved. So here in verse one of chapter 11 is a public announcement to all to follow him as he follows the example of Christ. This is a lot of responsibility on one man; however he is so sold out on God that he is willing to take the fall for everyone.

When you think about it, isn't that what Jesus Christ did for us? He came to be the example and with that He took on the weight of the world by carrying all of our sins as if they were His own. In the Bible He shows us how to handle every situation in which we could possibly find ourselves. Jesus Christ showed us how to truly be leaders of our lives, family, and others.

When you have been given the responsibility to be out front do you think that if those following you fail the spotlight shines on you first? What if you are in a leadership position and no one wants to follow your lead. Is it really them or is it you? When you lead you have to give others a reason to follow. Look at Paul's life: Many Christians were skeptical at first because of his past. However, Paul showed that he was truly serious about his faith and it got everybody's attention. As a result of Paul's tenacious conviction, he became a great leader and downloaded valuable character into those following him to make a tremendous impact on the world.

When I think about my boys, I think about whether I am impacting their lives in such a way that they will grow to be valuable leaders for others? It is interesting because outside of my house, it is not too difficult to get others to support and follow my leadership, humbly speaking; however at home is where it really counts because according to the Bible I am directly accountable for them. By the grace of God my wife and my boys do value my leadership; however as an individual I know that I still have room for improvement and I am more than willing to better myself.

Where do you stand on your leadership? Have you done a self-evaluation to see if the way that you lead is worthy of someone following? Who are you modeling your leadership after? If it lines up with Christ as the head, you are good keep pressing, however if not, it may be time to re-evaluate. Seek out leadership worthy of being followed so that you can be accountable to those following you, even the ones you don't know are watching. All roads should lead to Heaven, which is the final destination; you just have to make sure that you are on the right track so that others can follow in your footsteps.

God Bless

Defend Your Faith

"But in your hearts revere Christ as Lord. Always be prepared to give an answer to everyone who asks you to give the reason for the hope that you have. But do this with gentleness and respect." - **1 Peter 3:15**

When you think about loyalty and commitment there are few things that come to mind. I think about friendship, family, and relationships. I normally tend to be very careful with choosing friends or anyone allowed in my circle, mostly because I know how I am. I tend to be very loyal to the people that I have relationships with and I am very committed to being accountable to them. My wife knows that she is the one and outside of God, nothing will come between what He has helped us build.

Everyone may not always follow through with his or her commitments though. When the plot thickens that is when you get the chance to see who is really in your corner and who was just along for the ride. At that point, feelings get hurt and a real dose of reality kicks in. That uncertainty in loyalty and commitment, I believe, is a direct reflection of our relationship with Jesus Christ.

In the text the author starts out by letting everyone know that having loyalty and commitment is a matter of the heart. He says in your heart honor and dedicate your lives to Jesus Christ. I believe the reason is that again, out of the heart flow the issues of life. When we except Christ as Lord and Savior it is with the heart that we believe and are saved. So if it is cemented in your heart, it will be like that tree planted by the water; it shall not and will not be moved.

When you dedicate yourself to anyone or anything you are always prepared to give an account of why. Most often you may find yourself having to defend your reasons and when it is in your heart you can do that with passion and conviction. When your heart is in it, what other people think doesn't really matter. Here the author is saying that we should have that kind of relationship with Jesus Christ, yet we have to be careful how we communicate our feelings. When you think about it, if I can use this terminology, Jesus Christ is ride or die for all of us, so we ought to be loyal and committed to Him.

Some people have so many questions about Christ and who He is; at the same time some allow what other people say to cause their hearts and minds to shift what they think about Him. When we consider that Jesus literally gave all of himself for us without question, why do we have questions? Our relationship with our Heavenly Father directly correlates with our earthly relationships. If we choose not to allow ourselves to be committed to Him how could we commit to someone else? It is interesting because at some point in our lives we have allowed people to dog us out, yet we forgave them. Jesus has done nothing but love on us on the other hand. Meditate on that.

It is a matter of the heart.

God Bless

Christian or Disciple

> "And Jesus, walking by the sea of Galilee, saw two brethren, Simon called Peter, and Andrew his brother, casting a net into the sea: for they were fishers. And he saith unto them, Follow me, and I will make you fishers of men. And they straightway left their nets, and followed him."
> - **Matthew 4:18-20**

I was listening to a lesson for our youth at church; the presenter said that there were surveys done in the city where we reside and the topic was *do you go to a Christian church?* Less that 5% of the people surveyed said yes. So if 100 people were surveyed, that means less than 5 people go to church just in our area. There are many people who have been unreached, so that means that our mission field needs some attention. We all have a mission field, whether it is at work, your neighborhood, where you work out, you name it.

In this text Jesus is calling for disciples. Jesus was called a Rabbi, which means spiritual teacher. They would go from city to city teaching in the synagogues from the Old Testament. They have 12 young men, who were 15 years old, follow them for 15 years to mimic their every move. These young men would watch everything that the Rabbi would do so that they could be just like him. They wanted to walk like him, talk, even sleep like him if they could. After 15 years they would be qualified to be a Rabbi as well and duplicate the process with 12 more.

Jesus saw Simon and Andrew fishing and He instructed them to follow Him and without question they dropped everything to follow Jesus. In the original language fish meant to trap so Jesus didn't change their occupation just their purpose. He was now training them to trap men so that they could save them.

A Christian is used to label someone who believes in Jesus Christ and go to a Christian church they are a Christ follower. By definition a Christian is identified as people who associate with the cultural aspects of Christianity irrespective of personal religious beliefs or practices. If you are with a friend who robs a store and you both get caught, even though you didn't do anything you are an accessory to the crime. The reason you are an accessory is because you were associated with the thief. There are too many people saying that they are Christian but not living the lifestyle Christ intended for them to live.

A disciple is a follower *and* student of a mentor; one who accepts and assists in spreading the doctrines of another. This is what Simon and Andrew were called to do and so were we. The difference is that Andrew and Simon didn't question Jesus at all they just followed and many of us have too many reservations. The question on the table is are you just a Christian or are you a Disciple of Christ?

Time is not on our side and there are too many people who are lost. Do an assessment of where you stand and you decide which one you are. This was a hard reality for me because some times I choose to just be a Christian when I know I am a disciple so I expect it will be difficult for you as well.

God Bless

Call Them Out

> "If your brother or sister sins go and point out their fault, just between the two of you. If they listen to you, you have won them over." - **Matthew 18:15**

It is interesting watching children grow up because one learns so many lessons. I have witnessed my boys playing and the youngest would do something that he shouldn't do. So my oldest would immediately try to correct his action, and would tell me if his little brother ignored him. What I see in this situation is that my oldest child realizes that if he doesn't say something to his brother to correct him, he will eventually get in trouble. I have had told him on several occasions to look out for his little brother and not to allow him to do things that he should not do. As a father I am proud to know that he listened to what I told him and is applying it in the correct manner.

As Christians we tend to struggle with this issue. If we know someone who has gone astray, we would rather mind our own business and let him or her continue to fall. It isn't until they do something directly to us that something is said and then it still may not be handled the right way. In Genesis the question was asked, "Am I my brother's keeper" and the answer is "yes". We should be accountable to each other. How we handle the situation really does matter and how the other party responds to rebuke matters as well. We should all have the understanding that if we do anything contrary to the word of God and we claim to be Christian, others are going to confront us about it. If not, you may have to question where others stand.

No one wants to have fingers pointing at them telling them to do what they know they ought to do. The Bible says this: "You shall not hate your brother in your heart, but you shall reason frankly with your neighbor, lest you incur sin because of him" in Leviticus 19:17. The Bible requires us to pull a brother or sister aside and seek an explanation of their conduct and if they are wrong before giving them wise counsel, as along as we season our words with grace. If we don't pull them aside and say something, we put ourselves in jeopardy of sinning as well. This private meeting gives them the opportunity to set the record straight, to acknowledge their shortcomings, and to plan to fix them; it allows you to encourage and support them.

What we can't do is spread their business because that would just cause more damage. Jesus Christ was often wounded in the house of his friends and that led Him to say that a prophet has no honor in his own country. If we don't show compassion while being accountable to each other, who will? We are in a spiritual battle and we can't afford to destroy ourselves from the inside out. We are our brother's keepers and we have to handle each other the right way. Our Heavenly Father has instructed us to look out for each other and He has given us a proper way to handle it; our job now is to do it in the correct manner.

God Bless

Fight of My Life

"You are not able to go out against this Philistine and fight him; you are only a boy, and he has been a fighting man from his youth." -**1 Samuel 17:33**

I woke up early this morning, by the alarm clock that I forgot to turn off, even though it is my day off. The song that was blaring on the radio was Kirk Franklin's "This is It." Lying in bed listening to the words caused me to move to the Bible and I came across this text. The lyrics that kept repeating themselves in my head were as follows:

"Gonna cry now, go ahead and get it out of my system
Know I'm hurt now, but soon I gotta get back to livin'
Can't be here next year, givin' you these same tears
Hope you enjoyed it, 'cause it's the last time you'll take a piece of me

It starts right now, I don't know how I'm gonna get thru it
I'm broke right now, I pray somehow 'cause I can't do it
Can't keep livin' like this, there's gotta be more than this
Jesus, I'm ready, I'm ready for what you have for me"

The song goes on to say, "Are you going to wait for a sign, are you ready for your miracle? God's people, it's time to stand up and fight, let's get it. This is it!"

I began to think about the major battles that I have had in my life and sometimes the daily battles just to get through the day. There are so many things that we come up against on a daily basis that if we give power to them, we can find ourselves having the fight of our lives.

When I look at this text it reminds me of when I first came to the Lord. Just like David, I was young. The truth of the matter is that when you first come to the Lord, everybody is young in his or her faith. The giant Philistine Goliath had terrified the Israelites time and time again and David told them that he had enough: that he would fight him. Saul told David to go sit down somewhere because he was too young and inexperienced since Goliath had been fighting for years. Then, David said something that really inspired me. Young David said to Saul that while he was tending the sheep, sometimes a lion or a bear would come to take one of the sheep and he would follow it, grab it by its hair, and kill it, rescuing the sheep.

Here David was saying that he had faced situations in which he had to fight and the Lord gave him strength to do it. His battle wasn't against a giant, but he realized that a fight is a fight. Even though we've faced some really big situations in our lives, we all have had to fight some small situations as well and we won with the Lord on our sides. There is no reason to look at your situation and feel that your faith is not strong enough to fight "this one." The Lord has never let you down before. Even if you are young in your faith, you still have what it takes to defeat your enemy, no matter its size. All we have to do is make up our minds that we are not going to back down. Once we make a declaration like the lyrics above, we allow God to really fight for us. The Bible says in Exodus that the Lord will fight for us. We only need to be still. So look at your giant in the face and grab your five rocks and sling shot like David did and say "This Is It." You don't have to wait for a sign because the challenge in your face is the sign. So you have to decide to just stand up and fight.

God Bless

Obey Your Thirst

> "O God, you are my God, earnestly I seek you; my soul thirsts for you, my body longs for you, in a dry and weary land where there is no water."- **Psalm 63:1**

"Image is nothing. Thirst is everything. Obey your thirst." This is the slogan that Coca-Cola introduced to the world for the new image for their Sprite products. Donald Rifkin was the brains behind this catchy phrase and his inspiration came from a speech by Ronald Reagan.

When he was Governor of California he addressed the Boy Scouts of America and as he closed his speech, Mr. Reagan paused to take a sip of water. Noticeably refreshed, he returned to the microphone and the told the audience, "Now, I certainly have spoken on a number of different topics today. However, if you are to remember one thing, and only one thing, it should be this: Speeches are nothing. Thirst is everything. Always remember to obey your thirst."

Here we find King David crying out to the Lord while he is in the dessert because of a series of events that took place in 2 Samuel 13-18. One of his sons, Absalom, killed his brother Amnon because of what Amnon did to his sister Tamar. Amnon tried to rape his own sister. Absalom eventually gained some power and plotted to kill his father because of the blood that was shed. David found out and he fled to the woods and cried out to the Lord.

We know that David knew the Lord so he had a reliable resource in his desert situation. Since David had this kind of relationship with God he expressed it freely. He said that he was earnestly seeking God, that his soul thirsted for God, and that his body longed for Him.

To earnestly seek God meant that he did it early, not in the sense of the time of day, but in the sense of timing in his situation. This was a sign that he was diligently seeking God without delay. God quenched David's thirst before so He was confident that God would do it again. David, being in a dry land suffered from dehydration, which means to be deprived of the capacity to live or the power to endure. Thirst is basically a longing for or an eager desire for.

Many of us are spiritually dry, craving God but depriving ourselves of being satisfied by the only living water. We normally tend to deprive ourselves of the power of God working in our lives especially when we are in a desert or wilderness situation. The more we run away from God, the thirstier our souls become. We try to quench that thirst with everything but God, **which has the potential to kill our power to endure and our capacity to live.**

David counted on God while he was in the desert because God is the only one who knows the way through this wilderness experience. So all I am saying today is that we need to stay close to God and rely on Him alone. We need to read our word, pray, and exercise our faith daily in order for the power of God to manifest in our lives. In addition, when we are in a desert situation, we should quench our thirst and have the power to endure, based on our knowledge about God.

When we work out, we sweat a lot, so we lose water and salt. One could say that we are losing some of our saltiness. In the same manner, when we are going through and our faith is being worked out, we sometimes begin to fade or waver in our trust in God. The only way to regain what we have lost is to obey our thirst.

When we are going through and we finally decide to go to church, it seems as if the preacher was talking directly to us. Once we receive that message, we all of a sudden begin to feel better and our strength in the Lord is renewed. That is an example of "obeying your thirst." David tried and we have to get in the habit of doing the same thing.

God Bless

About the Author

I am Jesse R. Watson Jr., and I reside in Houston, Texas with my wife of eleven years and our three sons. I am an Electrical Engineer currently work in the power industry. Eight years ago I also accepted my call to ministry and I am now licensed and ordained.

www.ingramcontent.com/pod-product-compliance
Lightning Source LLC
Chambersburg PA
CBHW020938180426
43194CB00038B/220